CHANGING PATTERNS OF SECURITY AND STABILITY IN ASIA

CHANGING PATTERNS OF SECURITY AND STABILITY IN ASIA

edited by
**SUDERSHAN CHAWLA &
D. R. SARDESAI**

PRAEGER

PRAEGER SPECIAL STUDIES • PRAEGER SCIENTIFIC

Library of Congress Cataloging in Publication Data

Main entry under title:

Changing patterns of security and stability in Asia.

Includes bibliographic references and index.
1. Asia--Politics and government. 2. Asia--
Foreign relations. 3. Asia--Defenses. I. Chawla,
Sudershan, 1924- II. SarDesai, D. R.
DS35.C43   320.9'5'042   79-22977

ISBN 0-03-052416-4
ISBN 0-03-052411-3 pbk.

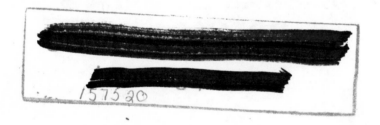

Published in 1980 by Praeger Publishers
CBS Educational and Professional Publishing
A Division of CBS, Inc.
521 Fifth Avenue, New York, New York 10017 U.S.A.

© 1980 by Praeger Publishers

0123456789   038   987654321

Printed in the United States of America

PREFACE

We want to thank all the contributors to this volume, who graciously agreed to join in this venture. We also wish to note that Professor Scalapino's article is published with the permission and the courtesy of the International Security Studies Program of the Fletcher School of Law and Diplomacy, which is about to publish a book on Security and Development in the Pacific-Indian Ocean Arena, containing Professor Scalapino's contribution.

We owe special thanks to Mary Curtis, editor-in-chief, Praeger Special Studies, for her unfailing cooperation and exemplary patience over the last several months.

Thanks are also due to Ellen Cole of UCLA's Stenographic Bureau, and Sandra Gann and Chris Iwanaga of California State University, Long Beach, for their cooperation in typing the manuscript.

CONTENTS

INTRODUCTION

It is neither difficult nor unusual for political pundits, editorial writers, defense experts, or professional diplomats to make a case for increased economic outlay toward defense because of a threat to national security. Equally, it is easy for professional politicians, economic planners, social activists, and others to plead forcefully for maximum expenditure on domestic development. It is a truism to say that defense and development needs are competitive. On the other hand, there is no doubt that a nation's security is enhanced by its internal political stability; itself dependent on the magnitude, modernization, and equitable distribution of its economic resources. Defense and development rival for a share of the same economic pie, yet they are interdependent also.

Although such competing considerations have prevailed historically, they have assumed a more emphatic dimension since World War II, and more so in Asia than in any other continent. The Marshall Plan and NATO made the rigors of a choice between guns and butter less severe for Western Europe. Correspondingly, though not equally, economic assistance from Moscow and the security provided by the Warsaw Pact enabled Eastern European nations to pursue their economic goals without the distraction of major defense development. In contrast, the political landscape in Asia has been impacted by conflict so heavily in the recent past that in the absence of any mechanism for collective security, defense needs of the nations in the region have drawn greater attention of the leadership than economic concerns, the poverty stricken status of most of the states in the area notwithstanding. If Europe was a cockpit of two world wars, Asia (including the Middle East) has been a potential tinderbox of global conflict in the last three decades.

During the colonial era, an externally imposed system of security pervaded most of Asia. Philip Darby's observations in regard to Southeast Asia may be usefully extended to cover most of the continent:

> The European state system, with its presumption of strong central governments, was superimposed on the existing landscape of fragmented authority and spasmodic conflict. Both by direct force and by restructuring relationships in the area, the traditional sources of instability were neutralized or at least frozen for a time. In part, the very development of formal empire can be attributed to the desire to establish conditions of political stability so that the business of trade and investment could proceed with a minimum of disruption.*

Such an edifice of intro-imperial security crumbled in Asia under nationalist assults in the 1940s and 50s. The withdrawal of colonial power also reopened old, historical sores among neighboring peoples, resulting in the eruption of local, bi-national conflicts. Externally, the extension of the Cold War to Asia and the communist victory in China made the rest of the continent, particularly Southeast Asia, an area of competition among all great powers of the world. Under these circumstances the political leadership in the newly independent states, already under pressure of the revolution of rising expectations of the teeming masses, had to allocate scarce resources to build security or to look beyond the region for military alliances.

Major changes in the external involvement, however, appeared at the end of the 1960s. Social unrest and changing values in the United States when it questioned itself of the legitimacy of its military intervention in Vietnam, frustration over the seemingly unending conflict, and the possibility of detente among the superpowers produced the Brezhnev and Nixon doctrines in 1969, both essentially aimed at reducing the superpower involvement and emphasizing regional security arrangements, although for different reasons. The growing popularity of Association of Southeast Asian Nations (ASEAN), and in 1971 its endorsement of Malaysia's neutralization proposal, underlined the indigenous awareness of the altered international scene.

Thus in the early 1970s it appeared as if the principal actors on the Asian scene would be Asians themselves, coexisting with each other, with minimal involvement of the external powers, whose roles would be that of guarantors of peace and security rather than principal players and protagonists.

Toward the end of the 1970s, however, the Asian scene presented a picture vastly different from what wistfully had been visualized. While Sino-American relations normalized, Sino-Soviet conflict surfaced with great fury. Soviet ally Vietnam marched into Cambodia in December 1978, overthrew the Pol Pot government, and installed a regime

---

*Philip Darby, "Stability Mechanisms in South-East Asia," *International Affairs* (London), IL, 1 (January, 1973), p. 26.

friendly to Vietnam. In February 1979 China invaded Vietnam as a reaction to the Vietnamese invasion and presumably to teach Vietnam a lesson.

At the other end of the continent, in April 1978, a military coup installed a Marxist-Leninist regime in Afghanistan, raising the fear that it might be active in exporting revolution to the neighboring states. In January 1979 Iran was convulsed in a revolution. The militarily formidable regime of Shah Mohammed Reza Pahlavi was overthrown by a religious leader seeking to establish an Islamic Republic. These events have raised the spectre of renewed great power rivalry in Asia, as well as tension and fear of war. It is these developments that provide fertile ground for a study of changing patterns of security and stability in the regions of South Asia, East Asia, and Southeast Asia.

The chapters that follow delineate the strategic interests and policy alternatives of the major powers—the United States, the Soviet Union, the People's Republic of China, and Japan—as well as their impact on the economic development of the region. Two separate chapters deal with the dominant power of the South Asian subcontinent, India, and that in the Southeast Asian region, Vietnam. Due attention has been given to the role of ASEAN, which has progressively drawn its membership closer in economic and related activities, though its potential for military cooperation is very doubtful. Finally, a special chapter is devoted to the Indian Ocean area where Soviet and American naval presence has increased in the last decade to the consternation of some of the littoral states, notably Indian and Sri Lanka, who have been foremost in urging the declaration of the Ocean as a zone of peace.

In putting together this volume, the editors have made certain that the viewpoint of the individual author is preserved, thus permitting presentation of a diversity of views and perspectives that enrich the value of the book.

CHANGING PATTERNS OF SECURITY AND STABILITY IN ASIA

· 1 ·

APPROACHES TO PEACE AND SECURITY IN ASIA: THE UNCERTAINTY SURROUNDING AMERICAN STRATEGIC PRINCIPLES

Robert A. Scalapino

In the aftermath of the Vietnam debacle, the United States has drifted uncertainly with respect to the basic strategic principles that should govern or at least influence its policies toward Asia. By some, this fact has been celebrated as a triumph of pragmatism over dogmatism, an evidence that Washington can operate effectively without strategic principles.

The results up to date scarcely warrant the latter conclusion. Unless a nation, and particularly a major nation, has a perception of the regional and global order that it would like to see achieved, its relation to that order, and the most promising among alternative strategies that can be pursued to reach toward the goals established, that nation will engage in an ad hocery that renders its policies unpredictable to friend and foe alike. Equally important, its policies will be without consistency, hence inexplicable to its own people. The result will be the type of confusion that lends itself to indifference at home and risk taking by others abroad. And if that nation, despite its various probelms, happens to be the most powerful nation of the contemporary world, its contribution to global instability will have been substantial, its good intentions notwithstanding.

This is not to assert that when a genuine effort to articulate a coherent strategy is made, the achievement of a consensus within America supportive of it will be easy, or that such a strategy can rest upon certain assumptions of the past. Pertinent in this regard is an ongoing debate in the U.S. administration over Africa, on that has

1

important implications for Asia as well. With respect to U.S. African policies, a struggle between two lines is taking place within the highest governmental circles, to borrow a phrase from the Chinese Communists. To put this debate in concise terms, we must understand the basic premises beneath the opposing views. The "minimalists" argue that the United States can afford a low-posture position despite the continuous and significant commitments of the Soviet Union directly and through its surrogate, Cuba, to shape both the regional relations and the internal politics of various African states. It is their thesis that in the long run, Soviet-Cuban intervention will prove counterproductive, given the extraordinary complexity of African politics, the mercurial qualities of leadership in the region, and the prominence of nonideological factors in shaping African political alignments.

Going beyond Africa, they pose some general questions about Soviet foreign policy. Where—outside of Cuba—they ask, has a Soviet alliance with a nation not bordering the USSR, hence not susceptible to the influence of its immediate military presence, lasted in the post-1945 era? Has not the Soviet record with respect to Indonesia, Ghana, Egypt—and above all, China, a neighbor it could not dominate strategically—cast legitimate doubts upon the ability of Moscow to operate as a global power via primary reliance upon its military strength?

Yesterday Somalia—today Ethiopia—but tomorrow? Is there any reason to expect lasting positive results from this type of intervention? Is it not logical to assume that as failures multiply, and elements within the Soviet Union recognize Soviet overextension and inability to manipulate the politics of radically different cultures, this nation will adjust its policies—after a considerable waste of its own resources?

What is the "internationalist" response, the argument of those who urge a countervailing commitment sufficient to be perceived both by the Soviet Union and by African states? First, the "internationalists" note that the Soviets have not committed themselves in a manner involving the masses of Soviet people in a direct and immediately perceived sense. Unlike the U.S. involvement in Europe during World War II and in Asia both then and subsequently, the Russians have not committed their own manpower in foreign wars on any significant scale. Thus their intervention up to date has not been excessively costly. Equipment and supply expenditures, to be sure, have cumulatively been a burden but one within tolerable limits. This type of commitment can thus be sustained, even if the percentage of failure is relatively high. Indeed, a single success may be sufficient to warrant continuance of the policy.

What are the risks of a nonresponse? To await passively for Soviet failure enables Soviet policy to continue the progress begun in Angola in recent times, and which has since been extended to other parts of Africa in a fashion similar to Soviet efforts in Europe and Asia immediately after 1945. Such an attitude thus heightens incentive for Soviet intervention, and at a time when we may assume that strategic issues have been hotly debated in the governing circles of the USSR from time to time. In sum, nonresponse constitutes a policy hand-tailored to the interests of the more militant Soviet exponents of a global high posture.

The Question of Asia

Against this background, let us turn to Asia. Here too, a fitful, half-acknowledged, semipublic debate has been taking place within as well as outside the U.S. government over strategic alternatives. Not two lines, but three, have been in conflict here if "pure" alternatives are isolated. The true minimalist line in Asia advances the principle of strategic withdrawal, based upon the thesis that neither U.S. national interests nor the general considerations of global security require our strategic presence in this part of the world. Most minimalists do not advocate an immediate withdrawal of all U.S. military forces and installations from Asia, but propose that this be done in stages. The first withdrawals have already taken place, they point out, with the removal of massive forces during the last stages of the Indochina War, including significant naval forces. The next stage has been scheduled with the withdrawal of ground forces from Korea. They would propose that our military commitments to Korea and Taiwan be completely eliminated. That would leave commitments—and installations—in Japan and the Philippines. Over time, these bases should be abandoned, they assert, with U.S. forces restricted to our Pacific possessions.

In their most complete form, the theses underlying the withdrawal strategy are elaborate, extending to political and economic as well as strategic considerations. First, it is asserted that the primary threat to the United States comes only from the Soviet Union at present, the other superpower being only the nation that can do physical damage to the American continent. The primary arena of the Soviet threat, it is further argued, is not in Asia but in Europe—and secondarily in regions like the Middle East. Thus it is appropriate to withdraw American forces from Asia and enable the nations of that region to find their own strategic balance, one likely to be directed against Russia.

It is further asserted that it is illogical for the United States to have military forces on the continent of East Asia and to contemplate a war of any sort involving this region, given the limitless manpower available there and the radically different cultural values, political objectives, and military capacities. By extension, this argument is also advanced with respect to South Asia, with the additional proviso that this is not a region of great strategic significance to the United States, nor one in which the United States can hope to play a major role with respect to political direction. This range of arguments derives in part from the experience of the Vietnam War and plays upon such concepts as the limits of American power; the inability of the United States to understand and act in concert with Asian peoples in the type of massive encounters envisaged in a strategic commitment; and the culpability of the United States in seeking to impose its values as well as its power upon other peoples.

Some minimalists would preserve the strategic commitment to Japan. They have fashioned an enclave theory by advancing the thesis that U.S. economic and political ties with Japan warrant military support for this nation of 110 million; but they have conceptualized a Japan whose primary links are with the United States and West Europe, and thereby removed it economically, politically, and psychologically from Asia. A general feeling prevails in the United States, however, which most minimalists share, that Japan will have to do a great deal more toward its own defense, thereby lessening U.S. responsibility in the strategic arena.

It is finally asserted that only an absence of U.S. military in the region is compatible with Asian nationalism. Indeed, the minimalist argument is that our economic and political relations with various Asian states will be enhanced as we move out of the region strategically.

The theme relating to the need for greater Japanese responsibility provides one of those linkages that enable connections and compromises between different strategic theories. A second theory, not totally disassociated from withdrawal, can be labeled the united front strategy. This strategy proceeds from some of the premises of the former, but diverges sharply at certain points in the implications which it draws. It begins with the assumption that the Soviet Union is indeed the principal threat to the United States today, but it sees the USSR as a threat in Asia as well as in Europe and regards it as important to meet Soviet expansionism on both fronts.

It also accepts the thesis that, in the past, the United States has made commitments that were too heavy, too unilateral, and partially misdirected. It envisages a reduction in U.S. commitments via the tactic of a united front policy, one that would connect the United States, Japan, and the People's Republic of China in strategic alignment against the Soviet Union. This alliance would not be a formal one based upon treaty guarantees, but it would be fulfilled through a range of economic, political, and strategic policies and "understandings," which include rapid recognition of the People's Republic of China irrespective of the terms required; the willingness to furnish military assistance to China if requested; an encouragement to Japan to move toward a much greater defense commitment; a wariness toward Japanese agreements with the Soveit Union; and support for a Japanese tilt toward China, including a major economic linkage.

Such a policy would also seek to bring as many of the smaller states of Asia as possible into a working relationship with the united front. There would be an effort here too to cut across ideological and political lines, with the hope that a meaningful relation between small nations and the three major powers would have its beneficial effects upon the divided states and regions of East and South Asia.

The final pure alternatives we may label the equilibrium strategy. Its proponents do not totally disavow the various propositions underlying the first two strategies. Most would accept the need to avoid the over-Americanization of conflict situations and to insist upon more equitable burden-sharing. Most would also regard as reasonable and necessary certain limitations on both the scope and nature of American strategic commitments, consistent with the relative strategic importance of various states and regions and their defense abilities; the limits implicit in American culture and the U.S. political system; and the changing nature of conflict in its multiple forms and interrelationships.

They would submit, however, that the Pacific-Asian region is destined to be ever more closely integrated, not to be treated as a series of unrelated parts, susceptible to enclavism. They would further argue that it is an area of vital and growing importance to the United States. U.S. economic interests in the region now exceed those in any other region of the world, including Europe. The implications of political developments in Asia are of equally major consequence to the United States, given the critical role that the nations of this region will play on the global stage, whether in international organizations or with respect to international agreements. No issue, be it maritime jurisdiction, resource allocation, energy, or nuclear proliferation, can be managed without an extensive input from these nations. And it is to be noted that all of the current states designated as major powers by virtue of their economic, political, and/or military power come into intimate contact with each other in this region making it unique among the regions of the world.

The equilibrium branch of the internationalists would further assert that the so-called natural strategic balance that the minimalists propose be found by the Asians themselves rests upon fallacious reasoning, since both the Soviet Union and the United States have a physical presence in the region as well as vital interests to be protected.

An American withdrawal of its strategic power would therefore precipitate an unnatural imbalance, one influencing the course of war/peace issues and, in broader terms, the outcome of negotiations on the widest range of fronts. In an era destined to be one of protracted, intensive negotiations among all parties, no nation—and particularly a major nation like the United States—can afford to neglect any element of strength needed at the negotiations table, including that of a strategic presence.

The equilibrium advocates regard the minimalist argument on alignment with Asian nationalism as simplistic and naive. Which Asian nationalists? Those that went down fighting the Communists in Cambodia and Vietnam—and are now dead or languishing in prisons and "reeducation camps"? The South Korean nationalists or the North Korean nationalists? Not even the Chinese Communist nationalists want the American strategic presence in Asia completely removed, and for reasons connected with their nationalism.

But the equilibrium supporters part company sharply with the united fronters on one very basic issue. They are opposed to the concept of a de facto alliance with the Chinese Communists against the Soviet Union. Such a policy, they believe, would have two extremely dangerous consequences. First, it would evoke sharp Soviet reaction, making agreements in such fields as nuclear weapon control and disarmament difficult if not impossible. We would move back to the era of the late 1940s and early 1950s. Second, it would be strongly destabilizing for Asia, supporting in the final analysis the rise of Chinese hegemony in the region.

Weighing the Options

Which strategy will prevail? In pursuing the Weberian method of posing pure alternatives, I recognize that no alternative will be adopted in its pure form, especially as a portion of the arguments underwriting one strategy can—with some modifications—be advanced in support of another. As noted earlier, withdrawal has taken place militarily on a considerable scale, but with the United States asserting that its strategic plans are based upon a maximum mobility, including the capacity to move significant military forces into the region quickly. It is admitted that U.S. military forces currently in Asia are not sufficient to meet treaty commitments, and that security in Asia has been downgraded to place prior emphasis upon Europe, but Carter administration spokesmen insist that the United States will stand by its treaty commitments and remain a major Pacific power. Indeed, these themes were reiterated strongly by Secretary of Defense Harold Brown in late February 1978 in a speech before the Los Angeles World Affairs Council. Brown asserted that the current level of combat forces would be maintained in Asia and that over the next five years, certain advanced weapons systems would be introduced in that region to strengthen U.S. military capabilities. He stressed the important role of the Seventh Fleet as a counterweight to a growing Soviet naval presence throughout the area, and emphasized the capacity—and intent—of U.S. forces to quickly react to any aggressive move by the speedy transport of American forces from existing bases, near and distant.

The Singapore *Straits Times* undoubtedly spoke for a large constituency when it remarked,

> Since the end of the Vietnam war and the advent of President Carter's policy of deescalating U.S. troop strength in Korea, non-Communist Asian countries have begun to be haunted by an uneasy feeling of insecurity. Despite repeated pledges and statements from Washington that the United States would continue to live up to treaty commitments and would not abdicate its responsibilities as a global power, there has always somehow been an unfilled credibility gap.[1]

Then it went on to add hopefully,

> But the speech by American Defense Secretary Harold Brown in Los Angeles on Monday, in which he stressed the theme of the United States continuing to be a major factor in the Pacific, should go a long way to reassure Asians that the United States was not turning away from them.[2]

While it is yet too early to be certain, and the elements of ambiguity and confusion in U.S. Asian policy remain substantial, the latest indications are that the withdrawal syndrome has reached its zenith, with the primary contest now between the united front and equilibrium strategies.

Meanwhile, the United States' military posture in regard to the Pacific-Asian theater will be based upon a one and one-half war concept, with the effort directed toward enabling response to a major conflagration in the European area while retaining the capacity to meet a lesser conflict situation in the Pacific-Asian region. The premium will be upon highly mobile forces in the latter region, both naval and airborne, with a lessening reliance on fixed bases, particularly those in populous areas. As a substitute, mobility will be combined with acquisition of the most sophisticated weapons systems available, so as to reduce reliance upon manpower. The use of American soldiers as a trip-wire defense and also as a guarantee of response will be a part of U.S. European but not Asian tactics.

WAR OR MERELY VIOLENCE?

Behind this strategy lies the fact that the United States government does not presently foresee a crisis in Asia that would require the use of major U.S. military forces. The official estimate of developments in various potentially explosive environments is as follows. On the Korean peninsula, relations between South and North are likely to remain minimal and hostile for the near future at least, but the combination of a rising South Korean power in all dimensions with the sustained credibility of the U.S. commitment (certified by the President personally to offset the unfavorable repercussions that followed the announcement of troop withdrawal) will suffice to prevent any large scale Northern attack. It is also noted that neither the Soviet Union nor China want another war on the Korean peninsula, especially in the likelihood of U.S. involvement. Some Americans and many Koreans have advanced a case whereby the North Koreans strike in full force, and taking advantage of the initiative, seize Seoul, capital of the South, then seek to end the conflict, having "readjusted" the border in the fashion of the 1967 Israeli-Arab war. This scenario is largely discounted in Washington as being far too risky for Pyongyang, given the certainty that devastating air-raids would be launched against northern installations.

Turning to the China-Taiwan issue, it is the position of the U.S. government—or at least of a majority of its spokesmen—that irrespective of the outcome of negotiations between the United States and the People's Republic of China, the PRC will not launch a military attack upon Taiwan in the near future. This presumption rests upon the thesis that the PRC is not militarily prepared for a successful invasion and cannot become prepared quickly; that the forceful seizure of Taiwan would alienate Japan, the United States, and many of the countries of Europe and Asia with which the PRC hopes to interact economically and politically; and that the main concern of the PRC strategically continues to be the Soviet Union. Hence, China will not take the military-political risks involved in an assault upon Taiwan, at least for the foreseeable future.

This analysis is probably correct. There are many steps in the economic and political realm that could be taken in an effort to weaken Taiwan that would be less costly, and it is likely that these would be attempted before any full-fledged invasion. It should be noted, however, that a persistent note of overoptimism has emanated from Washington regarding Peking's attitudes and policies. Once the belief was repeatedly voiced that China would help the United States achieve "peace with honor" in Vietnam, although it became clear later that during that very time, Chinese assistance to Hanoi was being increased.

Later, it was asserted that China would lean on Pyongyang so that a peaceful resolution of the knotty Korean problem could be achieved. To fortify that position, an overly optimistic analysis of the results of Kim's visit to Peking in April 1975 was forwarded, an analysis that suggested that Peking's insistence on a peaceful unification had prevailed over Kim's determination to use force. But this analysis omitted the fact that Kim himself had long used the phrase "peaceful unification." Indeed, it is the title of one of his collected writings.

More recently, Washington exuded high optimism over a formula to enable the U.S. to recognize the PRC without abandoning Taiwan, and various possible formulas were devised, only to meet with a hardening attitude from Peking, well exemplified in the August 1977 Vance-Teng meetings. At the fifth National People's Congress in March 1978, Hua Kuo-feng called again for preparations to go forward for the liberation of Taiwan, not precisely a conciliatory gesture. In sum, the idea—and behind it, the hope—that the People's Republic of China will help to effectuate U.S. policies for Asia dies hard in official U.S. circles. However, this does not necessarily vitiate the argument that the PRC is unlikely in the near future to attack Taiwan militarily. And clearly, that argument is enormously strengthened if a U.S. commitment to participate in the defense of Taiwan remains credible, since it is unthinkable that the PRC would risk a confrontation with the United States.

In terms of magnitude and long-term repercussions, the largest potential danger in Asia would be a Sino-Soviet conflagration. Here again the official U.S. perception—shared by most American scholars—is that such a conflict is unlikely. Neither side could possibly benefit from a full-fledged war, and the costs to each would be enormous. The evidence strongly suggests that the leaders of the Soviet Union not only rejected the idea of a surgical nuclear strike when this was at least technically possible, but that they have consistently shied away from the plan of trying to defeat 900 million people militarily and then face the prospect of governing them, directly or indirectly. The idea of China attacking a Soviet Union that is vastly stronger militarily is simply not believable.

The primary risk of war comes from a situation involving Chinese domestic politics, namely, a situation in which one side in an internal struggle for power might turn to the Soviet Union for aid. Whether the locale were Peking or some provincial arena, this would pose complex problems for Moscow, and it is precisely the scenario that worried Mao during his last years. But at the moment, the likelihood of this development seems slim, granting that it is the type of variable that is least predictable.

The United States has made it clear on occasion that it would not look kindly upon a Soviet attack on China. In the event of war, would it do anything more substantive? Under present circumstances, probably not. There is no sign that any sutstantial body of opinion in the United States would support U.S. involvement in a Sino-Soviet conflict, although shortly we shall explore further the position of the exponents of the united front strategy.

Is there a serious possibility of a Soviet-Japanese conflict? There can be no doubt that recent Soviet policies toward Japan have been tough, engendering strong antipathies within Japan at many different levels. Nor is there any evidence that Soviet policies here will undergo a basic change. Soviet concessions on the issue of the four northern islands seem unlikely. Fisheries and other matters concerning maritime jurisdiction are being compromised, albeit rarely in Japan's favor. And while the potential for extensive Japanese participation in Siberian development is great, economic and strategic considerations have combined to make progress slow and uncertain—although this may still emerge as the trend to offset negative elements in the relationship.

Despite the current mood and the problems underlying it, the possibility of a Soviet-Japanese conflict seems quite remote, given the military imbalance between the two nations. Even if Japanese rearmament were to move forward at a rate far greater than is presently indicated, Japan will be vastly inferior militarily to the Soviet Union for the indefinite future. To initiate a conflict with the USSR under these circumstances—even if one were to wave the psychological barriers within Japan to such a move—is inconceivable. And as long as the U.S. security guarantee is credible, the Soviet Union is hardly likely to take a similar initiative.

There remains Southeast Asia where another hot if undeclared war is currently being waged, and where various guerrilla struggles against established governments continue. It is in this region that the concepts of peaceful coexistence have had their sternest and, thus far, most unsuccessful tests. Despite various pledges of noninterference in the internal affairs of sovereign states, nations outside as well as within the area continue to give aid to guerrilla forces. In addition to the large-scale conflict between Cambodian and Vietnamese forces, military engagements of lesser dimensions have taken place on the Thai-Cambodian and Thai-Laotian borders. Meanwhile, the Burmese White Flag Communists claim to have liberated a portion of northeast Burma; the conflict with both Moslem and communist guerrillas continues in the Philippines; and in Malaysia, also, an insurgency ebbs and flows into its third decade. Further, unrest in Indonesia has emerged again, with the future there uncertain.

Consequently, Southeast Asia is a region where one can predict that a conflict of varying intensity will continue. Indeed, the primary issue is not whether there will be conflict, but whether that conflict can be contained below the nation-to-nation level or, barring this, below the level where major nations from outside the region participate. The chances of achieving this appear remote. Quite clearly, in the case of the old Indochina, nation-to-nation conflict has emerged; and while the current hostilities may be resolved, it is difficult to challenge the view that Vietnam's ultimate intention is to exercise hegemony over Laos and Cambodia. Hanoi's influence over Vientiane was already well established, and now Cambodia has followed. Under current circumstances, this condition involves both the Soviet Union and China. The Soviet commitment to Vietnam was and still is a factor in its containment of China. Thus, Vietnam's victories are USSR victories, even if they stem from the surge of historic Vietnamese objectives rather than any desire to accommodate the Soviets. But China is not anxious to see the formation of large units on its southern borders. Just as in the case of the Soviet Union with regard to Europe, China would prefer to deal with small, discreet political entities. Thus it can only view with apprehension the rise of Vietnamese imperialism.

This is not necessarily of benefit to nations like Thailand. The rival assistance of the Soviet Union and China to the Vietnamese Communists did not aid the non-Communists of the nation. Nor was the separate support given the Cambodian Communists by Peking and Hanoi of benefit to the Cambodian non-Communists. If the Thai insurgent movement gets support from rival sources, there is always the possibility of internal fissures, but there is also the possibility of a greater total amount of assistance, while a neutralist stance is affected toward all supporters.

Looking toward the future, it is logical to assume that the shadow of China will lengthen over Southeast Asia or at least its continental portions. China's cultural and geographic proximity, together with its massive size and its representation within the region by the overseas Chinese (not strongly pro-Communist at present but likely to accommodate to the prevailing tides of power) all suggest that if China can get its own house in order, its role in this region will probably be formidable. In comparison, the Soviet Union is a distant foreign power, and the United States a defeated one with scant stomach for further military involvement in Southeast Asia at this point.

THE POLITICAL REALITIES OF ASIA

Thus Washington's assumption that a war will not erupt in the

Pacific-Asian region that would centrally involve the United States is probably correct for the time being, although the fact remains that war—declared or undeclared—in the region can have an adverse effect upon U.S. interests. Beyond the stark war/peace issue, yet decisively influencing it, are other questions relating directly to security. The main ones are whether peaceful coexistence between and among states with different socioeconomic and political systems is feasible in this region; whether nuclear proliferation can be prevented; and whether any form of arms limitation or reduction is possible. It is quite likely that the ultimate decisions concerning U.S. strategy in combination with specific policies in the Pacific-Asian region will exercise a decided influence upon some if not all of these vital issues.

Let us start with the question of "peaceful coexistence," a phrase coined in Asia by Asians. In theory, most if not all of the existing Asian states have subscribed to its principles, namely, noninterference in the internal affairs of another state; an acceptance of differences in socioeconomic and political systems; and the acknowledgment of the sovereignty and equality of each polity along with an effort to create friendly relations.

Theory aside though, what are the current facts? As has just been noted, relations between and among Pacific-Asian states range from those of a hot war to alliance. Yet everywhere, flexibility or fluidity is the hallmark of this era. Wars are undeclared and alliances are porous and unstable, even when formal ties remain intact. In truth, the political configuration of the Pacific-Asian region can best be seen if one thinks in terms of four loose but discernible groupings, each with its fluid aspects and linkages to outside sources. Every grouping has an inner core and an outer, less firmly affixed mass, potentially susceptible to dislodgment. These groupings bear some relation to shared economic and political or ideological interests, but considerations of geopolitics, nationalism, reciprocal need, and ethnic-racial sentiment are of greater importance. The critical component units are nation-states, but parties and dissident groups cannot be excluded. And most importantly, as we shall see, relations between and among the separate groupings form an important aspect of the distribution of power and influence in Asia.

The first grouping can be defined as that of the United States-Japan-Republic of Korea-Taiwan-Australia-New Zealand, with looser ties to the Philippines and Indonesia. The distinction between the inner core and the outer mass of this grouping is extremely difficult to draw with precision, due to the combination of unpredictable, fluid U.S. policies and the instability characterizing some states within the group. It might be argued, for example, that Taiwan must be considered a less firmly affixed element, given the debate over normalization. Similarly,

United States-Republic of Korea relations have been weakened in recent times because of well-known developments. Even with Japan, economic and strategic issues have combined to render relations fragile as has been noted. And there was a time, under the Whitlam government, when Australia seemed inclined toward an Asian-centered neutralism, but that era has passed.

Some might argue that the Philippines should be included in the inner core, given the treaty and base agreements (which are likely to be renewed under somewhat altered conditions). Yet Manila's current bent seems toward increasingly close identification with another grouping, that of the Association of Southeast Asian Nations (ASEAN). However one may assign the states within the first grouping, there can be little doubt that its cohesiveness and inner strength are considerably less—at least on an isolated single-group basis—than prior to the Vietnam debacle, and this reflects the decline of American power and influence in the region as a whole.

A second grouping centers upon the Soviet Union, Mongolia, and Vietnam, together with a very few regional communist parties, notably those of Australia (CPA) and India (CPI), and some fragments like the Indonesian Communists resident in Moscow. The outer mass of the second grouping includes Afghanistan and India, although the latter state's affiliation is especially precarious, resting as it does primarily upon certain earlier military and economic commitments and the progressive estrangement of India from any other grouping under Mrs. Gandhi.

The current conflict between Cambodia and Vietnam has strengthened Soviet-Vietnamese-Laotian ties, but any long-range forecast here would be hazardous. On balance, however, Vietnam—and especially an expansionist Vietnam—needs a major power ally to offset the risk of Chinese reprisal, and the most logical ally is the Soviet Union. Yet, once again, the relative political weakness of the Soviet Union in Asia is underlined by a close examination of the second grouping. Whatever augmentation is taking place in its military power with the region, the political position of the USSR is infinitely weaker than it was prior to the Sino-Soviet cleavage, or even a decade ago—when relations with Japan were not so hostile nor those with India so uncertain.

A third grouping revolves around the People's Republic of China, and here most of the communist parties of Southeast Asia (as we shall consider) presently would be in the inner core, and the outer mass would include the Democratic People's Republic of Korea (DPRK) and Pakistan. Some would argue that North Korea ought to be excluded from this grouping and placed in a neutral status between the second and third groupings. Earlier, this argument was advanced with respect to Vietnam. In both cases, the data fails to support such views. While the DPRK can certainly be described as potentially movable, it clearly belongs to the outer mass of the third grouping, the most recent evidence being its support of Cambodia over Vietnam, an excellent litmus paper test of broader proclivities.[3] Since the Cultural Revolution, moreover, Pyongyang has tilted toward China on almost every critical issue, including its choice of intimates, and Soviet spokesmen make no secret privately of their distaste for Kim Il-sung, despite public support for the basic DPRK positions.

If one excludes its revolutionary potentials, however, the third grouping does not have much *inner* strength, this in part being a tribute to the xenophobic and isolationist tendencies of its leading component. If it is to be effective, therefore, it will have to count on some combination of domestic upheaval playing toward "its" communists and linkages with other groupings of the united front type discussed earlier.

A fourth grouping consists of the ASEAN nations, namely Indonesia. Thailand, Malaysia, Singapore and the Philippines. While the primary thrust of this grouping remains economic, predictably, security matters have never been absent from consideration, and, at the bilateral level, cooperation in this sphere is advancing. The fourth grouping has shown tendencies toward equidistance since the Vietnam debacle, but its general economic and political orientation is toward the first grouping, a fact that has not escaped the notice of all others. Within the group, however, noticeable differences of attitudes toward "the communist threat" have manifested themselves, something which reflects the domestic leadership and problems at any given time as well as the geographic facts of life. Most states of the region have normalized relations with the PRC, hoping thereby to stabilize that front and possibly even use China as a countervailing weight against the second grouping. Indonesia is the sole exception, an exception induced from history, geography, and the concern about an indigenous Chinese population holding great economic power.

In this fashion, most of the nations of the Pacific-Asian region can be classified. We have omitted Burma which clings doggedly to its ancient form of neutralism, coupling it with a seeming commitment to backwardness. Several of the states of South Asia might be listed with Burma—namely, Sri Lanka, Bangladesh and Nepal—to form a fifth grouping, that of the truly neutral states but for the fact that their category defies grouping. Hence, they must be treated as almost separate entities, although each of them is uniquely affected by both the domestic and foreign policies of India, their large neighbor.

Let us turn briefly to the relations between and among these various groupings. It is obvious that the greatest tension currently exists between the second and third groupings. When one weighs those factors that relate to the potentials for harmony versus conflict, the balance here swings decidedly toward tension and strife. Economically, these two groupings are more competitive than capable of fruitful interaction. Comprised of hugely populated nations that are backward in critical respects and in need of advanced technology, they must turn outward to the same sources if rapid progress is to be sought. Politically, while there is a sharing of certain ideological-institutional values and structures, it is offset by the fact that the two groupings mirror rival nation-building efforts, with historic ethnic-racial antagonisms now being reinforced by the increasingly close physical proximity in which they find themselves. Thus, the chessboard upon which these two groupings are distributed reflects the degree to which nationalism and power balancing has superceded political unity based upon a common ideology or stage of development. The imbalance of military power exacerbates the tension, since it is clear that the second grouping will generally predominate in this sphere indefinitely as a result of Soviet primacy. The third grouping, centering upon China, can only hope to see that power dispersed throughout the world, with its major concentration elsewhere, and/or look for a countervailing force.

A UNITED FRONT?

Thus we enter the complex question of relations between the first and third groupings and thereby return to the arguments of the united front exponents. There are certain potential ties between the first and third groupings that do not exist between the second and third. Economically, the interaction can be fruitful, especially between the advanced segments of the first and underdeveloped but committed China. Politically, however, the primary linkage is a negative one, namely the mutually shared concern over Soviet power. On other fronts—Korea, Taiwan, and Southeast Asia—there are few if any shared objectives beyond that of avoiding a major power conflict. In broader strategic terms, moreover, the identity of interests is a temporary one, as has been noted. The People's Republic of China is the least satisfied of the major powers with the Pacific-Asian status quo. Hence it aims at changes, both evolutionary and revolutionary, that will enhance its national position in the region as a whole. These include aid to various communist movements when and if they appear capable of achieving military victory; the effort to outbid the Soviet Union for the loyalty of North Korea; and, further here, the ultimate use of whatever means are necessary to assure friendly borders on both the Korean and the Southeast Asian fronts.

Unquestionably, the degree to which "united front" tactics will be pursued by the first grouping, including both the United States and Japan, its cardinal members, depends upon trends in relations with the second grouping and particularly the Soviet Union. As U.S.-USSR or Japanese-USSR relations deteriorate, the inclination toward a greater degree of rapprochement with China will grow. That is evident in current trends, especially where Japan is concerned. The Japanese government attempted to avoid a permanent tilt toward China, but under pressure finally signed the treaty of friendship, with its antihegemony clause in 1978. Japan also directed its primary economic efforts toward China rather than toward the USSR. Similarly, the United States, concerned over Soviet policies in Africa, the Middle East, and elsewhere, finds solace in a stronger China, and one that presents the Soviet Union with a second front of growing credibility.

Nevertheless, the united front position remains subject to the grave liabilities noted earlier. To adopt it as the primary strategy would create precisely the degree of tension between the first and second groupings—and particularly, between the United States and Japan on the one hand and the Soviet Union on the other—that would move international politics toward the renewal of global confrontation. Such as impasse could not possibly benefit the United States nor its broader constituency. No problem to which the Soviet Union is a party could then be resolved. While the Chinese prediction of a World War III fought between the United States and the Soviet Union in Europe, with China as an interested (and benefiting) spectator, could probably be averted, the coming era would scarcely be one of progress in resolving or containing international problems.

A united front strategy, moreover, would rapidly advance Chinese hegemony in eastern Asia, particularly in the continental area. Japan, despite the dire predictions of the Soviet Union today (and of China earlier) is not developing into a major military power even on a regional basis. And the United States, except in its commitment to South Korea and, in varying degrees, to the island nations of Southeast Asia and the southern Pacific, has no present intention of intervening militarily to support a threatened nation, nor the capacity to do so. Supported indirectly by the first grouping, therefore, China would be given powerful impetus to expand its influence, directly and indirectly, as its concern would be focused on the second grouping. And where is the Soviet Union prepared to intervene directly to block Chinese advances?

After a period of indecision and confusion, then, it is natural that U.S. policymakers are gravitating toward a renewed equilibrium strategy, but one with certain subsidiary, secondary united front elements. The threat of a united front will be used to indicate the dangers of Soviet intransigency and expansionism, and yet an effort will be made to retain a degree of flexibility, enabling dialogue to take place with both the Soviet Union and China and the resultant agreements to be based upon reciprocity and accountability.

The U.S. policy will further aim at keeping a relatively close relation between the first and fourth grouping, based primarily upon moral encouragement and private economic ties rather than massive economic and military commitments. Finally, the United States will seek to weaken the second grouping by appeals to certain elements, particularly India, for a stronger position of equidistance.

In sum, American strategic policy as it is now beginning to take shape, appears to aim at a close linkage between the first and fourth groupings while maintaining a more partial, looser linkage—or availability—to the third grouping.

SPECIFIC SECURITY ISSUES

If this be the new strategic balance toward which American foreign policy in Asia aims, what are its implications for nuclear proliferation? The danger of such a development is very real, and some have argued that it cannot be avoided under any circumstances. The issue here is not merely whether a given country, feeling insecure and threatened, acquires a nuclear weapons stockpile. It is also the threshold issue, namely, whether a nation moves toward having such weapons, so that in effect it is a situation of minus six months, minus three months, or indeed, minus a few days from the bomb.

Recent trends have clearly heightened the danger of nuclear proliferation via such countries as South Korea and Taiwan. Neither has regarded the American commitment as wholly credible, while each has perceived a major external threat. Renewed efforts by the United States may have reduced South Korean feelings of insecurity, at least temporarily. There is little as yet to reassure the government and people on Taiwan. Beyond these two nations, what other countries could conceivably be in a similar position and mood? One suspects that Vietnam might ultimately fall into this category, and possibly Indonesia. Despite recent pronouncements that defensive nuclear weapons are constitutional, Japan still seems a great distance from any such move, but one can envisage circumstances—the continuous rise of the Soviet threat and the declining credibility of the United States—where sentiment for a nuclear or near-nuclear capacity would rapidly grow.

Above all, nuclear proliferation will be a by-product of insecurity, an insecurity most likely to emerge out of a sharp imbalance of power in the Pacific-Asian area in combination with grave fissures in the domestic and regional settings. Thus far, the attitude of the PRC has not been helpful. Chinese spokesmen have frequently taken the position that they and others have every right to break the superpower "monopoly" on nuclear weapons, and on occasion they have argued that nuclear proliferation is not a menace since it will be conducive to lessening superpower influence and control.

This raises the general issue of arms control in its broader context. Here too, trends are not promising. Gimmicks such as nuclear-free zones are not going to resolve or even lessen the problem. In northeast Asia, for example, no one expects either the Soviet Union or China to abandon its nuclear weapons. Hence the concept of a nuclear-free zone for Korea or other parts of the region is meaningless. In Southeast Asia, such a declaration is unlikely to be acceptable given the present political configuration and the near presence of China and India.

It also seems clear that China will not agree to any meaningful SALT type agreement until its own nuclear weapon program yields what it considers a credible second-strike capacity. Already, it has emplaced medium-range ICBMs and, possibly, a few long-range ones. But its program has not moved as rapidly as was once hoped, and for a considerable period China will concentrate upon production, not control. Over time, this may complicate U.S.-USSR agreements, particularly if scientific and technological assistance flow to China from Western—including U.S.—sources.

The one issue that has immediate relevance but no immediate answers is arms transfers. Take the current Cambodian-Vietnamese conflict as an example. The Vietnamese are presumably far better armed—both with respect to quantity and quality—given the huge caches of American military materials and the substantial aid received from the Soviet Union. It is interesting to note, however, that recent reports speak of Cambodian acquisition of Chinese B-69 antitank rocket launchers and similar equipment.[4]

The militarization of Asia at large is one of the most striking—and potentially dangerous—phenomena of the post-1945 era. Southeast Asia at present owns a massive stock of military equipment derived from the major powers. The Korean peninsula is the most heavily armed sector of the world. Japan will rapidly acquire more sophisticated military equipment of a conventional type. The Soviet Union has the full range of its conventional and nuclear weaponry emplaced in Asia, directed primarily at China. The Chinese are now seeking to talk on two legs militarily, advancing their nuclear program as rapidly as possible but committing themselves to modernized conventional weaponry as well. Guerrilla forces, Moslem and Communist, have sought, and in a number of cases obtained, weapons from external sources. In South

Asia, India has become a middle-class military power with Russian assistance. Pakistan long possessed a considerable military arsenal, sustained in earlier times by the United States. In sum, most of Asia is more heavily militarized today than at any time previously, and the prospects are that its weaponry and manpower will only increase.

The only current restraints on external assistance, notably that from the major powers, is voluntary, and both the United States and the Soviet Union have generally been withholding their most sophisticated equipment on a reciprocal basis. Also, some caution is being exercised in the sales of offensive weapons in certain cases.

SOLUTIONS

Dramatic approaches to any of the problems noted may have a certain political pay-off, either domestically or internationally, but they are unlikely to have any practical consequences. The much vaunted nuclear non-proliferation treaty, although not without some value, will not stop nuclear proliferation, a fact now commonly acknowledged. Agreements upon across-the-board reductions in armed forces, such as proposed by North Korea, or calls for a total ban on nuclear weapon production, such as have been made by the Soviet Union and China, at various times should be recognized for what they are: propaganda (as the Soviet Union and China eagerly assert with respect to each other's statements).

It would be far wiser to work at a more modest level, and to begin by tackling problems that make meaningful disarmament so difficult, namely, the problems of perception of threat, peaceful coexistence, and arms transfer; while continuing the effort to limit or ban nuclear weapon testing on a universal basis and so prevent nuclear proliferation. The first two of these problems require that the Pacific-Asian states work in the political realm toward defining precisely the concept of peaceful coexistence accepted by all states in theory; provide mechanisms for the investigation of complaints; and allow international or regional forums to air grievances and consider sanctions. Progress in this field is likely to be as painful as it is essential, but until concrete measures are attempted, little progress in reducing tension can be expected.

In the field of arms transfer, the critical issue is whether there can be any enforceable agreements among the major powers, including China. Such agreements should start with the concept that when any nation is recognized as a sovereign entity by other nations, it shall be considered illegal and in violation of peaceful coexistence for any other nation to supply arms to forces seeking to overthrow that government. An agreement should further extend to the proposition that above a certain threshold of defensive weaponry, the security interests of any state are not being served, and further weapons should not be supplied.

Nuclear testing controls now hinge not merely upon American-Soviet agreements, but upon the acceptance of such agreements by other nuclear states, and that must be the next serious effort. Meanwhile, nuclear proliferation can be resisted only by a combination of a credible American foreign policy in Asia and the fullest cooperation of all of the nuclear powers.

In conclusion, one must frankly acknowledge that the Pacific-Asian region continues to be an essentially lawless region to which violence in various forms is endemic. The chances for preventing a large-scale war are reasonably good, as we have noted, but only because the potential costs of such a war to all the parties concerned appear too high to warrant the risks, not because of any major progress in achieving an identity of interests, perceptions, or goals. In such a setting, grandiose schemes for disarmament are at best the work of visionaries, not political leaders—and at worst, they are propaganda gimmicks which divert attention from what is necessary to real progress.

U.S. POLICY—A SUMMATION

The United States now appears to be emerging from a period of confusion and ambiguity following its defeat in the Indochina War. The absence of any Asian policy, in combination with various signs of withdrawal, profoundly alarmed the non-Communist countries of Asia in recent years and the People's Republic of China as well. One must be cautious, given the continuing evidences of ambiguity and amateurism to which the Carter administration has been prone; but it now appears that a modified equilibrium strategy will be pursued, with some subsidiary "united front" aspects, how strong depending on the course of American-Soviet relations in the period immediately ahead. Military policies will involve a heavier reliance on sophisticated weapons systems and mobility, a lesser one on fixed bases. The success of this strategy will hinge upon its political consequences as well as the adequacy of the U.S. assessment of Pacific-Asian conflict potentials. This highlights the fact that the economic and political aspects of security are at least as crucial as the military aspects, and here concrete policies have yet to be worked out in most instances. The economic underpinnings of the American-Japanese relation are fragile; political relations with traditional allies from South Korea to the Philippines have deteriorated; and attitudes toward the Communist states of Asia have been marked by vacillation and uncertainty. In sum, for better or worse, the United States is moving toward specific military policies for the Pacific-Asian region; it remains to develop concrete economic and political policies to underwrite the new equilibrium strategy, policies that accord with the political objectives of strengthening the first grouping and providing positive linkages to the others.

NOTES

1. *Singapore Straits Times*, February 23, 1978, p. 16.
2. Ibid., p. 16.
3. For a report of the 1977 Pol Pot trip to the DPRK and his warm reception, see *FBIS, Asia and Pacific*, February 24, 1978, D 3–4.
4. See the interview conducted by Jean Thoraval with Cambodian prisoners of war reported from Hong Kong, *FBIS, Asia and Pacific*, February 26, 1978, February 27, 1978, K 9.

· 2 ·

CHINA AND ASIAN SECURITY
Karel Kovanda

The first half of January 1979 has already seen the normalization of U.S.-China relations, the fall of Kampuchea to Vietnamese invaders, and the flight of the Shah of Iran. Wall posters in Peking have demanded the removal of Mao Tse-tung's corpse from his mausoleum. All these events are symptomatic of the tremendous changes that China has to deal with both at home and in her external relations; changes which in many instances started in the mid-1970s, and to which there is no end in sight.

From the flurry of developments, this paper will try to extract some underlying salient features. It will examine, first, the new Chinese emphasis on economic modernization, and then take up China's fear of the Soviet Union. These are the two principal motifs that set the tune of China's foreign policy. These two inquiries will be followed by discussions of China's extraordinary new relationship with Japan, of the setbacks she has experienced in Indochina, and of her efforts to safeguard the soft underbelly of Asia from expanding Soviet influence. Problems of the small countries of East Asia are of a different category. A brief concluding passage will be devoted to China's military posture in the light of the Soviet threat.

MODERNIZATION

A few months ago, the first wall posters appeared in Peking

22

criticizing Chairman Mao who had died in September 1976. They accused him of not having acted energetically enough against the Gang of Four, and of acquiescing in the suppression of people who mourned Premier Chou En-lai in April 1976, among other things.

The charges might sound a little esoteric to the uninitiated observer but are full of meaning for the Chinese. The Gang of Four was the nemesis of Chinese political life for the decade of the Cultural Revolution. These four extremist leaders, together with the former defense minister Lin Piao, are held responsible for the all-pervading chaos and tragedy of that period, roughly between 1966 and 1976. Accusing Mao of leniency toward them is just one step from saying the unmentionable, namely that he was in actual collusion with them. And considering the rate at which the domestic political atmosphere is changing in China, even the unutterable perhaps will have become commonplace by the time this reaches the reader.

The second allegation is equally serious. It refers to the so-called Tien An Men incident of the first days of April 1976. That was the time of the traditional Ch'ingming Festival during which the Chinese remember their dead. Hundreds of thousands, in fact millions, of people passed through Tien An Men, Peking's central square, to mourn the recently demised Premier Chou, and covered the central Monument to the People's Heroes with thousands of wreaths and poems. Eventually they were brutally attacked by paramilitary units. The whole event was subsequently termed counterrevolutionary and was blamed on Teng Hsiao-ping who lost his last vestiges of power. Teng Hsiao-ping was reinstated a year or so later; and now, the whole movement has turned into a legendary exploit of the revolutionary masses fighting the Gang of Four.[1]

The struggle for succession which many feared might be protracted and might plunge China further into chaos was in the actual event mercifully short. In one surgical strike, the four most prominent exponents of the adventurist line in Chinese politics, Chiang Ching, Yao Wen-yuan, Chang Chun-chiao and Wang Hung-wen, were arrested on October 6, 1976, a few short weeks after the death of Mao Tse-tung. Since then, China has been blessed with a level-headed, down-to-earth leadership, and the country has been exerting tremendous efforts to consolidate the domestic economic and political situation.

The recent wall posters are an indication of how far the changes have gone up till now. The observer in Peking has the feeling that far from coming to a halt, the rate of change is accelerating. China is gutting virtually all the dogmas of the Cultural Revolution, even though some lip service is still paid to them. Policy changes go even further back into the past to the period around the Great Leap Forward in 1958. The last of the leaders of the 1959 Tibetan uprising have been released. The Dalai Lama has been invited to return. All those stigmatized in 1957 as rightists have had their labels removed. Peng Te-huai, the defense minister who in 1959 opposed Mao's Great Leap Forward, and virtually all pre-Cultural Revolution leaders have been rehabilitated. Where this reevaluation of the past is going to end is anybody's guess.

The main directions for the future are, nevertheless, rather clear. The most important political gatherings since the purge of the Gang of Four, that is to say the Eleventh CPC Congress in August 1977 and the Fifth National People's Congress in February 1978 set forth an impressive program for bringing China up to the front ranks of the world's nations by the end of this century. The program for achieving it is called the four modernizations: of agriculture, industry, national defense, and science and technology. This program, coupled with a foreign policy based on the "three worlds theory," is already turning China into a kind of pivot for realigning the political forces in Asia, along lines very different from those prevailing even as recently as at the end of the Vietnam War in 1975.

Specific Goals

In examining China's role in Asian security, one therefore has to outline the changes programmed for China domestically and consider what forces might upset them. These domestic changes will then determine how much weight China will have to throw about in the international arena in terms of standing up to the Soviet Union, her principal adversary. Further, these changes will dictate how much freedom China will have to align herself in the process with any available ally, thereby following—and transcending—the three worlds theory.

The China of 1985, let alone of 2000, will be very different from the China of 1979 if the future her leaders envisage today materializes. The Fifth National People's Congress discussed and adopted a (back-dated) ten-year development plan for the period 1976-85. According to this plan, the country is to produce 400 million tons of grain and 60 million tons of steel per year by 1985. Agricultural output should exceed 10 percent a year. This would result in doubling industrial output even before 1985. These growth rates are high; but even during the 1966-77 period, throughout the Cultural Revolution, they were achieved in a third or so of China's 29 provinces, although at that time food management was considered a revisionist deviation, high productivity an impermissible neglect of ideology, and foreign trade toadying to foreign countries. Needless to say, all these attitudes have today been reversed.

While definitely impressive, and although they might yet be revised, these tasks (with the single exception of agriculture) are probably attainable. In addition to China's wealth of underused natural resources and the advantages of the socialist system, mentioned by Premier Hua in his speech to the National People's Congress, there are other major reserves in the economy.

Labor productivity is one. Lack of good management and assorted political distractions have helped keep its level abysmally low by any standards. This is obvious even to the lay observer who has toured a random sample of "visitable"—and thus by definition better—factories and has counted idle machines and surplus manpower. The ultimate proof of existing reserves—if one is needed—is provided by the economic indexes of the years of key political development. The year 1976 saw great turmoil, including the death of Chou En-lai, the temporary downfall of Teng Hsiao-ping, the death of Chairman Mao, the Tangshan earthquake, and the fall of the Gang of Four. In that year, production stagnated and in some cases even decreased. Hua Kuo-feng has remarked that the economy was on the verge of total collapse, and these words are taken very seriously in China. He said that the nation lost over $60 billion in industrial output and over $25 billion in state revenues between 1974 and 1976.

In the following year, during the first phases of post-Mao consolidation, industrial output picked up by a most respectable 14 percent, largely through increased productivity.[2] To a significant extent, though, this upturn had the value of making up for lost time rather than of a genuine advance.

In 1978 another decisive increase was posted. About 31 million tons of steel were produced, an increase of 28–29 percent over the 1977 level. The output of coal increased by over 20 percent. In that year the country had no obvious problems meeting the 10 percent industrial growth rate. Yet the extraordinary droughts just then were a factor in not meeting the production plan in agriculture. Although the 295 million tons of grain topped the previous year's results by 10 million tons (3.2 percent), this increase was lower than the average annual one necessary (4.8 percent) to meet the targets of the ten-year plan.

The extraordinary growth rate of industry is so far based on hidden reserves: raising low productivity, improving management, and utilization of existing capacities. These reserves are of course not endless. How far China could go before exhausting them, if the growth rate is maintained, will in the long run depend on new capital investment and construction.

The volume of capital construction is in fact anticipated to equal the total of the first 28 years after liberation. The ten-year plan counts on completing 120 large-scale projects by 1985. They will include 10 iron and steel complexes, 9 nonferrous metal complexes, 8 coal mines, 10 oil and gas fields, 30 power stations, 6 trunk railways, and 5 key harbors.

In streamlining production, and especially in constructing new capacities, China will to a considerable extent rely on foreign investment; the figure bandied about Peking is 10 percent. The development program that has been set in motion has been estimated to be worth some $600 billion. A week hardly passes without a new agreement on a capital investment complex being mentioned in the press. Thus Britain, for example, is to build a coal mine in Tatung; a consortium of Dutch firms will build a $2–3 billion coal-exporting harbor at Lien Yung Kang on the Yangtze river; four German companies will provide China with $4 billion worth of equipment and dig seven coal mines; and German companies are heavily involved also in building a $4 billion steel plant, the second largest in China, in Hopei province. The Japanese are building a $3–4 billion steel plant in Paoshan near Shanghai; and Japanese companies will also be involved in oil prospecting in the Pohai Bay, whereas American companies will participate in exploration and drilling in the South China Sea.[3]

There will be problems with this foreign involvement, and some will be touched upon below. But the fact remains that foreign participation on this scale—and the limits are as yet far from clear—will allow maintenance of the momentum of sustained growth, in accordance with the demonstration effect, that is to say, the capacity of the Chinese to disseminate and/or copy applicable features of the latest imported technology so as to improve the performance of the existing plant.

The Questions

Nevertheless, several factors call for prudence in economic forecasts.[4] Agriculture remains the mainstay of China's economy, and its problems will be more intractable than those of industry.[5] In China, 7 percent of the world's arable land feeds about one billion people. Agriculture still employs 80–85 percent of the country's population, whose standard of living is considerably lower than that of the people in the cities. Yet only so much can be done to increase agricultural production, even though the ten-year plan calls for today's annual yield of less than 300 million tons of grain to reach 400 million tons in 1985— marking a 5 percent increase each year—and 650–750 million tons by the year 2000.

There are probably reserves in labor productivity in agriculture as well, but these will be more difficult to tap than those in industry. Rural areas were always a little more immune to (though not totally isolated from) the Cultural Revolution frenzy. But the little private enterprise that had been allowed during more lenient periods was strongly discouraged, with obvious adverse effects on the peasantry's morale. Today, it is allowed again; and coupled with other measures designed to "relieve the peasants of unjustified burdens," one can expect an improvement in morale that should translate into production. These developments made a strong impression on the present writer during a 1978 tour of Szechwan province, one of China's chief granaries.

Agriculture, of course, stands as one of the main targets of modernization. Mechanization is to be one of its main facets. By 1985, 85 percent of major farm operations are to be mechanized. It is unclear, however, how mechanization per se will substantially increase the actual yields. It will release farmhands for other work but that surely is another matter. In the south, it might enable doublecropping of rice over a greater area; and in some parts of the north, especially in Heilunkiang, large tracts of virgin soil will be brought under the plough. For the greater part of rural China, though, its impact on future production is not really self-evident.

What would have a greater impact on yields is the application of chemical fertilizer and, north of the Yangtze, water. Important developments are projected in these areas too. Foreign firms have helped build 13 chemical fertilizer plants, for example, and the application of fertilizer per acre is expected to increase 58 percent by 1980. But already in 1973, chemical fertilizer accounted for 60 kilograms of nutrient per cultivated hectare, and higher usage was in many areas blocked by lack of water.

Water of course is a perennial problem. The year 1978 showed this again, with the provinces of Kiangsu and Anhwei experiencing their worst droughts on record for the last 60 and 100 years respectively. The single largest project designed to alleviate water shortage in several provinces will involve rerouting 5 percent of the waters of the Yangtze river (equal to half the flow of the Yellow River, China's second largest), which through a series of canals and lakes, locks and aqueducts, will be channeled north, some of them reaching Tientsin municipality and Hopei province.

The importance of rural development cannot be overstated. For one thing, it will have important bearings on China's foreign trade. In 1973 and 1974, and again in 1977, China imported around 7 million tons of grain a year, at the cost of $700 million–$1 billion.[6] Compared with the total production of 250–300 million tons, this is a drop in the bucket. There is an important distinction, however, between grain production and grain marketed. There is about 50 million tons of the latter, which is used to feed towns and grain-deficient areas. The imports obviously serve to complement marketed grain, and here even a few million tons make a tangible difference. The ten-year plan calls for all rural areas to be self-sufficient in grain, thus eliminating one claimant for marketed grain, and increasing the volume of grain for the market threefold. The chief beneficiary of this increase should be the urban population. But if it does not materialize, and if, nevertheless, the nutritional standards of the city dwellers are to improve in some proportion to the increase in industrial production they should bring about, the deficit will have to be made up by imports. It is not clear how great an increase in Chinese demand the world grain (and sugar) markets could accommodate, and at what prices. They would certainly be strained to some extent. For China, the cost of meeting the grain deficit could, in turn, easily amount to several billion dollars a year, diverting badly needed hard currency from more future-oriented purchases of foreign technology.

The only other alternative would, of course, be to wait even longer before improving the urban living standards—and this suggests the second potential problem for China's future. To this observer at least, the alternative seems untenable. After decades of hardship, one can no longer expect a Peking family of four, squeezed in living quarters perhaps as tiny as 100 square feet, to be forever content with a ration of eight pounds of meat and ten eggs per month; and with grain, oil, cotton, industrial goods, and often even hot showers, rationed as well. This was possible while the emphasis was on political struggle and while the awareness of the outside world was severly restricted. Now the struggle is over: "the Cultural Revolution has been victoriously concluded," beamed Chairman Hua at the Eleventh CPC Congress. The tourist traffic in China, the influx of foreign experts building various projects, the sight of overseas Chinese in their modern attire, the introduction of foreign films (much more widespread than notices in the papers indicate), and, last but not least, letters home from the thousands of Chinese that have started leaving the country to study abroad, will all function as a critical mirror. People will now be satisfied with what they have even less than before, when they were unaware of what people had. elsewhere. One already senses an undercurrent: a gradual broadening of interest from affairs of state to the affairs of the kitchen.

Additionally, the Tien An Men incident of 1976 wonderfully vindicated mass spontaneous action, something which with sufficient provocation may conceivably reappear. The present leadership of the country thus cannot ignore the low standard of living any longer without courting the danger of something like a Poland in the winter of 1970.

The third question mark about the future concerns the leadership itself. Ever since the extremist ringleaders, the Gang of Four, were purged in October 1976, a broad campaign has been under way to remove from positions of power those people who had been under their sway. The process has been a protracted one and is only now coming to a close. The thousands of purged officials represent a considerable potential force, resentful of the present leaders.

There are two other groups that have grounds for anxiety. One consists of the several thousands of middle-level managers and bureaucrats who owe their jobs to political patronage rather than to professional ability. Many of them realize their inability to meet the more stringent demands that the modernization drive must put on management, and that they could lose their jobs—be discharged, perhaps, by the very workers subordinate to them now, whose own participation in management will have increased. They perceive, rightly, the new developments as threatening and are digging their heels in.

Finally, there are millions of the Red Guard generation: people in their twenties and early thirties who spent their university years in the fierce political debates and fights of the Cultural Revolution—but who in the process were cheated out of an education. They are now being leapfrogged by their juniors who have the superior educational opportunities that have opened up only recently and that include, for the very best, studying abroad. True, even the Red Guard generation has ever increasing opportunities for extramural study, and advancement is based on knowledge no matter how it is acquired. But self-study, evening courses, TV courses, and so forth, require much more self-discipline, and at a period of life when time itself is at a premium. Thus here is another considerable group of people who, even while generally applauding the new emphasis on performance in the national economy, cannot but feel bitter over the years they lost and will never be able to make up. In particular, the millions among them who were sent down to the countryside will be eager to get back into the action, which is in the town. During the Spring Festival of 1979, they demonstrated their considerable force.

Any major change in the top leadership—occasioned, for example, by the death of Teng Hsiao-ping who after all is in his mid-70s—thus might throw open the question of whither China. An appeal to the three constituencies of unreconstructed party hacks, incompetent managers, and disgruntled former Red Guards might conceivably allow a pretender seeking to change the emphasis on modernization to make his move. Such a move would meet with fierce opposition and would in all likelihood fail; but in the slight chance that it succeeded, if only in the short run, the curve of steady growth projected for the country's future would be shaken up again.

Despite the existing question marks, it would be incorrect to extrapolate China's history of political turmoil into the future without examining its causes. The turmoil was often initiated by Mao himself in the extraordinary attempts to regain the power over the party which during the early 1960s he had largely lost to the likes of Teng Hsiao-ping. The suffering of the people as a result was unimaginable, and they themselves would deter any adventurer from trying again. The leadership today is doing its best to inspire confidence in the future, and this is not always easy with a people that had often turned cautious or cynical. But in so doing, the leadership is casting an increasingly critical light on the past 20 years. The *People's Daily* has discussed the whole period since 1958 as having been replete with subjectivistic errors, such as "specious communism, exaggerated achievements, setting targets that were too high, and issuing wild orders to try to realize them."[7]

The lessons of those years have been exceedingly bitter. It would be imprudent, not to say condescending, to assume that China has not learned them.

SOVIET UNION: THE ODD MAN OUT

The second axis of China's foreign policy concerns the Soviet Union. The bitter enmity between the two countries has now lasted twenty years. During this time, it has proved to be the most consistent feature of China's external relations. Her relations with every other country, from Albania to the United States, have gone through shifts and switches, sometimes by 180 degrees; but vis-à-vis the Soviet Union, such changes as have occurred have almost all been in one direction only—deterioration.

The rift has persisted throughout all the changes in China's leadership. Differences started germinating at the time of the Great Leap Forward in 1958, which was Mao's brainchild, and broke into the open in 1960 when the Soviets abruptly cut off all aid and withdrew their technicians. Liu Shao-chi was in firm control then. In 1966 the Cultural Revolution erupted, and Liu soon found himself under fierce attack. The street with the Soviet Embassy was renamed Antirevisionist Struggle Street. In 1969, the two powers clashed on the Ussuri river, and Defense Minister Lin Piao soared to what two years later turned out to be neck-breaking heights. The Chinese allege that he was killed in an aircrash in September 1971 when trying to flee the country for the Soviet Union. This is perhaps the only official suggestion that any of the leaders might have wanted to change China's anti-Soviet orientation.[8]

It never did change. Contrary to the forecasts of some pundits, the anti-Soviet edge of China's foreign policy remained as sharp as ever even after the death of the founding fathers, and after the purge of the Gang of Four in 1976.

In no way can the Sino-Soviet split now be considered a passing phenomenon. On the contrary, with the benefit of hindsight it is actually necessary to reinterpret the decade of the 1950s, the period of cooperation between the two countries, as something of an aberration. During their 300-year history, Sino-Russian intergovernmental relations have been hostile as a rule, friendly as an exception.[9]

These relations are today worse than ever, China feels directly threatened by the Soviet forces stationed on the common border of the two countries and in Mongolia. After the invasion of Czechoslovakia in 1968, their strength rapidly increased to reach today's 44 divisions. That invasion helped transform Chinese opposition to the Soviet Union into the very centerpiece of the country's foreign policy. After the years of hostility toward all powers in the region, from India to Japan to the United States, China at that time started gradually shifting gears. The result was the "ping-pong diplomacy" and the unprecedented opening to the whole world, which was given a quasi-theoretical expression in the so-called "three worlds theory." The Soviet Union is presented here as the sworn enemy not only of China but of the whole world.

The Three Worlds Theory

The theory was outlined by Teng Hsiao-ping at the United Nations General Assembly session in 1974 but was elaborated in detail only in November 1978, as a peculiar Chinese contribution to the sixtieth anniversary of the Russian October Revolution.[10] In some respects, it has been overtaken by the pace of Chinese diplomacy; it is still, however, regularly referred to as the basis of China's foreign policy, and it will therefore not be amiss to present its main points.

The first world, as designated here, consists of superpowers. Only two countries have ever achieved superpower status: the United States and the Soviet Union. The distinctive features of a superpower are these:

> Its state apparatus is controlled by monopoly capital in its most concentrated form, and it relies on its far greater economic and military power than other countries have to exploit, oppress and control other countries; each superpower is after exclusive world

hegemony, and to this end is frantically preparing for another new world war.

China is too weak to aspire for superpower status: but Chinese leaders repeatedly emphasize that even after the country achieves its modernization goals and becomes a socialist power in its own right, it will never be a superpower, that is, it will never try to subjugate other countries and prepare for war.

Of the two superpowers, the Soviet Union is "the more ferocious, the more reckless, the more treacherous. It is the most dangerous source of world war." This is the result of at least four different historical conditions.

First, the Soviet Union had to catch up with the United States and is therefore more aggressive and adventurous. To attain global supremacy it has to try and wrest various areas of the world from U.S. control. Meanwhile, the United States "has overreached itself and all it can do at present is to strive to protect its vested interests." Its overall strategy is defensive whereas the Soviet Union is on the offensive.

Second, the Soviet economy is by far inferior to that of the United States. The Soviet Union therefore must rely predominantly on its military power and on threats of war in order to expand. Every statistic confirms that the expansion of Soviet armed forces has been much more rapid than that of U.S. forces.

Third, the Soviet Union features a "state-monopoly capitalist economy" unequaled in any other country. State power has degenerated into a "fascist dictatorship." "It is therefore easier for Soviet social-imperialism to put the entire economy on a military footing and militarize the whole state apparatus." Soviet political socialization imbues the people with values of militarism and Great Russian chauvinism, extolling expansions of the past to justify those of the present.

And finally, Soviet social-imperialism is the result of "the degeneration of the first socialist country of the world." Among various left-wing parties and countries it still has a certain legitimacy, derived from the prestige of Lenin. Its aggression is always couched in terms of "meeting internationalist obligations," "supporting national liberation movements," and so forth.

The main force in the struggle against imperialism, colonialism and hegemonism is the third world. The concept of the Third World as understood in the west usually includes developing countries. China's concept is similar but not identical. For China, the third world includes developing countries, but also socialist countries; socialist, that is, according to Chinese evaluation and thus excluding those countries under Soviet sway. The two categories largely overlap: China and

North Korea, for example, are both socialist and developing. Yugoslavia and Romania, however, which are both socialist countries even by Chinese standards, have definitely transcended their earlier less developed character but are still classified as members of the third world. And China will continue to consider herself a member even after she becomes powerful and developed.

Governments of the third world come of course in every hue of the political spectrum, from true revolutionaries to outright agents of social-imperialism. By and large, however, they together still constitute the main force of opposition against imperialism and hegemonism, or so at least the Chinese argue.

A theory is a theory, with its inevitable generalizations. When it comes to concrete foreign policy which deals with countries individually, one might expect that the different regimes of the third world would be accorded different treatment; that China could, for example, allow distinction between revolutionary and reactionary regimes. But in fact, only outright "agents of social-imperialism," that is, Cuba and Vietnam, are singled out and villified. All other countries, no matter what their domestic policies, are invited to be friends with China.

The second world countries are "in between": nations of Western Europe and Japan, that is, the industrial countries of both East and West, except for the superpowers. They are said to have a dual character. On the one hand, these countries are also involved in exploiting the third world. On the other hand, second world countries are themselves exposed to superpower bullying and control. In actual practice, this fact is by far the most important. The greatest threat to the second world also comes from the Soviet Union.

And what is the world supposed to do, faced as it is with the threat of Soviet hegemonism and of a new war? The three worlds theory outlines three main tasks: First, warn people of the world of the danger of war. It would help, of course, if a socialist revolution broke out in America and the Soviet Union, but even China does not really expect one. Thus in the last analysis, they will end up settling their ever increasing competition on the battlefield. Any other analysis, including efforts at promoting détente, is just so much wishful thinking.

Second, people should fight to put off the outbreak of war. In their war preparations, the superpowers "are bound to encroach upon the sovereignty and interests of other countries" and thus aggravate their conflicts with these countries. Not always will they end up on top, and the setbacks they will inevitably experience will upset their war timetable. War can thus be postponed.

In the light of the assertion that the outbreak of war can be postponed, the entire thesis of war's inevitability assumes a rather different meaning. I think this thesis should not be interpreted as though China believed war to be as inevitable as tomorrow's daybreak. Rather, it is in the same category as other Marxian predictions which their authors consider scientific, even though they are practically unverifiable. Thus equally inevitable, according to the Chinese, is the eventual victory of communism the world over, or the disappearance of differences between nations. These events may take hundreds of years to come about; but who will ever take their authors to task if they don't?

With the allegedly forthcoming war, the same thing holds true. If it breaks out, the prediction is confirmed. But as long as it does not, it proves that the people of the world have been successfully waging their struggle to postpone its outbreak, which still must come—sometime. One has the sense that emphasis on the war's inevitability has been decreasing in China, as indeed it should, for such an emphasis could actually lead to a rather defeatist attitude: "What's the point of economic construction when the coming war will destroy everything anyway?" The rising skyline of Peking belies the talk of a coming war as being increasingly ritualistic. The country counts on living in peace, at least until the end of the century.

The third task for the present is all-out opposition to détente, or what China refers to as the policy of appeasement. If there is one thing that will not curb Soviet expansion, the Chinese say, it is efforts to accommodate it. Instead, it is necessary to forge as broad an alliance as possible against the two hegemonist powers.

The three worlds theory represented a very considerable shift from China's foreign policy of previous years. During the sixties, for example, China still considered her conflict with the United States to be at least as serious as the one with the Soviet Union, and found herself virtually encircled by hostile or at least unfriendly powers. China was opposed to all pro-U.S. regimes and she promoted revolutionary forces in various countries. The emphasis on the imminent world revolution that would "defeat U.S. imperialism and its running dogs" has now disappeared—in part because U.S. imperialism was in fact defeated in Indochina.

The three worlds theory still calls for struggle against both of the superpowers; but, in reality, very few are the instances when American policy is still denounced today. For all practical purposes, China is ready to include the United States with the countries of the third and the second world in a common front directed against that enemy of the whole world, the Soviet Union. The shift culminated with the U.S.-Chinese communique on normalization. Both countries foreswore any hegemonist intentions—an extraordinary thing for a supposedly hege-monist power (the United States) to do. And it was just as extraordinary for China to accept this pledge at face value; it is a stance that the three worlds theory would, strictly speaking, not consider possible.

A similar shift is noticeable with respect to second world countries. Though they are supposed to have a dual character, one side of which is evil, never does the Peking press talk about them critically. The facet of their being a (minor) oppressor of the third world is entirely disre-garded.

Thus while the three worlds theory amounted to a major step in reorienting China's foreign policy from one of enemies all to one that singles out the two superpowers as enemies, practical diplomacy of the late 1970s has gone even further, focusing on a single target. For all practical purposes, the three worlds theory has become outmoded, barely a year after it was enunciated in any detail, and replaced by the simplest "world is good, Soviet Union is bad" approach.

This shift in China's foreign policy can be formulated in other words too. The simple East-West, communist-imperialist (or free world, if you wish) division of the world no longer pertains. Every country has to become aware of this and draw the right conclusions. What is necessary is a large-scale restructuring of world alliances. The Western camp has to realize that the Communist bloc, its former adversary, is split right down the middle into two exceedingly hostile camps. One of these, the Soviet Union, remains the West's implacable enemy, no matter how sweetly it talks. The other, China, is the West's ally, no matter what memories of the past still haunt the present.

Unreconstructed anticommunists and diehard conservatives are, therefore, preferable to sophisticated liberals. The anticommunist has at least preserved his healthy skepticism about the Soviet Union. The conservative is suspicious of détente, and quite rightly; for détente, far from leading to a peaceful world order, is in fact a fiction—a shortcut to war. That the anticommunist and the conservative are opposed to China as well is an unfortunate carryover from the past; one which, since it is so unfounded, will in time pass: especially with study of the three worlds theory.

If China can ally herself with the West and with the third world, and if the third world does not divide into progressive and reactionary camps (despite the Soviet efforts here), the Soviet Union will end up isolated. That, argues China, is the only way to prevent it from launching a war and the only way to establish a peaceful world order. This in other words amounts to a policy of containment—which in practical diplomacy China is doing her utmost to promote.

JAPAN: PARTNERSHIP FOR THE FUTURE

In Asia as elsewhere, China tries to make friends with almost all countries, no matter what their political system, to broaden the anti-Soviet front or at least to prevent the expansion of Soviet influence.[11] With Japan, she tries harder.

Japan occupies a privileged position. It is Asia's only second world country. Economically, China and Japan are two different worlds. Yet for a thousand years, China has represented a civilization that the Japanese have looked up to and freely borrowed from; this is an often repeated truism. Now, it might be China's turn to look up to and borrow from Japan's century of experience with modernization.

In 1972, Japan recovered from one of President Nixon's "shokkus" with exemplary resilience. Soon after Nixon signed the Shanghai Communique, Japan went a step further and, in September 1972, established diplomatic relations with China. Several other agreements followed. Virtually overnight, China dropped the attributes of imperialist and militarist that customarily used to be hurled at Japan.

Japan was caught in a delicate balancing act. Normalizing relations with China was natural and normal. Nevertheless, in the light of the Sino-Soviet dispute it was bound to affect Japan's relations with the Soviet Union as well. At least since 1969, the latter had been interested in creating a so-called Asian collective security system: a network of bilateral treaties that would bind Asian countries loosely with the Soviet Union, directed essentially against China. Sino-Japanese diplomatic relations dispelled any lingering hopes that this concept could get off the ground.

The Soviet case was not helped at all by its refusal to discuss—and often even to acknowledge—Japan's outstanding territorial claims to its northern territories, four tiny islands north of Hokkaido, that the Soviet Union has been occupying since the end of World War II. China, by contrast, earned easy points by vociferously and unequivocally supporting that claim.

The Sino-Japanese declaration of 1972 not only normalized relations between the two countries but also called for a peace and friendship treaty to be negotiated between them. Such a treaty was expected to formally seal the wounds of the past decades of animosity and hostility. This action would leave the Soviet Union as Japan's only major former adversary without a peace settlement. And most significantly, the treaty would open up a new perspective for the future, especially in economic ventures. Japan's domestic political issues were one reason why negotiations of what seemed a fairly straightforward document took many years and in 1975 actually broke down. A second significant reason was that China insisted on inserting a so-called antihegemony clause: a formulation that for the first time in diplomatic history would explicitly include this three worlds theory concept in a treaty. Because of its barely concealed anti-Soviet orientation, Japanese politicians found it difficult to accept the clause.

Only in 1978 were negotiations resumed and the treaty eventually concluded—complete with the clause in question. The final text included another article specifying that the treaty is not directed against any other nation. Each party can thus interpret it pretty much as it wants: with China emphasizing that everybody knows the only hegemonist is the Soviet Union, and Japan saying that the clause is just as much a Chinese commitment not to seek hegemony herself.

The wording is otherwise very innocuous and general; and if one were to consider only its letter, the treaty would appear as little more than an exercise in symbolism.[12] The treaty partners see it as more, however. It is the cornerstone for an all-around future partnership. China, for example, was for a long time not prepared even to discuss any long-term economic arrangements with Japan before concluding the treaty, just as Japan shies away from such cooperation with the Soviet Union until the northern territories issue is settled.

In February 1978, though, economic experts of the two countries signed a $20 billion trade agreement for 1978–85. According to this agreement, China will export oil and coal to Japan and import industrial plants, technology, and building material. Apart from the Paoshan steelworks near Shanghai, mentioned earlier, Japan will expand and modernize the Anshan and Wuhan steelworks, build a copper smelter, four petrochemical plants, a facility to manufacture synthetic leather, and a plant for color TV tubes. Other projects are under discussion.[13]

For Japan, the significance of this trade agreement is obvious. The country is in dire need of diversifying its oil supplies. Chinese oil from the Tach'ing oil field has a high paraffin content, and this would make necessary the construction of additional refining facilities in Japan; but other oil, for example from newly tapped fields in the north of Kwangtung province, is very light. By 1985, Japan will be importing 40–50 million tons of crude annually.

The main beneficiary in Japan seems to be the steel industry, whose exports to China may end up topping those to the United States (7 million tons). The big new China market might help alleviate some of the problems Japan is experiencing in trade relations with the United States and with Western Europe. Exports to China, coupled with the ripple effect inside Japan, might provide the necessary stimulus to put the country's economy on an even keel.

If the trade agreement of February 1978 seemed impressive, its subsequent expansion was no less than amazing. Soon after the Sino-Japanese Peace and Friendship Treaty was signed, the agreement was extended until 1990, and expanded from $20 to $90 billion.

No less important are the political ramifications of the treaty. It expresses a substantial commitment of the two countries to each other, a foundation for generations of peace between two former adversaries and a piece of the groundwork for a new Pacific system in which the two countries will play an active and leading role.

In this system, the United States, Japan, and China will eventually be linked together much more closely than they are today. Mr. Ohira might well intend to promote his "multidirectional diplomacy" and wish to be friendly with both China and the Soviet Union. However, it will turn out to be easier to go in some directions than in others. In the long run, the logic of things will gradually nudge him ever closer to China. His protestations that the friendship treaty is not directed against the Soviet Union might even be sincere. But should Japan wish to embark, say, on some new cooperative project in developing Siberia, the Chinese will be sure to indicate that this would amount to aiding its enemy in a critical area and not be considered friendly.

But then, Japan faces the same danger as China does, according to Peking. This is how the three worlds theory puts it:

> The massive Soviet military buildup in the Far East, aimed as it is at China, is directed also against the United States and Japan. . . . The Soviet Union thus constitutes a growing threat to Japan and is intensifying its infiltration of the country.[14]

And yet Japan's military might is quite incommensurate with its economic stature. China has repeatedly stressed that she would like to see a Japan with stronger military forces. Self-defense capabilities and militarization are two entirely different things, the Chinese argue. In a similar vein (and in another shift from past positions), China argues that Japan must maintain its most important relationship with the United States, relations with China itself coming second. Statements, for example, of the Japanese opposition Socialist Party, that Japan should dissolve the security alliance with the United States are viewed in Peking with scorn; this would, however, turn into alarm if that party were any closer to power. It is symptomatic of Peking's view of the Pacific security system that the Chinese press spoke approvingly of the establishment of a Japanese National Committee for Japan-United States-China Friendship.[15]

Its goals are to promote and popularize the significance of the Sino-Japanese friendship treaty and of the Shanghai Communique. If it were up to the Chinese, a third document would undoubtedly have been included—the U.S.-Japan security pact.

INDOCHINA: A SETBACK

Southeast Asia today is still one of the world's greatest trouble areas, as it was ten years ago. After a blitz attack by 14 divisions with 100,000 men, Vietnam in January 1979 effectively conquered Kampuchea (formerly known as Cambodia) and installed a regime of its own liking.

About one year before that, on December 31, 1977, Democratic Kampuchea severed diplomatic relations with Vietnam, and its government issued a statement addressed to "all friends, near and far." It revealed that the country had been involved in a conflict with Vietnam virtually since the first days of the new Kampuchean regime in April 1975, and that in September 1977 this conflict erupted into a major conflagration. In this and in following statements, Kampuchea outlined a longtime pattern of alleged Vietnamese attempts to control all of Indochina in one way or another. The last of these statements was a "black book," issued as Pnompenh was falling, in which Kampuchea traced these Vietnamese designs back to the fifteenth century.[16] At least since the war against the French, Vietnam was interested in creating an Indochinese federation; Ho Chi Minh even floated the idea to Chinese leaders—who at the time were noncommittal. Kampuchea argued that (even before the blitz) the armed clashes between the two countries amounted to Vietnamese aggression against Kampuchea, aimed at furthering that old project. Vietnam denied this, declaring that, first, it was the Kampucheans whose rabid xenophobia and nationalism were responsible for the outbreak of hostilities; and second, that the federation idea had long been discarded. Nevertheless, in the same breath they talked about a special relationship binding the three Indochinese countries as a consequence of their previous common protracted struggles.[17]

It is unclear just what this special relationship was supposed to mean. Laos, for instance, is today barely more than a Vietnamese protectorate. Now that Vietnam has installed an even more docile regime in Kampuchea as well, the Indochinese federation idea is obviously alive and well, in fact if not in name.

Sino-Vietnamese Tensions

In 1978, during the first weeks of the Kampuchean-Vietnamese conflict, China maintained a degree of impartiality, publishing statements of both sides in her press. China even offered to mediate. However, the extraordinary reception the Kampuchean prime minister, Pol Pot, had been accorded during his September 1977 visit to Peking made it quite clear which of the belligerent parties had China's real sympathy. This could hardly have come as a surprise. During the 1970s, the prospect of a Vietnamese-led Indochinese federation was no longer one that China viewed noncommittally: it had become an anathema to her, just as it was to Kampuchea. While for the latter and especially its rulers, it was a question of life and death; for China it was a question of paramount strategic importance.

The point was straightforward: Vietnam had changed. No longer was it a revolutionary ally. Ho Chi Minh was dead; the war against the United States had been won, and the country had been unified—faster than even China had expected. Hanoi had completely eliminated the one-time National Liberation Front of South Vietnam. While the war lasted, Vietnam had maintained a studied neutrality in the Sino-Soviet rift. The help of both sides was essential for the war effort, and Vietnamese leaders did their utmost not to antagonize either side. Once the war ended, however, some well-known pro-Peking personalities of the Hanoi leadership faded out of sight; and while Vietnam had only praise for the Soviet Union, its press attacked Peking by innuendo, through historical parables. These signals were not lost on the Chinese. China in turn cut down on aid—which had been dispensed quite generously during the war (the Chinese talk about $10 billion worth of wartime assistance)—and in July 1978 cut it off altogether.

Any Indochinese federation under the leadership of Vietnam would have thus been under the leadership of an increasingly pro-Soviet Vietnam. The Soviet Union itself would of course delight in such a turn of events and sooner or later would include such an entity in its own anti-Chinese considerations. China had to do her level best to prevent this from happening, lest she found herself in something of a Soviet noose, or really pincers, with the Soviet forces to the north and Soviet-supported Vietnamese forces to the south of the country. Vietnam's military machine is Asia's third largest, with vast combat experience and with some relatively modern American hardware at its disposal, probably better than a lot China has, the lack of spare parts notwithstanding. China therefore supported the Kampuchean regime as best she could, short of outright military involvement.

Logically, China would have come out in support of any country menaced by Vietnam. While ideological affinity certainly played a role in China's support of Kampuchea, it was strategic considerations that compelled her to back Pol Pot's regime—a regime that resembled

Jonestown, Guyana, more than today's China and that the Chinese privately characterized as being unwholesome.[18]

To further heighten tensions between the two countries, one more source of conflict surfaced at this time. In May 1978 a leading official in Peking mentioned how disturbed the government was over the massive exodus of ethnic Chinese from Vietnam. After a few months, China closed the border to unauthorized returnees—but not before 160,000 people had already poured in. The reasons for this exodus were unclear, and the contrasting claims of the two sides are both unsatisfactory. Vietnam claimed that people were leaving after the expropriation of private commerce in the south of the country, which had been egged on by rumors of a possible war, allegedly spread by the Chinese embassy in Hanoi. Yet an overwhelming majority of the repatriates originated from the north of Vietnam, not the south, and why China would be interested in fomenting such rumors is anybody's guess. China on the other hand claimed that ethnic Chinese were being victimized in Vietnam and were fleeing persecution; and while there definitely is evidence of stricter, indeed discriminatory, control by Vietnamese authorities, instances of brutal treatment in Vietnam proper (as opposed to clashes on the border) were few and far between. The Vietnamese at any rate deny these charges altogether. In fact, while they recognize the presence of more than 1 million ethnically Chinese citizens of Vietnam, they deny the Chinese claims that most of them are citizens of China.

The story behind the conflicting citizenship claims is rather complex and not particularly relevant to this paper. The whole issue has been blown out of proportion, and could be settled in a relatively painless way if this were the only problem between the two countries. It is significant, though, that on the citizenship issue, Vietnam is reneging on a position it had maintained before unification: twenty years ago it denounced and declared illegal Ngo Dinh Diem's forcible Vietnamization of Chinese in South Vietnam. Other cases of such reversals exist, and they do not help Vietnam's credibility. They concern, for example, Vietnam's position vis-à-vis the islands in the South China Sea, claimed by both Vietnam and China, and its border with Kampuchea.[19] Vietnam generally argues that its earlier stance was dictated by the exigencies of war and that, with the war ended now, it feels no longer bound by its word.

After Chinese pressures on Vietnam intensified, Vietnam joined the Council for Mutual Economic Assistance (COMECON) and signed a friendship treaty of some military implication with the Soviet Union. One might ask whether the pressure has not actually been counterproductive. However, as mentioned above, the two countries can surely read each other's signals better than the West can. China probably came to the conclusion that nothing would stop Vietnam's drift into the Soviet orbit, and simply decided to cut her losses.

The Soviet-Vietnamese friendship treaty clearly has a military side to it. One may assume, for example, that it opens the door of the Cam Ranh Bay military installations to the Soviets, Vietnam's protestations to the contrary notwithstanding. China at least considers Soviet use of it as an accomplished fact. Her press has pointed out that, as a result,

> the Kremlin's base of operations has moved from Vladivostok more than 2,000 nautical miles southwestward. Accordingly, its Pacific Fleet had been steadily reinforced to a total tonnage of 1.25 million, compared with 700,000 in 1965. The fleet, made up of over 750 ships of different types, has far outnumbered the US Seventh Fleet.[20]

The immediate import of the treaty was manifestly directed against Kampuchea. The Chinese point out that when the Soviet Union signed a similar treaty with India in 1971, it allowed that country to engage Pakistan in the war of Bangladesh—a pattern that Vietnam merely repeated with respect to Kampuchea. Even if this was the limited immediate objective of the treaty, its long-term implications are definitely disquieting. It shows that the Soviet Union, conscious of China's intentions of isolating it, will use all its power to do the same to China. As for Indochina, it has already succeeded.

Thus the basic contours of the Sino-Soviet rivalry are traced out in Indochina as well. Nowhere else in the world do the interests of the two Communist adversaries clash so close to home, and nowhere else is their conflict so menacing for China. The Sino-Soviet division line is, however, superimposed in Indochina over an intricate matrix of historical loyalties and enmities. For two thousand years Vietnam has fought China, and Kampuchea has fought Vietnam for five hundred years. (The Kampucheans even call the Mekong delta Kampuchea Khrom, or South Kampuchea.) During the Indochinese wars, Indochina as a whole was pitted against a succession of foreign intruders: the Japanese, the French, the Americans. During this time, the underlying historical fissures were camouflaged (or papered over) in the higher interests of the common struggle. But China is an old power on the Indochinese scene in her own right, and so the Sino-Soviet conflict has rather easily accommodated itself along the traditional division lines which have resurfaced. Vietnam naturally allies itself with whoever is against China, Kampuchea with whoever is against Vietnam.

Sino-Vietnamese enmity reached a new high in early 1979. Friction between the two countries had gone through cycles of abortive negotiations, border clashes, and protest notes. In June 1978, China closed Vietnamese consulates in the country after Vietnam had been reluctant to grant reciprocal privileges. The propaganda barrage between the two countries was unrelenting. China stopped all her aid to Vietnam and recalled her technicians; but unlike the situation in 1960 when the Soviet Union acted in a similar way toward China, the Chinese did not even press for repayment. In early 1979 a border war broke out.

For several years, skirmishes on the border were becoming more frequent.[21] China insisted that they were taking place on her side of the border, and that Vietnamese personnel were responsible for them. China had held her fire, in an effort to go the last mile in solving the outstanding problems peacefully. In the second half of 1978, however, she was regularly issuing protest notes to Vietnam, punctiliously detailing the circumstances of every incident. Notes were issued almost every week, and every one contained a final clause warning Vietnam of its responsibility for the possible consequences of its provocations.

The consequences came on February 17, 1979. Right after Teng Hsiao-ping returned from the United States, China decided to counterattack Vietnam with the massive forces she had been assembling in the border region over the preceding months. The counterattack was to be limited in space, time and scope, and in many ways was to be a repeat of the 1962 strike against India. It was a businesslike operation; accordingly, Peking displayed no jingoism, no mass meetings, no war hysteria.

Over the next two or three weeks, the Chinese took three Vietnamese provincial capitals and another score or so villages and strategic points. This done, China announced that the limited objectives of the punitive strike had been accomplished and on March 5 started withdrawing her troops. The process was completed on March 16, a month after the counterattack started, although Vietnam claimed that China had not in fact withdrawn totally.

Consequences and Implications

Militarily, the conflict ended undecisively. The final test of strength never came: Vietnam refused to engage its regular troops which were saved for a defense of Hanoi that was never necessary, and countered the People's Liberation Army (PLA) only with its armed militia and local army units. China could claim she gained what she had wanted—and since that was never spelled out in the first place, the claim was beyond challenge. Vietnam, on the other hand, could enter another chapter into its glorious history of struggle against foreigners and argue that if the Chinese left, it was because of their own stiff resistance.

In the last analysis, however, the strike was as much a diplomatic effort as a military one. Diplomatically, China did not emerge unscathed, but definitely seemed to have made most of the opportunity.

To say the least, Vietnam's feathers were ruffled. While it considers itself the world's third military power, Vietnam did not manage to prevent an incursion into its own territory, for whatever reasons. "The myth of Vietnam's invincibility has been shattered," crowed the Peking press.

The Soviet Union attacked China forcefully—but only in words. It probably lost some of its credibility with its other client regimes in the Third World. As China's incursion demonstrated, the Vietnamese-Soviet pact did not guarantee unconditional military support for Vietnam, and as such it differs from pacts between the Soviet Union and countries of Eastern Europe. The superpower seemed utterly powerless to soften the blow Vietnam was getting; though Vietnam, on the other hand, might have preferred not to rely on the Soviet cushion.

Nevertheless, there was an element of risk involved on China's part. China never could have been absolutely sure that her calculations of the Soviet reaction were correct. The Chinese leadership was prepared for the possibility of a stronger Soviet reaction. Teng Hsiaoping himself told Senator Jackson that 300,000 people had been evacuated from sensitive areas in Sinkiang, and some areas in Heilunkiang in the Northeast were evacuated as well, according to the talk of Peking.

Another lesson was taught to the West. Explicitly or by innuendo, the Chinese press contrasted the forceful stance of Peking in dealing with the "Cuba of the East" to the nonexistent response of most Western nations to the original Cuba's adventurism in Africa and elsewhere. This forceful stance was presented as the only real and worthwhile alternative to the toothless process of detente.

Resurrecting the issue of Kampuchea, diplomatically almost dormant at the time of China's incursion, was another objective in which China succeeded admirably. China never specifically linked her own action against Vietnam with that country's invasion of Kampuchea. Her eventual withdrawal, for example, was never conditioned by a similar Vietnamese withdrawal. Yet the two foci of war were connected both in press commentaries and in diplomatic efforts. In the United Nations, China welcomed all initiatives that would link the two issues, and supported a Security Council resolution that called for the withdrawal of all foreign troops from all countries concerned—thus forcing the Soviet Union into a corner from which it could escape only by using its veto. The new Kampuchean regime's drive for international respectability slowed down noticeably. India, which after the fall of Pnompenh had expressed its readiness to extend diplomatic recognition virtually for the asking, disagreed with the Soviet Union on the issue when

Premier Kosygin visited that country in March 1979. And the loyalist guerrillas might have gotten a new lease on life when Vietnam was forced to withdraw at least some units from Kampuchea.

There was a debit side to China's counterattack as well. Its obvious resemblance to the 1962 Chinese drive into India dealt a stinging blow to the uneasy process of Sino-Indian reconciliation. To add insult to injury, it was launched just as Indian Foreign Minister Vajpayee was travelling in China, which he consequently left in a huff. And Laos which hitherto had been sitting on the ever more uncomfortable fence between China and Vietnam fell conclusively into the Soviet-Vietnamese camp. The Indochinese federation, which China had tried to forestall through every means, is now turning into a reality. It will be led, however, by a Vietnam that is weakened, chastened, and more isolated than ever.

SOUTH ASIA: EFFORTS

South Asia consists of a remarkable collection of Third World countries. Any doubts that the entire concept of a "third world" might be too broad and thus not very useful (doubts that the Chinese, however, do not seem to share) will be reinforced here.

Strategically, this is one of the world's most sensitive areas. In the nineteenth century, Britain controlled a series of outposts here, which linked the home country with the Indian Empire and Hongkong further on. The Soviet Union might be viewed as attempting to establish something similar: not perhaps to exploit a particular country but to further its entire global strategy.

At the end of 1978, a hard-nosed sober review of Soviet activities appeared in the Chinese press.[22] It detailed Moscow's activities in the area during that year and offered an overall picture of its southward thrust. This thrust, the commentary noted, is aimed at a strategic breakthrough from Soviet Central Asia to the Indian Ocean, "thereby outflanking Western Europe and menacing East Asia." That would enable the Soviet Union "to turn eastward and meet its southwestward advance from its Far Eastern territories halfway." The thrust is intended "to undermine the U.S. position in the West Pacific, threaten the oil supply to Japan and to encircle China." In addition, it would "facilitate [the Soviet] move to the West and combine with Soviet gains in the Middle East and Africa." The Soviet Union would then gain control over passages from the Indian Ocean to the Mediterranean and to Europe.

But how can this Soviet threat be thwarted? The united front concept that the Chinese advocate would presumably lead to the forming of a strong chain of countries that would contain Soviet expansion. The idea is a very difficult one to carry out though. Obviously, the chain is only as strong as its weakest link. It would suffice for the Soviet Union to break it in one place, and the entire containment strategy would end in shambles.

The Soviets, for example, offered the Republic of the Maldives a pitiful sum of $1 million for use of the Gan military base left behind by the British. The Maldive government refused the offer; but it is impossible to ensure that every government will at all times be immune to Soviet offers, and there is not much that China can do about it.

She tries. Her answer to the problem is to cultivate friendship with all regimes in power, hoping that this will discourage pro-Soviet tendencies in the present and future governing units. In 1978 China established diplomatic relations with Oman and Jordan, and such ties with Saudi Arabia might follow in 1979. But it is the right-wing, authoritarian governments that are most likely to be anti-Soviet, and which thus enjoy China's support. Regardless of how corrupt a country's regime may be, regardless of how beneficial a profound change would be for the country's people, forces that seek such changes are generally considered suspect until they prove themselves innocent; for there is never any guarantee that a new regime will not be more pro-Soviet. And indeed, such suspicions were dramatically borne out in 1978 by the coups in South Yemen and Afghanistan, after which both countries turned into virtual Soviet outposts.

By supporting every regime in power just because it is in power, China lays herself open to charges of supporting the world's Chiang Kai-sheks. When the local strongman is overthrown, the insurgents have often one reason less for friendship with China. Sometimes, China finds herself in an outright embarrassing spot: the first noncommunist country that Hua Kuo-feng chose to visit was Iran, even then embroiled in the civil strife which has since engulfed the whole country and driven the Shah, that old friend of China, into exile.

This then is one of the main weaknesses of the three worlds theory: inability to offer a precept for opposition to Soviet hegemonism that would be compatible with social and political change within the members of the united front that China is trying to forge.

Of China's relations with her non-Communist southern neighbors, those with India and the Association of Southeast Asian Nations deserve special mention.

China and India

China's relations with India have been at a low ebb at least since the border war between the two countries in 1962. It bears noting that today, aside from the Soviet Union and Vietnam, India is the only country with which China has a major border problem. Since the early 1960s, the Chinese have perceived India as a link in the chain of hostile countries that surround them. Their friendship with Pakistan can at least partly be viewed as a counterbalance to their testy relations with India. The 1971 war of Bangladesh increased Chinese suspicions. If the United States in that conflict "tilted" toward Pakistan, in Henry Kissinger's memorable utterance, then China positively leaned over. In the belief that Bangladesh would turn out to be an outright Indian puppet, she even took the unusual step of vetoing its UN membership. (Once it became clear that these fears were unfounded, relations between China and Bangladesh quickly improved, and during his 1978 trip to that country, Teng Hsiao-ping talked about traditional friendship between them without the slightest embarrassment.)

China's suspicions about India were exacerbated by the Indo-Soviet Peace and Friendship Treaty which was signed before the Bangladesh war. It was one of the first such treaties (to which similar ones with Afghanistan and Vietnam, among Asian countries, were added in 1978), and China viewed it as an ominous sign that the Soviet Union had merely repackaged its "Asian collective security system."

The final affront, in China's eyes, was the incorporation in 1975 of Sikkim, a semi-independent buffer kingdom on the Sino-Indian border, as just another Indian state. China considered this step as yet another proof of India's expansionism, in line with the Sino-Indian border conflict and the dismembering of Pakistan.

Since China's foreign policy turnabout in the late 1970s and since the Janata party was elected to power in India, there have been shifts in both countries' positions. So far, however, the signals have been mixed. Prime Minister Desai voiced a determination to revert his country's foreign policy back to "genuine nonalignment"—only to follow this up by a cordial visit to Moscow which, for China, indicated that the Soviet Union remains a favorite friend. China has praised India's efforts to settle various outstanding problems with her neighbors, but at the same time has helped Pakistan build the strategic Karakoram road that provides a direct road link between Pakistan and China and will be the key to the control of the whole of Kashmir, should it ever become a reality.[23]

There are signs, however, that Sino-Indian relations are warming up. Indian Foreign Minister Vajpayee finally visited Peking in February 1979, the first Indian minister to arrive in 19 years. One can now expect an expansion of trade and cultural exchanges, and China might even recognize Sikkim's new status; so far, though, Sikkim appears even on new Chinese maps as an independent country. The bitter legacy of the border issues will also be dealt with through negotiations. Such an approach, emphasizing the soft issues, would restore some measure of trust between the two Asian giants. Significantly, referring to Sino-U.S. normalization, Prime Minister Desai said he hoped "it will also lead to agreement with other nations."[24] India will always be unlikely to fit snugly into China's strategy of containing the Soviet Union.

China and ASEAN

Thailand, Malaysia, Singapore, Indonesia, and the Philippines, members of the Association of Southeast Asian Nations (ASEAN), geographically form an enormous goblet around Indochina. These are the dominoes of yesteryear; but now that Kampuchea has fallen prey to Vietnamese regional hegemonism, who knows whether the goblet will be sturdy enough to contain Vietnam's possible further expansion. This is the main consideration that guides China's thinking in this area.

China has always given vocal support to ASEAN as a whole, in contradistinction to the Soviet Union and Vietnam which, until recently, had viewed it with considerable suspicion and animosity. China would like to see as strong an ASEAN as possible, in line with her general support for all regional organizations not controlled by the Soviet Union. She would also naturally like to see ASEAN adopt as anti-Soviet and as anti-Vietnamese a foreign policy as possible. This is one motive behind the unequivocal support China lends to the Association's concept of turning the area into a zone of peace, freedom, and neutrality. And while ASEAN countries might harbor their suspicions about China's motives, they do as a whole feel more comfortable dealing with China than with the Soviet Union.

China's bilateral relations with the indiviudal members are, however, more complex. They are quite cordial with Thailand, fair to middling with Malaysia and the Philippines, but Singapore and Indonesia do not even maintain diplomatic relations with Peking. China herself is eager to improve these relations. Teng Hsiao-ping even visited Singapore in the fall of 1978. This was the first official visit of a top-ranking Chinese leader to a country where China does not have an embassy. Nevertheless, progress in removing obstacles to friendship has been comparatively slow.

There are two main problems: overseas Chinese, and security. All told, there are perhaps 12 million overseas Chinese (*hua-chiao*) living in ASEAN countries. China's position toward them is that they should voluntarily choose to be citizens of their country of residence and should at any rate obey local laws. They should not, however, be forced to naturalize and, if they opt to maintain a Chinese passport, China is obliged to protect their legitimate interests.

In practice, however, conditions of the overseas Chinese population vary considerably from country to country, as does their strength in absolute and relative numbers. Conditions are easiest perhaps in Thailand where, as in Burma, the tolerant Buddhist religion poses no obstacles to intermarriage and even assimilation. Thailand has gone furthest in extending full citizenship to its ethnic Chinese. In Islamic countries, that is, Malaysia and Indonesia, the cultural fissures are deeper, and the Chinese communities which resist mixing under the best of conditions are quite separate.

In Indonesia they constitute barely 3 percent of the total population, but they are distinctly outside the political mainstream. In 1965, the country experienced major anti-Chinese riots, in the wake of an abortive communist coup d'état, and the Indonesian authorities ever since have considered their ethnic Chinese as a security threat. Their unresolved position has so far stood in the way of Indonesia's reestablishing diplomatic relations with China. Dr. Mochtar Kutsumaatmadja, the country's foreign minister, has repeatedly stated that his government will be ready to consider that step only after completing a registration process of its Chinese population. In the course of it, Indonesia's Chinese population will have to choose the citizenship of one or the other country, and thereby eliminate the stateless condition among a considerable portion of the people.

Since over three quarters of Singapore's population is ethnically Chinese, the term "overseas Chinese" which carries connotations of a minority status hardly applies here. But the strongly anti-communist leaders of this barely 20-year-old country are wary of its citizens' divided loyalties ("Are we Chinese or Singaporeans?"). They have to consider the political and cultural impact a Chinese Embassy would have on the local population. Singapore has often stated that it will be the last ASEAN country to establish diplomatic relations with Peking.

The second issue which concerns Southeast Asian leaders is China's support for communist insurgents operating in Burma, Thailand, and Malaysia. This is a relic of China's earlier foreign policy of promoting revolution around the world, or at least wherever she could. Today this policy seems strangely out of place, and yet in this rather isolated instance, China still clings to her ideological offspring. In the fall of 1978, Teng Hsiao-ping refused to withdraw China's support for these movements, allegedly because it involves a "very big principle" and would have "very serious international implications." Most of the insurgents, let us not forget, are themselves ethnic Chinese, which does nothing to allay the suspicions of local politicians vis-à-vis Chinese communities in general. In Malaysia, Teng reiterated the old argument of separating state-to-state from party-to-party relations, demonstrating a kind of logic which his hosts found disingenuous. Nor did this position win him any more converts for the cause of normalization in Indonesia and Singapore, although these two particular countries do not have any Chinese-backed insurgents to deal with.

By contrast, Vietnamese Premier Pham van Dong, who had visited the same countries a little earlier, renounced all support for these movements. In the last analysis though, it is the acts, not the words, that count. As for Vietnam, it is unclear whether it had in recent years been offering much support anyway. Thus the statement of the country's premier, welcome as it was, had a rather hollow ring to it. On the other hand, the invasion of Kampuchea on behalf of a hastily organized opposition was far more ominous and significant. In addition, Vietnam has a record of going back on its word. And while China gave no word, neither does she seem to be giving the local communities much more than moral encouragement. The Chinese press occasionally echoes statements of the Thai, Malay, and North Kalimantan— Malaysia's Borneo—insurgents (nothing has been heard from Burma for a long time); and a leader of the illegal Indonesian Communist Party residing in Peking makes an occasional appearance. Material and military support, however, seems to have ceased.

The year 1978 was one of intensive diplomatic jockeying on the part of the area's Communist countries of ASEAN's heart and mind. The area welcomed Li Hsien-nien and Teng Hsiao-ping from China, Ieng Sary from Kampuchea, Pham Van Dong from Vietnam, and even Soviet Deputy Foreign Minister Firyubin. On the whole, it appears that China made a better showing; and after the invasion of Kampuchea, this certainly could be the trend of the future.

ACCOMMODATING THE PAST

Countries whose policies are most closely based on the outdated concept of the East-West conflict will have the most difficult time finding a place in the new world order the Chinese are trying to forge. In Asia this concerns the two Koreas and Taiwan. These countries felt themselves most threatened by the Sino-American rapprochement. In addition, the two Koreas are for historical reasons not certain about the Sino-Japanese friendship treaty (up till now, Pyongyand has to the best knowledge not even mentioned it in its press), and North Korea is quite uncomfortable about the irreversibility of the Sino-Soviet split.

Relations with the Koreas

Over the years of the Sino-Soviet contention, North Korea has managed to pursue an admirably independent line. It has tilted this way and that, depending on the circumstances. Today its relations with China are excellent. It openly sides with China in foreign policy, even if its language is slightly different (North Korea attacks "dominationism" rather than "hegemonism" which is in the Chinese vocabulary), and went as far as to give unequivocal support to Democratic Kampuchea. When Hua Kuo-feng started traveling abroad, North Korea was the first country he visited, in May 1978, as a symbol of the two countries' close ties. In September that year, Teng Hsiao-ping took part in celebrating the Democratic People's Republic of Korea's thirtieth anniversary. Its friendship, however, can never be taken for granted.

For North Korea—or at least for its president, Kim Il Sung—the main goal is to reunify the country, preferably under Kim's own wise leadership. North Korea emphatically opposes the idea of the country being permanently divided. As Kim Il Sung said to East Germany's party leader Honnecker, the Korean question will never be settled after the German model.

But any international order brings with it a measure of stability, and stability decreases the chances for reunification on Kim's terms. Thus from the North Korean perspective, any change that it cannot control and which leads to greater stability in the region is, latently at least, a change for the worse. The country has never really adapted to the shifting international relations of the 1970s ties or even of the 1960s. Not the Soviet Union but South Korea is its archenemy, and it still views the United States as a major adversary. As for Japan, only after Teng Hsiao-ping's visit in September 1978 did the North Korean press stop referring to it as an imperialist country: now it is merely a reactionary one. Because of Korea's deep-seated mistrust of Japan, North Korea has great trouble adjusting to the new realities of the Sino-Japanese friendship treaty. The treaty might facilitate Chinese-South Korean contacts through Tokyo. Sooner or later, North Korea fears, this could lead to the black day of "cross-recognition," whereby North Korea's allies could establish ties with the South and South Korea's allies, ties with the North. At that point the day of reunification would be more distant than ever.

Curiously, Sino-American normalization was welcomed in Pyongyang—albeit for the wrong reasons. The North Koreans took special note of the U.S. pledge not to seek hegemony. The situation, as then appraised by the North Korean *Rodong Sinmun*, was

an interesting matter that should be welcomed. . . . If the US does not want to seek hegemony in Korea, it should first of all do something good concerning the reunification of the country. The US should not oppose reunification, it should not instigate the puppet rulers of South Korea to launch war, and should withdraw its troops.[25]

Of course, North Korea and the United States might not exactly see eye-to-eye on what constitutes hegemonism; more importantly, China's view might be still different.

For public consumption at least, the Chinese also consider the presence of U.S. troops in South Korea as the most objectionable aspect of the country's regime. This, however, is an anomalous position. In general, China views the withdrawal of U.S. troops from any part of Asia as an indirect threat to her own security, at least inasmuch as it leaves a possible opening that the Soviet Union might choose to exploit.

South Korea is the only exception to this pattern. This is the only part of the world where China openly calls for the withdrawal of U.S. troops, echoing the North Korean position. Measures such as rescheduling the withdrawal of ground troops or establishing a United States-Republic of Korea joint military command are soundly denounced as dirty tricks aimed at perpetuating the division of the peninsula. China's altogether different position when other parts of the world are concerned invites the question, though, how genuine is her call for withdrawing U.S. troops from Korea?

With all the risks involved in second-guessing real Chinese intentions, my tentative answer is that China might welcome the withdrawal—but not right now. Her feelings about the issue are certainly mixed. While such a step would meet a key North Korean demand, and would perhaps add legitimacy to the South Korean leadership (which China, incidentally, no longer describes as "puppet"), it would on the other hand weaken the regional defenses and the U.S. commitment to the region; and strategic defense considerations are of topmost priority. Safeguarding against any and all possible increases in Soviet power takes precedence over any other foreign-political considerations, and certainly over Korean reunification.

One might go a step further and ask whether China really believes in the feasibility of reunification. And again the answer seems to be yes—but not right now.

China is just as aware as the next observer of the rigid nature of the North Korean regime. Hua Kuo-feng, after all, personally took a close look at it. It is true that for every other instance of a country divided, China favors reunification also. In other cases, though, reunification would be to China's benefit (Taiwan) or to the detriment of Soviet interests (Germany, and even Japan—"one Japan and one percent of Japan," as Teng Hsiao-ping called the Soviet-occupied northern territories). Korean reunification, however, falls into neither of these categories. China is also doubtless aware of the risks such a development could create for stability in East Asia, especially the security risks this would pose for her newfound friend Japan.

However, China has to tread carefully with her valuable but erratic North Korean ally. Peking, therefore, vociferously supports Kim Il Sung's reunification proposals, and the Korean issue is one of the very few on which Peking is still critical of the United States. But with his sober eye, Teng Hsiao-ping has repeatedly declared that he doesn't believe there are "any serious tensions" on the peninsula, and that reunification might take decades, or even a century, to achieve.

That just might not be fast enough for Kim Il Sung. Therefore, while talking the same language as Kim does, China has been all along putting a damper on some of his wilder ambitions. When Kim Il Sung toured China in 1975, in the aftermath of the North Vietnamese victory on the battlefield, he was widely believed to be looking for Chinese backing for a similar path in Korea. He never got it.

At the same time, China is very conscious of the stupendous economic successes of South Korea and would be interested in economic contacts at least, if she could get around North Korean objections. At this moment, with China's foreign policy in considerable flux in the aftermath of normalization with the United States, it is unclear to what extent North Korea is indebted (literally) to China and how much maneuvering space China, therefore, has with respect to South Korea. For the time being at least, China's interest in South Korean experiences in only platonic.

The Soviet Union, by contrast, does not have much to lose, and its options in dealing with the South Korean regime are broader. It has occasionally sent out feelers indicating interest in contacts with that country.[26] On such occasions, China gleefully points an accusing finger at the Soviet Union but is not beyond doing her own exploring.[27]

More substantial changes in China's position will depend on the emergence in North Korea of a new leadership, one a little more pragmatic and a little more flexible. In this eventuality, China would look for new possibilities for the peninsula. These would include humanitarian efforts to reunify families and elementary contacts of civilized countries such as postal, cultural, and commercial links between the two Korean states; toward this objective, tentative—but abortive—steps were taken in 1972, and China herself is now seeking to establish such ties with Taiwan. This enterprise might even involve support for the cross-recognition concept that the North Koreans dread so much, and for an eventual confederal arrangement for both states. It appears that at China's behest, Romania's President Ceausescu made some suggestions along these lines to North Korea in 1978, only to be resolutely rebuffed.

Changes in the North Korean leadership might well be forthcoming. The country has been having considerable economic difficulties in recent years and politically too is in a sticky corner. It is the only country in the world that anachronistically has military treaties with both Peking and Moscow. When the underpinning of these two treaties, the Sino-Soviet treaty of 1950, is formally abrogated in the spring of 1979, North Korea will find itself linked to both the adversaries while trying to keep out of the crossfire.

The Taiwan Situation

The problem of Taiwan is another one of a country divided, but it differs from that of Korea in one fundamental aspect: there is no question whatsoever that China's public stance in this case is not identical with her real intentions. If conditions on the Korean peninsula were to change, China might be able to recognize the existence of two Koreas, albeit perhaps qualified as "temporary." With Taiwan, no recognition of independence can be granted under any conditions. The eventual goal is the liberation of Taiwan, that "sacred territory of the Motherland," and reunification of the country.

It was this goal that blocked recognition and normalization of diplomatic relations with the United States for so long. Now that normalization is an accomplished fact, China's goals have been recognized as legitimate by virtually all of the world's powers. What happens next? Can one expect China to launch a "liberation invasion" and shatter East Asian security?

After the Shanghai Communique of 1972, the United States in vain sought Chinese assurances that the process of reunification would be peaceful. Just as steadfastly, China argued that the means to be employed were purely a Chinese internal matter which, as the tortuous official translation has it, "brooks no foreign interference." The military option cannot be foreclosed, argue Chinese leaders, because

> if we pledge not to use arms, it would become a major obstacle to reunification. It would allow Taiwan to behave more arrogantly. It would even make unification by peaceful means, by talks, more difficult.[28]

Well before the U.S.-China normalization was announced on December 16, 1978, that year was shaping up as something of a watershed in China-Taiwan relations. In the light of normalization, some events of that year offered a preview of things to come.

One of the little-noticed episodes was the first unofficial—but officially sanctioned—"people-to-people" contacts. In September 1978, Chinese physicists took part in a Toyko seminar on high-energy physics, although Taiwanese scientists had announced plans to attend as well. It is unclear whether they talked to each other; but previously, it had been inconceivable that China would even participate in any event side by side with Taiwan. The scientific gathering in Toyko thus meant a major switch in Peking policy. Its significance was more than transitory and indeed was not lost even on low-level cadres in Peking.

The promise for the future was spelled out quite clearly in statements and actions around January 1, 1979, when normalization with the United States came into effect. The National People's Council's Standing Committee issued a "message to compatriots in Taiwan,"[29] in which it reiterated that in dealing with the island, China "will take present realities into account," "respect the status quo on Taiwan and the opinions of the people." This was later spelled out in greater detail: China will respect the existing social and political system of the island, aiming, it seems, for some kind of confederal arrangement. China's reunification policy, said the standing committee, will be reasonable "so as not to cause the people of Taiwan any losses." The "Message to Compatriots" also suggested establishing transportation and postal services, arranging tours and visits, and academic, cultural, sports, and technological exchange. It found "every reason" to develop trade.

According to one report,[30] the port of Amoy is already being readied for mainland-Taiwan trade, the benefits of which for both partners are obvious. The successes of the island's economy are so well known in Peking that wall posters have even appeared registering wonder that Taiwan is doing so much better than the mainland.

Taiwan is shunning any talks, though, at least for now. Chiang Ching-kuo, Taiwan's president, declared shortly after the normalization announcement that he will never, under any circumstances, deal with the communists. Taiwan, he said, will remain "the spiritual fortress of the free world to fight against communism." Taiwanese leaders fear that any negotiations would be only "a means for the communists to achieve what they cannot win on the battlefield." How long this position will be tenable is unclear. U.S. recognition of China and withdrawal of its recognition of Taiwan was quite unthinkable eight or ten years ago, and the transformation since might signify what could happen in the next eight or ten years. China hopes that U.S. politicians will themselves attempt to bridge the gap between the two parts of the country.

Now that Taiwan has been abandoned virtually by all, the logic of the new international order which pits all against the Soviet Union might lead to exploration of close ties between that nation and Taiwan. Such a suggestion was indeed floated in Taipei after the normalization announcement. Logical though it might be, deep-seated historical animosities will block this avenue, certainly for a long time. Yet in charting her policy toward Taiwan, China will also have to take this possibility into account, however remote it might seem. It is the one eventuality in which China would feel compelled to use force against Taiwan.

Barring that, a military assault by the mainland is one alternative simply not in the cards. China has even stopped her thrice-weekly shelling of the offshore islands, and apparently has even been removing troops from the coastal areas facing Taiwan.[31] The last thing that China needs is a war, and this includes a war with Taiwan; it would, in addition, be a war for which she lacks the resources. The half-million-strong Taiwan army, armed to the teeth, would be a formidable match for the PLA which, to start with, does not have the necessary amphibious vehicles to attempt a forced landing. The question might still look differently in the twenty-first century; by which time, however, significant changes are bound to have occurred in the relations between the two parts of the country.

"China must certainly liberate Taiwan" is a cry that will ring for some time yet to come. But a picture with that title at a military art exhibition in Peking depicted crates of Mao Tse-tung's works, rather than guns, being floated to the island to achieve that goal.

DEFENSE

Air Force Marshal Sir Neil Cameron, British Chief of Staff, noted during his summer 1978 trip to China that China and the West face a common enemy. His hosts were very pleased to hear this observation expressed aloud. In other instances, Western officials in occasional outbursts of enthusiasm have likened China to a NATO of the East. They point out that she is holding down 44 Soviet divisions and that she thus gives considerable indirect aid to Western defense efforts. The International Institute for Strategic Studies has, for example, suggested that as a result of the confrontation on its eastern borders, the Soviet Union could rely only on 99 divisions to reinforce its Warsaw Pact allies in the case of a conflict with Europe instead of 141 specified in previous estimates.[32]

Yet the argument that China is "holding down" a considerable portion of Soviet troops is perhaps a misrepresentation of the situation. This thesis actually supports the Soviet cry of a Chinese threat and gives it merely a different value judgment. In reality, it is the Soviet Union that has adopted an agressive military posture. It is worth remembering that as recently as 1966, Soviet military strength on the Chinese border amounted to only 16 divisions. In the intervening dozen or so years their number has increased by a factor of 2.5 at least, excluding forces of the Mongolian People's Republic with which they are closely coordinated. It could hardly be argued that this increase in force levels was occasioned by an increase in Chinese aggressiveness. Keeping forces on the border is at the Soviet Union's discretion, and thus the Red Army is holding down the People's Liberation Army rather than the other way around.

The confrontation on the border (the world's longest border of hostilities, one might call it) is at once a strategic one—pitting the two countries against each other as enemies—and a local one—that is, concerning the border itself. As mentioned earlier in this paper, fruitless negotiations on the border problem have been going on intermittently since 1964. The Soviet Union, Vietnam, and India are the only three countries with which China has reached no agreement.

In actuality, there has been some give-and-take on the border, mostly to the detriment of the Chinese; armed clashes have sometimes erupted and left high casualties.[33] There is of course a constant danger that any one of these clashes might trigger a large-scale war.

Chinese forces in the four military regions adjacent to the Soviet and Mongolian border (Shenyang, Peking, Lanchow, and Sinkiang) amount to 17 armies with three divisions each. While this would indicate a rough parity of men between the two adversaries, parity here is numerical only. For one thing, the Shenyang Military Region covers the entire Northeast, and that of Peking covers the capital itself, Tientsin, and Hopei and Shansi provinces, apart from the Inner Mongolian Autonomous Region on the actual border. Their military tasks are thus far greater than border defense only. Secondly, the PLA is inferior to the Red Army in everything except morale.

Superior morale is the basis of the Chinese military doctrine of "people's war." In the last analysis, men are more important than weapons, as Chairman Mao stated in several of his well-known aphorisms. The enemy, according to this doctrine, would be lured deep into China's hinterland in case of a conflict. The army, closely integrated with the people and supported by paramilitary forces, would deal with it at its own discretion, piecemeal, in a long war of attrition. The doctrine was developed during the long years of war against Japan, but even then its effectiveness was questionable: the Chinese and U.S. evaluations of that war understandably differ, but China certainly underrates the U.S. role in defeating Japan. If a people's war were to be waged today, by a China that is isolated, its outcome would be very uncertain.

It would have tremendous costs: extreme casualties and probable dismemberment of the country. Soviet military leaders have read their Mao as well and need have no illusion that they can conquer the entire country; detaching vast tracts of it and turning them into puppet states would be sufficient. There exists, for example, a Soviet long-term historical interest in Sinkiang in China's Northwest: an enormous, sparsely populated area that is relatively poorly defended, and whose inhabitants are ethnic minorities, almost all of them (such as the Ugihur, Kazakh, Kirgiz, Tadzhik and Uzbek) straddling both sides of the frontier. Militarily, a push through the Ili Valley would allow for a somewhat uncomplicated seizure of Urumchi and the Turfan basin, once the first line of defense was broken. While the economic consequences of losing Sinkiang could be borne, the ensuring vassal state would bring Soviet forces that much closer to China's heartland. Its creation would in addition represent a substantial political blow to any Chinese government which, by proving itself incapable of defending the country's integrity, would provoke the question of its own legitimacy.

Even worse would be a thrust against the northeast, another area long coveted by Russia. With its 100 million people, rich mineral resources, a substantial industrial plant and a relatively well-developed infrastructure it would be a prize worthy of any geopolitician's dream. A simultaneous attack against Peking would deal the coup de grace to China's northern defenses. The enormous political pressure resulting from this would suffice to install a quisling government in the rump of China that would remain.

Such are the nightmares of China's military leaders. They are compounded by the fact that the equipment used by the defense forces is almost uniformly inadequate and out of date. China has no match for the Soviet mechanized, armored, and paratroop divisions stationed on the border.[34] The PLA ground forces consist of over 3.5 million men, roughly equivalent to the Red Army (for a population almost four times as large). But most of their heavy material is derived from 20-year-old Soviet models: the T-59 tank from the Soviet T-54, the light amphibious T-60 tank from the PT-76, and so on forth. Even the best that China has, the light T-62 tank of her own construction, is outclassed by modern Soviet equipment. Antitank weaponry is also inadequate.

In a large-scale conflict, air cover would be ephemeral. The Soviet airforce would control the skies with its MIG 23s, 25s, and even 27s, against which the best China could pit would be MIG 21s and their underpowered derivations.

Neither would the Chinese navy stand a chance. China may have the world's third largest submarine fleet, for example, but has only one or two nuclear-powered submarines and no submarine-launched ballistic missiles. The detection capability of Chinese submarines is archaic. The surface fleet is largely defensive, and an oceangoing capability is not even envisioned. The surface-to-surface Styx missiles are also obsolete as is the navy's anti-submarine capability.

The one bright spot in the country's defense is its strategic program. This area was among the least affected by the turmoil of the Cultural Revolution and the political upheavals that followed and has now reached the threshold of credibility. Its main problem is a reliable delivery system as an ICBM is still in the development stage, the options for now are: 30–50 IRBMs, about as many MRBMs, or the TU-16 bombers which, however, cannot be counted on to penetrate the Siberian defenses. Some commentators have pointed out the lack of a tactical nuclear force which, they argue, is needed to make up for the weakness in conventional armament and to defend the North-East.[35] But if China were attacked by such a weapon, she would surely respond by unleashing her strategic force; as for China using it first, this her leaders have reiterated they will not do.

The other major weakness of the PLA is in what one might call the state of the military art: training, logistics, coordination. "Hard training produces proficiency, crack troops and combat capability," said Wei Kuo-ching, the PLA Political Commissar, at a PLA political conference in the early summer of 1978.[36] Rather than repeating a truism, he was indicating what the PLA lacks. Only in the last year or two did the army stop spending most of its time reciting the Works and working in the rice fields. In 1978, military academics were reactivated in the country's 11 military regions as was a military staff College and a military War College for lower and higher ranks respectively. The Chinese army has the oldest active generals in the world, as the process of gracefully retiring them is slower than it should be. The absence of sophisticated communications equipment has so far precluded exercises beyond divisional level and especially those combining ground and air forces.

The people's war doctrine came to a test in Korea where conditions of frontal movements constrained to a narrow peninsula showed its limitations. Defense Minister Peng Te-huai, the commander of the Chinese troops in Korea, was eager to draw the necessary conclusions from this experience. The question of PLA doctrine, however, was not only a military one but an important political one as well; and in the ensuing political struggle with Mao, Peng Te-huai lost out. With his fall in 1959, modernization of the PLA which he had advocated was shelved as well, for almost 20 years. As a result, China found herself in the 1970s ready to fight a war with material from the 1950s.

Not surprisingly, defense is one of the four targets of the present modernization drive.[37] Marshal Peng Te-huai has quite logically been rehabilitated. If the Mao Tse-tung–Lin Piao doctrine of the people's war has not yet been laid to rest, along with other favorite theories of the same order, it is only because nothing at the present can replace it. Nevertheless, attention is being paid to "modern conditions of war," to "education and training from the point of view of strategy," and even to "useful military experiences" of other armies.

Some of the constraints limiting PLA's modernization are techno-logical: China simply does not have the know-how to produce certain steels, fuels, optics, and communication equipment. This is where foreign markets that the country is exploring on an ever broader scale will be quite essential.

If the description of China as the NATO of the East were applied in all its consequences, it would lead to much greater military cooperation between China and the Western world, which is precisely what China wants. But for now at least, Germany, Japan, and the United States are not ready to trade arms with China—although the United States does not object to its European allies selling China defensive weapons. The Chinese shopping list is endless. It includes most prominently the British Harrier jump jets; antiaircraft and antitank missiles from France and Italy; helicopters from Italy, Germany, and Britain; antiaircraft guns from Italy. China hopes that eventually even the United States will be more lenient in helping her fill her defense needs.

The other major constraint on the modernization of the PLA is of course economic—or perhaps political. There are many hands outside the military reaching out for every extra ton of steel produced and every extra yuan earmarked for foreign purchases. Balancing out the nation's priorities is of necessity an ongoing concern of its leaders. It appears that for the present at least, modernization of exclusively military areas has been put on the backburner. Higher priority is given, for example, to the industrial base and to science and technology. These areas, however, will have an impact on military modernization as well, and military leaders might be satisfied with that for the moment.

In 1956 Mao made the point that to strengthen national defense China must first of all strengthen economic contruction.[38] The article in question is not by accident one of the most widely read since the fall of the Gang of Four.

In the years ahead, certain critical defense sectors will be moder-nized, as already indicated by the pattern of imports. For an across-the-board modernization, however, the PLA will have to wait until the mid-1980s or so. The question is will that be early enough? But inasmuch as China's role in Asian security is based on China's own security, the modernization of the PLA and, more broadly, China's general economic progress are among the keys to peace in that area.

NOTES

1. See *New China News Agency* (November 23, 1978) (hereafter: *NCNA*).

2. For a fascinating analysis of the interplay between politics and industrial output on the provincial level, see Robert M. Field et. al., "Political Conflict and Industrial Growth in China: 1965-77," in Joint Economic Committee of the US Congress: *Chinese Economy Post-Mao*, vol. 1: *Policy and Performance*, Washington 1978, pp. 239-83. (hereafter: *Chinese Economy*).

3. For a list of major business deals with China, see *Far Eastern Economic Review* (December 29, 1978, p. 41) (hereafter: *FEER*).

4. For a more pessimistic analysis of China's economic prospects see Robert F. Dernberger and David Fasenfest, "China's Post-Mao Economic Future," *Chinese Economy*, pp. 3-47.

5. For a discussion of Chinese agriculture that, however, does not include problems of labor force nor obviously the most recent important changes in policy, see Henry J. Groen and James A. Kilpatrick, "China's Agricultureal Production," in *Chinese Economy*, pp. 607-52.

6. For details see Frederick M. Surls, "China's Grain Trade," in *Chinese Economy*, p. 653-70.

7. *People's Daily* (December 27, 1978).

8. I read, however, an interesting poster put up in Peking at the end of 1978 in which a Chinese participant of the March 1969 border clash suggested that it had been provoked by the Soviet Union precisely to bolster Lin Piao's chances at the Ninth CPC Congress which met a month later, and elevated him to the position of Mao's heir apparent.

9. As if to underline this point, the Chinese are publishing a four volume work detailing the history of Czarist agression against China, *NCNA* (December 25, 1978).

10. See *Peking Review* 45 (1977): 10-41.

11. Excluded from this system are only those countries of the world whose very legitimacy China questions or denies: South Korea, Taiwan, Israel, and South Africa come to mind.

12. For the text, see *Peking Review* 33 (1978): 7-8.

13. For a schedule of trade, and for a list of other projects under discussion, see *FEER* (March 3, 1978), pp. 40-41.

14. *Peking Reveiw* 45 (1977): 30.

15. *NCNA* (November 28, 1978).

16. See *FEER* (January 19, 1978), pp. 19-22.

17. Ibid.

18. They would have much preferred to aid a sensible nation-front government, headed, say, by their old friend Sihanouk, and were nudging their extremist Kampuchean friends in this direction. Ironically, they succeeded when it was too late, in early January 1979 Sihanouk led a Kampuchean delegation to the UN Security Council debate on the conflict, but by then Kampuchea had all but fallen.

19. The number of border incidents has skyrocketed from 121 in 1974 to 439 in 1975, and from 900 in 1976 to 1,108 in 1978. Between August 25 and December 15, 1978, 200 border incidents occurred. Vietnamese armed personnel penetrated into 100 areas of the Kwangsi Chuang Autonomous Region, nibbling away at Chinese territory. *People's Daily* (February 27, 1979).

20. *NCNA* (December 29, 1978).

21. For a more detailed review of the situation before the Vietnamese invasion was launched, and for further references, see Sheldon W. Simon, "New Conflict in Indochina," *Problems of Communism* (Sept.-Oct. 1978), pp. 20-36.

22. *NCNA* (December 29, 1978).

23. China effectively considers Kashmir a part of Pakistan, whereas Jammu, the

southern part of the disputed state, which is under Indian control, is always carefully referred to in the Chinese press as precisely that—Jammu.

24. UPI from London, January 1, 1979.

25. *NCNA* (December 23, 1978).

26. A South Korean government minister visited the USSR in September 1978 for the first time ever, and was accorded all due courtesy. A Soviet provincial paper, *Kazakjstanskaya pravda*, on that occasion referred to the country by its official name, Republic of Korea.

27. During his trip to Japan, Teng Hsiao-ping is reported to have talked with Kim Jong Pil, a former South Korean Premier.

28. Teng Hsiao-ping to Japanese correspondents on September 6, 1978. See FBIS-China, September 12, 1978.

29. *Beijing Review* 1 (1979): 16–17.

30. *FEER* (October 13, 1978), p. 5.

31. *Los Angeles Times*, January 2, 1978, quoting Leonard Woodstock.

32. DPA from London, August 31, 1978.

33. In Sinkiang, the Soviet Union has reportedly nibbled away at the frontier and, between 1970 and July 1977, occupied over 1,000 square miles of disputed territory. Of the 3,861 square miles of disputed territory in that region alone, the Soviets are now in control of 3,475 square miles, *The Times*, London, October 11, 1978.

On the other hand, the USSR is reported to have lifted the blockade on Chinese vessels passing through the confluence of the Amur and Ussuri rivers around Khabarovsk, Neville Maxwell in *The Times*, London, September 29, 1978.

Recent border clashes included one in August 1977 in Sinkiang and one in the summer of 1978 on the Ussuri river.

34. For a detailed analysis of the two contending forces which, unfortunately is not at my disposal at this writing, see Drew Middleton, *The Duel of the Giants: China and Russia in Asia* (New York: Scribner Publications, 1978).

35. E.g. Rene Saint-Vincent, "La defense chinoise après Mao," *Defense Nationale* (July 1977), p. 99.

36. *NCNA* (June 8, 1978).

37. For a review of the situation see Georges Tan Eng Bok, "La modernisation de la defense chinoise et ses limites," *Defense nationale* (May 1978), pp. 69–84, from where most of the information in this section about the PLA is drawn.

38. "On the Ten Major Relationships," in *Selected Works of Mao Tsetung*, vol. 5, Peking: 1977, pp. 284–307, esp. pp. 288–89.

· 3 ·

THE SOVIET UNION AND
ASIAN SECURITY
Robert C. Horn

O ver the course of the past decade the Soviet Union has had an
increasingly active role in Asia. Not only has this nation accelerated its competitive efforts vis-à-vis the United States and the People's
Republic of China in areas where this rivalry was already highly
significant by the end of the 1960s—such as in India, noncommunist
Southeast Asia, and Japan—but the Soviet leaders have also undertaken
qualitatively new initiatives. These have included putting forward their
own security scheme for Asia and signing peace and friendship pacts—
with important military provisions—with India and later with Vietnam
(pacts which were soon followed by major conflicts involving Moscow's
new allies). This overall Soviet offensive in Asia has taken place in the
context of wide-ranging and enormously significant changes in the
configuration of world politics since 1969. Perhaps most importantly,
Sino-Soviet relations worsened dramatically beginning with the clashes
along the Ussuri River in March of that year. Not only was there
greatly heightened military tension, but Beijing (Peking), with its
"reappearance" from the withdrawal of the Cultural Revolution, was
rapidly emerging as a major threat to Soviet interests on the diplomatic
front. Moreover, numerous hints were observed by Moscow of a
change in relations between the People's Republic and the United
States. This evolving relationship, furthered by Kissinger's secret visit
to Beijing in 1971, Nixon's state visit in 1972, and other developments
up through the diplomatic recognition of January 1, 1979, posed and
continues to pose ominous implications for a broad range of Soviet

interests. Finally, the United States indicated, through Nixon's Guam Doctrine of 1969 and the lessening role in Indochina which culminated in the Paris Accords of 1973, a substantially reduced profile in Asia.

When these developments on the superpower level are combined with changing governments, policies, and relationships in and among the various countries and regional subsystems in Asia, it is apparent that the Soviet Union has been faced with new opportunities and new challenges. It is the purpose of this chapter to analyze Moscow's response to these changing conditions, to assess the extent to which the Soviets have been successful in the pursuit of their interests, and to evaluate the factors which have been conducive to or obstructive of the establishment of Soviet influence[1] in Asia. Before moving to an examination of these factors in South Asia, Southeast Asia, and Northeast Asia, we need to examine first the nature of the premises and goals with which the Soviet Union approaches Asia and, second, the overwhelmingly significant Sino-Soviet relationship.

THE SOVIET PERSPECTIVE

A number of basic premises have been the foundation stones for the Soviet Union's policy in Asia since the 1950s. Like all other Soviet policies, actions here are intended by Moscow to enhance Soviet security primarily and to increase Soviet power secondarily (and relatedly). More specifically, the general line of Soviet foreign policy, peaceful coexistence, has meant continued competition with the capitalist system—the United States in particular—in the economic, political, and ideological spheres. The crux of this competition has been precisely in the need to keep it peaceful. Thus, another operational principle of the Soviet approach to the various regions of Asia is the absolute necessity of avoiding a confrontation with the United States. Fundamental also to Moscow's perspective is the conviction that the drive for genuine independence and even some form of non-alignment or neutralism in the Third World as a whole and in Asia in particular can coincide with Soviet interests and lead to the creation of a sort of alliance between the Soviet Union and these states or a "zone of peace" as described by Nikita Khrushchev at the Twentieth Congress of the Communist Party of the Soviet Union (CPSU) in 1956. A final premise of Soviet behavior in Asia has been to approach that area in a pragmatic—if at times overly optimistic (and, the Chinese have charged, opportunistic)—manner rather than a rigid, ideological one. As Soviet policy makers have become more knowledgeable about Asia and the Third World since getting actively involved in the 1950s, "the politicians have led the scholars [not to mention the ideologues] in reorienting

Soviet policies and attitudes."[2] Thus, it is not surprising that the most likely beneficiaries of an ideological Soviet approach, local Communist parties and guerrilla movements, have been given short shrift in Russian policy. Moscow has built its policies and expectations on dealing with regimes in power and on state-to-state relations.

Among the goals of the USSR Asian policy, the most basic is that of persuading Asian states—and non-Asian powers such as the United States—that the Soviet Union is not only a world superpower but also an *Asian power*. What Moscow seeks here is to be accepted as a legitimate and major voice in the region's affairs and as a full and responsible member of the Asian subsystem. This has been part of the Soviet approach since the 1950s and it has become even more explicit in the 1970s. A second goal of Soviet policy, and the one that was Moscow's primary aim when its involvement in Asia began to grow in the post-Stalin years, is that of reducing and limiting Washington's influence. It may well be the Soviet Union's increasing belief that the United States does not have long-term vital interests in Asia and is not an integral part of Asia (as is the Soviet Union and, for that matter, China and Japan).

In the late 1950s—and perhaps even as early as the Bandung Conference of 1955—a third goal became prominent among Soviet objectives, that of containing the influence of China. The People's Republic of China is clearly a permanent part of Asia, aspires to leadership of the medium and small states there and, at least in Soviet eyes, to political and ideological leadership of Communist countries in Asia. Chinese influence in the various regions of Asia historically and potentially makes Asia that much more crucial a forum for Soviet interests. Another, and more recent, goal is the limitation of growing Japanese influence. Soviet concern has mounted in proportion to expanding Japanese involvement. Just as the Soviet Union is not anxious to see expanded Chinese influence replace a dwindling American role, it is not happy about a new Japanese role filling that supposed vacuum either. The rapidly expanding Soviet navy has provided Moscow with further goals in Asia (the Soviet interests there being one cause for the naval buildup in the first place). Bases or at least docking and repair facilities as well as free access through such bodies of water as the Straits of Malacca in order to increase the Soviet presence in the Pacific and Indian Oceans and the Persian Gulf—these have become necessary and major objectives of Soviet policy. Finally, the Soviets have economic interests in the various regions of Asia and they seek expanded opportunities for trade. They are particularly interested in new markets for their own products in order to balance the much greater importing done by the Soviet Union from the region.[3]

A mixture of these goals and the collision of them with external events has determined Soviet behavior in Asia over the past two and one-half decades. It is a major argument of this chapter, however, that the objective of the containment of China and of its influence in Asia has since 1969 been Moscow's real priority. For not only do Moscow and Beijing compete throughout Asia, but their rivalry permeates their roles in world politics. Moreover, the direct Sino-Soviet relationship is the fundamental fact of political life in Asia today. It is that relationship which must be examined next because it provides the key part of the framework for the discussion of the Soviet Union's Asian policy which will follow. It is the major thread that runs through all of Moscow's behavior in Asia.

THE SCOPE OF SINO-SOVIET RIVALRY

As the term "cold war" was a convenient—if imprecise—label for the international politics of the 1950s and 1960s, so has "detente" become the catchword to describe the world political scene in the 1970s.[4] This trend of relaxing tensions has been evident in the bilateral relationships between the Soviet Union and the United States and between the latter and China. However, this shift has clearly not taken place in the third side of the major power "triangle"—that is, in relations between the Soviet Union and China. To the extent that there has been a noticeable change in their relations since early 1969, in fact, it has been in the opposite direction. The 1970s have seen the development of a more hostile and more globally competitive relationship between Moscow and Beijing.

In the direct, territorial aspect of Sino-Soviet relations, hostilities reached a new height in 1969 with the succession of border clashes which began on the Ussuri River in early March and erupted sporadically for the next several months there, along the Amur River also in the Far East and on the Sinkiang border in China's Northwest. Soviet military deployments grew to 21 divisions in mid-1969 from 15 one year earlier.[5] Coupled with the military buildup were harsh political denunciations and thinly veiled threats. These culminated in the summer in Soviet intimations of the application of the so-called Brezhnev Doctrine of limited sovereignty to China and the hints that the Kremlin was considering a preemptive strike against China's nuclear facilities.

The immediate crisis in Sino-Soviet relations was relieved by the Kosygin-Zhou Enlai (Chou En-lai) meeting in Peking in September of that year. Tension, however, remained high. The deployment of troops to the border region was accelerated by both sides. The USSR strength reached a peak of 45 divisions in 1973 and has stabilized at 44 (as of mid-

1978) while China's troop strength in the border area jumped from 60 combat divisions in 1968 to 90 by 1971 and to a peak of 109 by mid-1973. (In mid-1978, it still stood somewhere between 100 and 110.)[6] Moreover, there have been recurring incidents along the border. While none of these has reached the level of the 1969 clashes, the capture in March 1974 of a Soviet army helicopter and its crew and the crossing into China by a small contingent of Soviet troops in May 1978 have been significant flareups of the border issue. In late 1978 there were reports by American military figures that Moscow was bolstering its air and ground forces in the Far East and that the Soviets had held major military exercises near Khabarovsk, along the Chinese frontier. Just prior to China's invasion of Vietnam early in 1979 both the Soviet Union and China engaged in threatening troop movements and build-ups as well as reorganizations on their respective sides of the Sinkiang border. At the same time, however, the Soviets and Chinese have undertaken intermittent border negotiations in Beijing. These have gone on for two months or more at a time through mid-1978, but have so far yielded no apparent progress.[7] Border differences as well as border tensions seem likely to continue.

Most experts would agree that it is China that has presented demands making improved relations impossible. Moscow has seemed interested—as evidenced by the periodic offers to China of various agreements or understandings—in bringing about some normalization of relations, albeit with no territorial, ideological, or political concessions to Beijing. In this context, the death of Chairman Mao Zedong (Mao Tse-tung) in September 1976 must have appeared as a golden opportunity to the Kremlin leadership.[8] With the passing of the Chairman, who had injected so much of his own anti-Soviet hostility into Chinese policy, the USSR hoped that more "rational" elements would prevail in Beijing. If the "Soviet card"—better relations with Moscow— was to be played, the Soviet Union would have to play down the dispute, minimize Sino-Soviet differences, make careful gestures to the Chinese, and allow progressive tendencies to emerge in China. From the time of Mao's death up to the spring of 1977, Moscow's policy, with some minor qualifications, was marked by substantial restraint. In contrast, however, there was no change in Chinese policy toward the Soviet Union. Finally, in mid-April the Soviet media and certain spokesmen began to resume the attack. On May 14, *Pravda* published a 2,500 word editorial signed by "I. Alexandrov"—a pseudonym believed used by the top CPSU leadership—that was a thoroughgoing indictment of China, accusing her specifically of preparing for war, with the USSR first but eventually the West and Japan as well. It contained warnings to the West regarding China's threat to world peace, the necessity of avoiding any appeasement of Chinese expansionism, and, explicitly, the danger of Western military assistance to the PRC.

Since May 1977, Moscow's anti-China polemics have continued and have matched the anti-Soviet diatribes from Beijing.[9] The Soviet leadership has been ever ready to interest the Chinese in some agreement that would lessen their confrontation. This was seen when Moscow responded to the April 1979 announcement of Peking's intention to cancel the 1950 Sino-Soviet Treaty of Friendship, Alliance, and Mutual Assistance by proposing again to sign a joint statement of principles to govern the relations between the countries. On the whole, however, the Kremlin has concluded that China has retained "Maoism without Mao." In foreign policy, Maoist anti-Sovietism is being continued. Those areas where Maoism is being "revised" are internal and incline toward economic development and military modernization for China, trends which only add to Moscow's apprehension.

Beijing also challenges Moscow in a broad range of Soviet foreign policy interests. One of these, which was one of the first areas of competition, is in the context of ideology and world communist movement. The Chinese offered ideological "orthodoxy" as an alternative to Moscow's "revisionism." Leadership of a not insignificant movement was at stake. Yet China's challenge in this area has in most respects largely declined, mainly owing to the "normalization" of Chinese foreign policy that began in 1969 and, most particularly, the reapproachement with the leading imperialist state, the United States. Beijing has been robbed of much of its appeal as a militant and principled revolutionary.[10] One area, however, where Beijing's challenge has continued is where this ideological area is crossed by security concerns. For the Soviet Union this is Eastern Europe, and China has been active in that region strengthening bilateral ties and encouraging independence from Moscow. Party Chairman Hua Guofeng's (Hua Kuo-feng) visit to Romania and Yugoslavia in August 1978 was particularly upsetting to the Soviet Union, and repeated warnings were issued by Moscow to all concerned.

With the mid-1971 revelation that Henry Kissinger was in Beijing arranging for the visit of President Nixon, a new—and perhaps the most critical—arena was added to the Sino-Soviet competitive relationship. Where before the Soviets had been able to deal with their two major adversaries separately, they now confronted a situation where this would be much more difficult and, moreover, where those adversaries could discuss and perhaps coordinate their approaches to the Soviet Union. Soviet fears in this regard seemed only to be confirmed by certain developments that followed Nixon's 1972 summit in Beijing. The increasing coincidence of skepticism regarding détente shared by Chinese leaders and certain U.S. political figures has been particularly disturbing. The visit of U.S. Senator Henry Jackson, then a presidential aspirant and a leading spokesman against détente, to China in mid-1974 was characteristic; he extolled the "real détente" which China and the United States were moving toward as well as China's wariness of Soviet pressures in Europe and elsewhere. The visits since of President Ford, ex-President Nixon, and more recently, Secretary of Energy James Schlesinger—a major skeptic on détente with the Soviet Union—and Zbigniew Brzezinski, the national security advisor only further confirmed Soviet fears. The announcement in mid-December that China and the United States would establish full diplomatic relations at the beginning of 1979 was perceived as another stage in this process. Moscow accepted the recognition as realistic—if belated—as it did the ending of the American alliance with Taiwan. The key in the Soviet perception, as it has been ever since Nixon's visit, is to what use this new relationship will be put. The words of Leonid Brezhnev to a Congress of Trade Unions in 1972 still characterize the Soviet assessment:

> First of all, the very fact of the reinstatement of contacts between two states, and the normalization of relations between them is an absolutely natural phenomenon. The Soviet Union has always opposed the imperialist policy of isolation of the PRC, has always been for due recognition of its role in the international arena. The appraisal of the present contacts between Peking and Washington depends, however, on the foundation underlying them. . . . The decisive word will be pronounced by the facts, by the subsequent actions of the USA and the PRC.[11]

Given Moscow's suspicions of U.S.-China collusion against Soviet interests, what "facts" have the Soviets probably seen since the December announcement? First, Moscow was uncomfortable, despite Washington's disclaimers, with the reference in the U.S.-China agreement to joint opposition to the seeking of "hegemony," Beijing's code word for Soviet policy. Second, the Soviets perceived—and Chinese statements explicitly confirmed—that China sought to involve the United States in the creation of a broad front against the Soviet Union in Asia and elsewhere. The anti-Soviet statements of Chinese Vice-Premier Deng Xiaoping (Teng Hsiao-ping) during his visit to the United States in January 1979 only served to fuel further Soviet suspicions of U.S. support of China's anti-Sovietism. More "facts" were China's subsequent invasion of Vietnam and the accelerated talk of major Chinese purchases of military equipment from Western Europe. Clearly, the Kremlin sees little reason for optimism in this area of Sino-Soviet rivalry.

Western Europe, like the United States, has emerged as a new arena for the Chinese challenge to Soviet interests. Beijing has conducted a diplomatic offensive in this area, especially vis-à-vis West Germany, Great Britain, and France since about 1972. China has particularly courted leaders of the conservative parties in Britain and Germany. In all contacts, China has stressed the need for European unity and military strength in the face of the threat from the Soviet Union. China has emerged as perhaps the world's foremost spokesman for NATO, for a continued U.S. military commitment to Europe, and for the European Economic Community. Moscow has denounced them all for years. Quite perceptively, if with some exaggeration, the Soviets have argued:

> Forgetting their erstwhile "revolutionary character," the Chinese leaders are openly sympathizing with reactionary forces in Western Europe. At every available opportunity Peking representatives are trying to convince West Europe leaders of the need to unite western countries, saying that China sees "the first step towards Europe's independence" in the development and expansion of the Common Market.
>
> In striving for a "strong Western Europe," the Maoists would like to create, above all, an effective counter-weight to the USSR.[12]

The most recent and, from the Soviet perspective, most significant indication of collusion between West European countries and China has been the negotiations regarding arms sales to the latter. Plans are under way for France to sell defensive antitank weapons and for Britain to sell the jump jet Harrier plane and diesel engines for Navy vessels. Although the United States has said it will not sell arms to China, it has announced it will not object to other NATO countries doing so. Given the degree of Sino-Soviet tensions and China's manpower advantage, it is obvious that the Soviets cannot view with equanimity any sales which will close China's 10- to 20-year lag in modern weapons. In the words of Georgi Arbatov, head of Moscow's Institute for the Study of the USA and Canada, "Whoever is [pushing Europe to sell arms to China] should think again. It is not persuasive to say there's a difference between defensive and offensive weapons. Both can be used offensively." Then, in the Soviet version of linkage, he went on to warn the United States, "If you want détente in Europe ... you will be very unwise to send arms from Europe to the Far East for use against us."[13]

The final area of Sino-Soviet rivalry—other than the Asian arena which will be the focus of the remainder of this chapter—is the Third World. Sino-Soviet competition has been an important fact of international politics for the Third World states since at least the end of the 1950s. In the 1970s it has taken on even greater relevance as China has sought to challenge Soviet interests wherever that country has chosen to get involved. Beijing's verbal attacks have been most pronounced on Soviet policies in Africa and the Middle East—particularly in Angola and the Horn. The Chinese denounce Moscow with regularity for the Soviet Union's "unscrupulous use of Cuban proxy forces and agents to launch outright military intervention" and for its efforts to create social upheavals in order to subvert governments and "replace them with regimes subservient to it."[14]

In most areas of the Third World, of course, China is too distant and too lacking in economic and military capabilities to offset completely Soviet efforts. The various regions of Asia, however, are the exception to this. These areas are located next to China, and the PRC has a history of involvement in, if not hegemony over, most of the countries there. Moreover, China perceives its own interests and future as integrally related to its Asian environment. It has available a wide variety of means in trying to extend its influence, from military, political, and economic to cultural (particularly via the overseas Chinese present in many of the countries). Moscow has its own security concerns in Asia—where over two thirds of its territory lies—and has important goals there, as was discussed. Thus it is hardly surprising that it is in Asia where, along with the crucial superpower level, the stakes in the Sino-Soviet rivalry are the highest and this rivalry is the most intense.

A COLLECTIVE SECURITY SYSTEM FOR ASIA

In June 1969, General Secretary Brezhnev issued a call for the development of an Asian collective security system. This proposal has been little elaborated upon by the Soviets since then and has for periods of time disappeared from Soviet commentary. When it has been put forth, it has received a very unenthusiastic reception from Asian states. It has nevertheless shown a stubborn resilience. A decade later it still characterizes Moscow's overall approach to the pursuit of its interests in Asia. This is the case because the proposal in essence calls for active Soviet involvement in the security affairs of Asia. Thus it is an effort to move toward the foreign policy goals of making the Soviet Union a major and "natural" power in the region. Given Moscow's competition with the United States and China, it is also an approach toward containing and reducing the influence of Washington and Beijing while creating the opportunities for the expansion of the Soviet Union's own influence.

In view of these goals, the current U.S. posture in Asia looms as a threat to Moscow's security proposal and interests. Former president Ford's Pacific Doctrine, announced in Honolulu after his December 1975 visit to China, defined in strong terms—since supported by U.S. policy—an American commitment to, and stake in, the maintenance of an "equilibrium in the Pacific" and the stability and security of the states of the region. There was to be no withdrawal from Asia to a "fortress America." The Soviets were quick to express their disappointment with Washington's decision not to disengage more completely from Asia. Dmitry Volsky, writing in the Soviet international affairs journal, *New Times*,[15] attacked the U.S. policy for being a "coverup for a shopworn expansionist strategem" and one that sought to place greater "emphasis on involving Asian political forces" to carry out American plans. What was even more ominous for Soviet interests was the perception of Volsky and subsequent commentators that the doctrine pointed to increasingly close cooperation in Asia between the United States and China. In Volsky's words, "The Maoist leaders now not only accept the imperialist military presence in Asia, but are helping the Pentagon to build it up." This involvement of Beijing in any Washington-proposed "structure of peace" in Asia is based on

> the reconstitution with Maoist help of the system of pro-Western military-political alliances, on modernized colonialism, and on the confrontation with the countries of the Socialist community and the leading non-aligned states.

To the extent that this perception is accurate, it certainly would not be in the Soviet Union's interest for the United States and China to suspect increasingly that she is seeking to expand her influence in Asia, and that they themselves, therefore, must stand firm and together, in opposing such efforts. To support such a Soviet perception there is the fact that, while Ford claimed that the United States, China, Japan, and the Soviet Union are all Pacific powers with security concerns that intersect in Asia, he went on explicitly to foresee cooperation only between the first three and made no mention of the Soviet Union in the remainder of his address. Perhaps in answer to the obvious question of whether it was the Soviet Union against which such cooperation would be directed, Ford made the direct and symbolically important statement that "we share [with the PRC] opposition to any form of hegemony in Asia or in any other part of the world." Such a loaded anti-Soviet phrase would hardly have been used carelessly by Ford in his doctrine (or by Nixon in the Shanghai Communique of 1972).

A major Soviet study of collective security in Asia, written by a staff member of the International Department of the CPSU Central Committee and published in 1976,[16] warned that only this approach would prevent the formation of alliances of some powers against others. These alliances, especially one among United States-China-Japan, would lead unavoidably to instability and conflict. The study dwells particularly on the harmful and dangerous effect of U.S. policies which allow Japan to seek the expansion of its military and political power in Asia, and Beijing to seek to involving Tokyo in its anti-Sovietism. *All* Asian states must be involved in Asia's security, hence the importance of Moscow's collective security approach.

This contention concerning the overall Soviet role continues. The treaty between China and Japan and the United States-China normalization both contained antihegemony clauses, and the Soviets reacted strongly to each. For their part, the Soviets have hailed their own bilateral treaties—especially those with India and Vietnam—as stepping-stones to a collective security system. A recent Chinese assessment denounced these moves and this Soviet approach:

> An important move in the Kremlin's Asian strategy is to knock together an "Asian collective security system." With Hanoi now at its command, it thinks the time has come to revive its project. . . . It hopes to build up a network of treaties and eventually bring these countries together into a "collective security system."
>
> The Soviet Union is noisily vilifying China as being guilty of "hegemonism" and "expansionism" and trying to poison China's relations with other Asian countries. At the same time, it is positioning its forces and rattling it sabre in the Asia-Pacific region. . . . Of course, the Kremlin has China in mind in pushing expansionism in Asia. But its more important objective is to enlarge its sphere of influence and push out the influence of its arch rival, the United States, from Asia and threaten the peace and security of Japan and other Asian nations and that of Southeast Asian nations in particular.[17]

Naturally, broad approaches such as collective security proposals have not constituted the only efforts to establish influence of the Soviet Union and its competitors in Asia. Indeed, bilateral efforts have received greater emphasis and been more crucial. How the Soviets have sought more concretely to strengthen their presence in the region through bilateral relations, and the factors that have determined Moscow's successes and failures, comprise the remaining sections of this chapter.

MOSCOW AND SOUTH ASIA: SUCCESS
AND THE LIMITS OF INFLUENCE

Moscow's extensive involvement in South Asia in the post-Stalin period dates from the Khrushchev-Bulganin trip in 1955. Both out of a recognition of India's potential as a Third World leader and as a response to the inclusion of Pakistan—India's chief adversary—in the Western-sponsored Southeast Asia Treaty Organization and the Baghdad Pact, the Soviet government chose India as the major focus of their policies in the region. Moreover, as Sino-Indian relations cooled following the 1955 Bandung meeting, Soviet-Indian relations helped to exacerbate and began to symbolize growing strains in the ties between Moscow and Beijing. The extent of Soviet assistance to India and the Soviet Union's implicit support of that country in its 1959 and 1962 border clashes with China became serious points of dispute as Sino-Soviet differences escalated into public view. Moscow clearly seemed to place a higher priority on its relations with New Delhi than on those with Beijing.

Nevertheless, by 1965 the Soviets were indicating a willingness to tolerate some cooling in the relationship with India as they began also to court Pakistan. As the cold war waned, Moscow recognized (as did Pakistan) that new opportunities existed for reducing U.S. influence in such treaty states as Pakistan. The limitation of China's role in Pakistan provided a second basic motivation for Soviet initiatives toward Islamabad. In addition, Moscow was somewhat disillusioned with India due to internal political and economic trends and to the country's military weakness as exhibited in the 1962 clash with China. India seemed too "weak a reed" on which to base Soviet regional interests exclusively and Moscow hoped that, by striking a balance in relations with India and Pakistan, it would be able to exert maximum leverage in an area of substantial importance to Soviet security.

This basic Soviet policy framework—of seeking a balance in its ties with the two states, while giving India slightly greater emphasis in general and a higher priority when the situation comes to a "crunch"—has continued through the 1970s. Moscow played a neutral role in the 1965 conflict between India and Pakistan, and Premier Kosygin successfully undertook to bring about an agreement between the two, at Tashkent early in 1966, to end the conflict. The Soviet Union qualified its pro-Indian stance on Kashmir and initiated aid programs—including military aid—to Pakistan. By early 1969,[18] however, Soviet policy seemed to be less than successful. Further mediation efforts had failed totally and Indo-Pakistani relations had worsened; political instabilities in each country aggravated their mutual relations. Indian dissatisfaction with Soviet arms supplies to Pakistan was growing, while Moscow had had no success in weaning Pakistan away from China. From the Kremlin's perspective, there was now the strong probability of "losing" in both states of the subcontinent: having its previously significant role in India reduced and yet not gaining a more influential position in Pakistan. When this is added to the facts that by mid-1969 the Chinese threat had increased and the heretofore unimaginable possibility of Sino-American cooperation had been hinted, it is clear that Moscow faced a "crunch."

Given this framework, it is not surprising that the Soviet Union began to mend its relations with India in an effort to restore that preeminent relationship while still hoping to have some influence on Pakistan. By September 1969, movement by both Moscow and New Delhi was discernible. The Soviets sought support against China, and India looked for a reliable friend vis-à-vis Pakistan; China's close relationship with, and substantial assistance to, Pakistan, in addition to the threat China herself represented to India, provided the crucial linkage that brought New Delhi and Moscow together. The continuation of Sino-Soviet and Indo-Pakistani tensions plus the growing instability in Pakistan in 1970–71 only furthered this process. The Treaty of Peace, Friendship and Cooperation signed between the Soviets and the Indians in August 1971 was a logical culmination of these trends in the subcontinent. Although Moscow indicated its desire to avoid a military clash between India and Pakistan—growing out of Pakistan's civil war in the Eastern wing of the country (now Bangladesh)—by August India's security needed further support. With Washington and Beijing lining up behind Pakistan, it was time to make public Moscow and New Delhi's previously reached agreement.[19]

The Indo-Soviet treaty played a highly significant role in the India-Pakistan war over Bangladesh in December 1971. To be of 20 years duration, the treaty cited support for such things as Indian nonalignment, equality and noninterference in internal affairs, and cooperation in various fields. Moreover, the signatories agreed not to undertake any commitment against each other and to start immediate consultations if either was attacked, "with a view to eliminating this threat and taking appropriate effective measures to ensure peace and security for their countries." The treaty essentially enabled India to take the action it deemed necessary, with the confidence that Soviet support would deter Chinese or American intervention. This worked to India's advantage in a major way as its armed forces thoroughly defeated Pakistan's and aided in what proved the birth of Bangladesh. The United States and China were made out to be the losers (it might also be remembered that it was Pakistan that had facilitated Henry Kissinger's mid-1971 secret mission to Peking that got U.S.-PRC relations moving, a development viewed uneasily both in New Delhi and in Moscow). Finally, the outcome of the war left India in a predominant position in the subcontinent.

Perhaps the greatest irony of Soviet security policy in Asia is that its greatest success—the Indo-Soviet treaty and India's Bangladesh victory, aided by Soviet treaty, and India's Bangladesh victory, aided by Soviet arms, naval movements, warnings, and UN vetoes—left Moscow without appreciably greater influence in India. Indeed, the story of Soviet policy since the 1971 war has largely been one of "a search for the spoils that go with victory."[20] New Delhi's position in the subcontinent was now so dominant that its dependence on Moscow was substantially reduced. To be sure, Soviet-Indian relations have remained close and been an important factor in the international politics of Asia. This was particularly true in the remainder of Indira Gandhi's tenure as prime minister. Her periodic visits to Moscow continued and in November 1973 Brezhnev journeyed to India (a visit so historic that its fifth anniversary was highly publicized in 1978 by the Soviet media). Large numbers of other visits and exchanges took place, trade continued to grow, and Soviet economic and military aid programs remained very significant inputs into India's economic and military development plans. Indian and Soviet foreign policies coincided on most major issues. Irritants in the relationship, such as Moscow's displeasure with India's detonation of a nuclear device in May 1974, were overshadowed by the areas of agreement. The United States remained largely disinterested and Sino-Indian relations remained strained.

The end of Mrs. Gandhi's Emergency Rule (which the Soviets had supported), brought about by the Janata victory in the March 1977 election, has introduced a new element of uncertainty into the Soviet-Indian relationship. During the campaign, Morarji Desai, who was to become Prime Minister, criticized the one-sided nature of Indira Gandhi's policy. "Genuine" nonalignment had to be restored, and the "special relationship" with the Soviet Union ended. Desai, who for more than a decade, and during the election campaign particularly, had been characterized in the Soviet media as a reactionary, seemed to confirm Soviet fears when he entrusted the external affairs ministry to Atal Behari Vajpayee, a member of the right-wing Jan Sangh party. Moscow was sensitive as well to China's encouragement of any slackening in the Soviet-Indian relationship which the change in government in Delhi might bring about. "A break in the friendly relations between the Soviet Union and India is what the Chinese hegemonists would like to see most today," wrote one Soviet commentator.[21]

Despite Chinese hopes—in Moscow's view—that "the change of

government would weaken Soviet-Indian ties,"[22] there has been some change but no radical alteration in relations. Desai and Vajpayee went to Moscow in October 1977 and with their hosts reaffirmed the importance of Soviet-Indian relations. While to the Soviets this visit "was a vivid demonstration of the friendship and good-neighborly relations between the Soviet Union and India,"[23] to outside analysts it more closely resembled "a deft downgrading of what was once an intimate relationship to the level of mere friendship."[24] The new Indian foreign policy was indeed one of no special relationships with any state while continuing the important relations with the Soviet Union.

Soviet policy in India is currently not only confronted with a renewed Indian sensitivity to "true nonalignment," but also to changes in U.S. and Chinese policies toward New Delhi. The Carter Administration has taken a far greater interest than its recent predecessors in India and in Indo-American relations. Many of the outlooks of Jimmy Carter and Morarji Desai are similar. Relations clearly have improved, particularly with Carter's New Year's Day, 1978 visit, although the two states are still divided on a number of issues—particularly the prickly one of U.S. supplies of enriched uranium for India's Tarapur atomic reactor. After a great deal of negotiating and a lengthy delay, a promised shipment of 16.8 tons finally arrived in India in April 1979. Despite this, it appears that there will be no further shipments unless India reverses her position on international inspections and safeguards to accept them. This issue seems likely to prevent Indo-U.S. ties from becoming much closer (despite the American cut-off of aid to Pakistan in May 1979 in response to reports of Islamabad's building an atomic bomb.)

In the area of Sino-Indian relations there has also been movement which Moscow undoubtedly is watching carefully. India was prepared to make an initiative toward China in 1978, but Vajpayee's visit had to be postponed when the foreign minister became ill. In February 1979, however, he did make the trip and the talks began productively. As Vajpayee later reported to the Indian parliament, the meetings were cordial, numerous areas of agreement were found, and China gained "a new respect for our policy of genuine nonalignment." To be sure there were differences, particularly over the border question which had merely been "unfrozen" by the talks and concerning which it would take "maturity and reciprocal efforts" over a "long haul" to bring about a satisfactory resolution.[25] However, a serious if only temporary blow was dealt to this new stage in the long-hostile Sino-Indian relationship when Beijing undertook its invasion of Vietnam while Vajpayee was still in China. Forced to cut his visit short, the external affairs minister returned to New Delhi, where he seemed to spend most of his time defending his trip and negotiations; and he denied that he had gone at

U.S. insistence or that he had any knowledge of China's plans and expressed his regret at the Chinese action. The Soviets quickly sought to capitalize on the damage done to hopes for a significant improvement in relations between Beijing and New Delhi. Soviet Premier Kosygin arrived in the Indian capital within three weeks of the Chinese invasion and took every opportunity to condemn the Chinese. An especially prominent theme was of seeing China's invasion of Vietnam as an example of China's attitudes and policies toward its neighbors—that is, China might also want "to teach a lesson" to India at some time in the future.[26] Thus, despite some fine points of difference in the Soviet and Indian approaches toward China and Southeast Asia, it is clear that China's actions played directly into Moscow's hands. The Kremlin's urgings of caution to New Delhi in its pursuit of a normalization with Beijing will, at least for the short run, carry a bit more weight.

Finally, mention also must be made of Moscow's efforts to strengthen ties with the other states of South Asia. The Soviets moved quickly after the 1971 war to restore relations with Pakistan, and ties have been cordial if not close since. Soviet-Bangladesh relations were initially very warm, but regime changes in Dacca have led to a substantial cooling. The Soviet Union has also made approaches toward Nepal and Sri Lanka and relations there are also satisfactory if not warm. Afghanistan is the only country of the region where developments have engaged Soviet interests and involvement on anything approaching the scale of the engagement with India. The bloody military-led coup in Kabul in April 1978 brought a regime that has sought increasingly close ties with the Soviet Union. The Soviets have undertaken substantial military and economic aid programs, sent a large number of advisers, and signed a twenty-year Treaty of Friendship, Good Neighborliness, and Cooperation, concluded during the December visit to Moscow of the new leader, Nur Mohammed Taraki. Taraki has declared himself a Marxist-Leninist, and although he describes his foreign policy as pragmatic and nonaligned, Soviet-Afghan relations have become quite close. Moscow may well be developing a significant stake in the Taraki regime. The March 1979 antiregime uprisings by Muslims in Afghanistan were vociferously condemned by the Soviets, who accused Pakistan, Iran, Britain, the United States, and China, of aiding the "Afghan reactionaries."[27] Moscow also stepped up its military aid to Kabul, including the provision of sophisticated helicopter gunships (and perhaps Soviet pilots).

In sum, despite the problems and differences in Soviet-Indian relations, this relationship probably represents Moscow's greatest "success story" among its efforts in non-Communist Asia. Despite the new Janata government, Moscow's relations with New Delhi are probably closer than its ties with any other non-Communist capital in all of Asia. Still, the Soviet Union's actual influence, or leverage, seems greatly limited. As long as the interests of the two coincide, their cooperation will be close. Where their interests are different, however, their policies diverge. An illuminating example of this is the issue of Asian collective security: India's reaction has been so cool that the Soviets chose not even to mention it during Desai's 1977 visit or Kosygin's 1979 trip.

THE INDIAN OCEAN: SOVIET-U.S. NAVAL RIVALRY

Since 1968, the Soviet Union has engaged in a dramatic strengthening of its naval power in the Indian Ocean. It now deploys more ships for more days and undertakes a far greater number of port calls than does the United States. When Moscow dispatched an aircraft carrier task force into the area in April 1979, it increased the Soviet naval force in the Indian Ocean to about 24 vessels, as compared to about 11 for the United States. The USSR goals in this display of naval power are several: greater control over the only ice-free sea passage between European Russia and her Eastern ports; the protection of her economic and military complexes in the southern USSR; and the furtherance of her efforts to establish influence with those countries, such as India, bordering this strategic body of water.

While defending its own peaceful intentions in the area, Moscow has been quick to denounce Washington's military expansion, which only builds up tension and fuels the arms race.[28] In 1971 the United Nations General Assembly passed a resolution on the Declaration of the Indian Ocean as a Zone of Peace. This resolution called for:

> eliminating from the Indian Ocean all bases, military installations, logistical supply facilities, the disposition of nuclear weapons and weapons of mass destruction and any manifestation of great power military presence in the Indian Ocean conceived in the context of great power rivalry.

The Soviets have repeatedly cited their support for this concept of the Indian Ocean as a "zone of peace" provided that the stipulation of the removal of all foreign military bases—that is, primarily U.S.—is met. The U.S. decision in early 1973 to upgrade base facilities at Diego Garcia has been the particular target of Soviet accusations.

The Soviet Union has substantial support from India in the campaign against U.S. naval power in the area. This may well be due to

Delhi's perception that the only way to curtail greater Soviet involvement and a superpower arms race is to have Washington decrease its
own activity. In any case, successive Indian governments have expressed concern over, not what the Soviets may do, but what the
United States has already done in establishing a presence.[29] One
country which has denounced Moscow's policy as hypocritical is, not
surprisingly, China. According to one Soviet analysis:

> As the world is increasingly protesting against American air and naval
> bases in the Indian and Pacific Oceans China has not made a single
> move to support the just demands of the littoral states, although the
> Chinese leaders like to pose as champions of those states' interests.
> With their tacit approval, the USA is setting up other military
> installations as well. The Chinese leaders try "not to notice" the
> appearance of new imperialist strongholds.[30]

For the last few years Moscow and Washington have been engaged
in talks on the demilitarization of the Indian Ocean. The difficulties of
definitions are enormous—between port calls and a semipermanent
base, between transit and stationing, and so forth. Nevertheless, the
talks have gone on sporadically. As Moscow has recognized,[31] both sides
have practical reasons for seeking an accord—for the Soviet Union, the
reasons cited above, for the United States the similar one of the
importance of the Indian Ocean as a transport route for oil and other
raw materials. The Russians would prefer a solution that included the
liquidation of military bases and a mutual reduction of Soviet and
American military presence there. Yet they would be willing to accept
Washington's gradual, step-by-step approach of freezing military activities by both sides—a move toward "an actual reduction of the level of
military activity" and, most importantly, toward "corresponding measures with respect to military bases."

That this issue of the Indian Ocean is still an important one was
seen again in Kosygin's March 1979 visit to India. Both countries
criticized reports that Washington was seeking to upgrade its naval
presence in the area, and both called for a zone of peace. The joint
communique signed at the end of the visit expressed regret at the
suspension of the U.S.-Soviet talks and urged its immediate resump-
tion. Thus, while the question of superpower rivalry is no longer as hot
an issue as earlier in the 1970s, it still remains an important facet of the
Soviet Union's Asian policy.

NON-COMMUNIST SOUTHEAST ASIA: MINIMAL RETURN

Since the end of the 1960s, the Soviet Union has undertaken a major offensive in its efforts to extend its influence in Southeast Asia.[32] Given interests the Soviets had perceived there historically, the various changes in international and regional relations that were becoming significant gave Moscow additional incentive to escalate its efforts in the region. The Soviet Union certainly feared a situation where either the United States would hang on to its influence behind a smokescreen of withdrawal or China would asume the role of the dominant power in the region. The Soviets also came to see Japan's rapidly expanding economic presence as an equally serious development. Significantly, this acceleration of Soviet activity has become intertwined with the growing effort of all the regional states to deal with these same international changes as well as their own domestic issues.

With the opening of relations with Malaysia and Singapore in the latter 1960s, the Soviet Union had established formal diplomatic ties with all the states of Southeast Asia except the Philippines. Long—and to the Russians undoubtedly frustrating—negotiations finally established Moscow-Manila ties during President Marcos's visit to the Soviet Union in May 1976. A major instrument in the Soviet effort to foster closer relations beyond the diplomatic and official level has been the familiar "carrot" of economic aid and trade offers. Here, in an area where Moscow can compete somewhat with Washington and Tokyo and where it has a clear advantage over Beijing, the Russians have won only limited successes. Both Burma and Malaysia have resisted substantial Soviet proposals, and hence only modest beginnings have been made. The same, but on a smaller scale, for both offers and acceptances, is true of Singapore, Thailand, and the Philippines. It is only in Indonesia that a significant aid program has been undertaken. Indonesia was of course the recipient of large-scale Soviet economic (and military) assistance in the Sukarno era; but ever since 1965, economic relations have been as strained as the overall political relationship. In December 1974, however, the Soviets were able to conclude an economic and technical cooperation agreement with Jakarta. Indonesian policy in this respect was partly the result of a political desire to demonstrate its nonaligned credentials and partly an economic reaction to the "softer" Soviet loan terms. Near the end of 1975, a further step was taken in the announcement that the Soviets would build two hydroelectric plants in Indonesia (at a cost exceeding $100 million). Nevertheless, this cooperation has been limited as Soviet bloc offers have not proven lenient enough or large enough to meet Indonesia's massive economic needs. The Suharto regime has thus continued to look primarily to the United States, Western Europe, and Japan for its assistance.[33]

Soviet efforts to expand trade with the countries of Southeast Asia have also met with only limited success. Not only has total trade risen just slightly since the beginning of the 1960s but, much more significantly for the Soviet Union, that country has been unable to develop substantial markets for its goods. Moscow's balance of trade with Southeast Asia has shown a chronic deficit.

Current Soviet emphasis is concentrated on the Philippines, Thailand, Singapore, and Indonesia. The Russians have expressed enthusiasm for any moves by these states which tended to loosen their military ties to the United States. The closing of U.S. bases in Thailand in mid-1976 was welcomed by Moscow as was the early 1979 Manila-Washington agreement, which turned over the Subic Bay naval base and Clark Field air base to Philippine sovereignty. The first Soviet ambassador arrived in Manila in January 1978, and in October of that year Soviet Deputy Minister Firyubin visited the Philippines. Thailand also has recently received a new Soviet ambassador (in mid-1978, as did Malaysia at that time) and has had other important Soviet visitors including Firyubin (who also visited Indonesia). While economic ties with Thailand have remained small-scale, Bangkok recently signed a trade agreement with some East European states. In the most significant development in Soviet-Thai relations, Prime Minister Kriangsak of Thailand journeyed to Moscow in March 1979 in the first visit ever of the top Thai political leader to the USSR. Although the visit was primarily concerned with the situation in Indochina—especially Thai anxieties about the intentions of their newfound Vietnamese "neighbors" and the effects of the Vietnamese invasion of Cambodia—a major focus also was on bilateral relations. The joint communique underlined the "friendly atmosphere" and "spirit of mutual understanding" in the talks as well as "the coincidence or closeness of the two countries' positions on many current issues."[34] Singapore's Foreign Minister Rajaratnam visited the Soviet Union in April 1976, where he and Foreign Minister Gromyko "declared for broader mutually profitable cooperation in trade, economic, and political fields."[35] Soviet interest in the city-state, both for trade and for ship repair facilities, continues unabated.

Viewing the region as a whole, Moscow has been suspicious of the Association of Southeast Asian Nations (ASEAN)—comprised of Indonesia, Malaysia, the Philippines, Singapore, and Thailand—ever since its formation in 1967. The prime danger of this organization in Soviet eyes is that it could take on a U.S.-influenced military character. The Russians undoubtedly realize that their skepticism toward ASEAN impedes the development of relations with the member states, and in recent years have tempered their accusations and warnings. How far they have been willing to go, however, is seen in their talks with Thailand's Kriangsak. The USSR *"duly notes"* (rather than "accepts" or "agrees with") said one Soviet analysis, the statements of the leaders of ASEAN countries that they strive to promote economic and cultural cooperation *and that this association is not military in character.*[36]

The organization's 1971 proposal to make Southeast Asia a "Zone of Peace, Freedom, and Neutrality"[37] has also been greeted warily by Moscow. Probably perceived as a scheme which would preclude the Soviet Union (and perhaps the United States) but not China from the region, the Soviets have preferred their own collective security system approach. Yet in recent years this has also undergone subtle change. Soviet criticism of the neutralization idea has softened, direct espousing of collective security has become less frequent, and the Russians have been suggesting that there were close parallels between the two approaches. At the CPSU's Twenty-fifth Congress in February 1976, Brezhnev asserted that the Soviet Union is continuing "to participate actively in searches for ways to strengthen peace and security on the Asian continent," but he made no reference to any collective security system.[38] Again, in the talks with Kriangsak, the Soviets indicated their middle position of lessened hostility but continued wariness: "*The Soviet Union views with understanding* [rather than "supports"] the idea of creating a zone of peace in Southeast Asia which was advanced by a number of countries of that region."[39]

Through virtually all of the Soviet offensive in Southeast Asia during the 1970s, Moscow has been faced with a Chinese offensive of even greater magnitude. Prime Minister Tun Razak of Malaysia journeyed to Beijing in May 1974 to formalize Sino-Malaysian diplomatic relations, and Marcos and then Thai Prime Minister Kukrit of Thailand came soon afterward for the same purpose. In November 1978, Vice-Premier Deng Ziaoping (Teng Hsiao-ping) made a much heralded trip through Malaysia, Singapore and Thailand, in which he levelled scathing attacks against the Soviet Union and Vietnam. There have also been visits to the Philippines, made by other Chinese leaders. To China itself, again, there came Lee Kuan Yew of Singapore in May 1976, Kriangsak in March 1978, and Prime Minister Datuk Mussein bin Onn of Malaysia in May 1979. In its relations with non-ASEAN countries, the PRC remained closer to neutral Burma than any other state, and Ne Win's trips to China now number at least a dozen. In addition to these bilateral efforts to establish their own role in Southeast Asia and to warn against Soviet designs—and also to encourage a continued U.S. presence that includes a military commitment—the Chinese have also been supportive of regional security efforts. Beijing's outspoken support of ASEAN and its "zone of peace, freedom, and neutrality" proposal has been in marked contrast to Moscow's suspicious attitude.

The PRC has also endorsed the 1969 Indonesian-Malaysian declaration of sovereignty over the Straits of Malacca, a policy which the Russians have opposed. This is not to say that Beijing does not face serious obstacles, too. These include the emotion-laden overseas Chinese issue and Chinese support of communist guerrilla movements in various states. The Soviets regularly accuse China of seeking to subvert Southeast Asian regimes—both through local Chinese insurgents and insurrection in the countryside. These issues have particularly hurt Beijing's relations with Jakarta, as well as Rangoon, Kuala Lumpur, and to a lesser extent Bangkok.

A final concern for Moscow is that Washington's withdrawal from Southeast Asia does not seem to be taking place, at least not with the rapidity that the Soviets would like. Beginning in February 1978, the Carter Administration seemed to pick up the themes of Ford's Pacific Doctrine and to stress the continuation of the U.S. commitments to Asia.[40] In May, Vice President Mondale visited the Philippines, Thailand, and Indonesia (as well as Australia and New Zealand) in order to counter widespread concern in this region that Washington was cutting back its political, military, and economic commitments. Mondale's trip seems to have had the desired effect and the United States followed this up by appointing a China expert as ambassador to Thailand, proposing new military aid to Bangkok, subduing its human rights campaign against martial law in the Philippines, continuing large-scale economic assistance to Indonesia, and signing the new bases agreement with Manila.

Despite all its efforts, the Soviet Union is still viewed with considerable suspicion in Southeast Asia. Moscow tends to be seen as an outsider in contrast to Beijing with whom the Southeast Asian states will have to coexist permanently. To a great extent, the loosening of ties between the United States and some of these states has redounded more to China's benefit than to the Soviet Union's. Perhaps most discouraging for Moscow is the case of Indonesia where, notwithstanding that its relations with China have remained "frozen" since 1967, the Soviet Union has been able to make little progress in even reestablishing a presence, much less an influence. In any case, all states of the region are striving to avoid being dragged into the middle of the Sino-Soviet conflict. The Soviet veto in the Security Council early in 1979 of the ASEAN proposal for withdrawing of all foreign troops from Indochina (Vietnamese troops from Cambodia as well as Chinese troops from Vietnam) not only antagonized the ASEAN states but also made clear the reality of this great power rivalry in the life of Southeast Asia.

INDOCHINA: HOW LONG-LASTING THE NEW ALLIANCE?

Indochina had been the focus of continuing and major conflict from the end of World War II up to the 1975 communist victories there. Since 1975, a number of factors have made possible a close relationship between the most important state in Indochina—Vietnam—and the Soviet Union.[41] For one thing, Hanoi could turn only to the Communist bloc for the necessary economic assistance to rebuild and develop the war-ravaged and backward country. The Soviet Union continued to be the Socialist Republic of Vietnam's (SRV) major aid donor—on a massive scale—and also major trade partner, and has been its main arms supplier as well. Diplomatically, the SRV found itself almost isolated, especially in Southeast Asia, in 1975. The Soviet Union was seen as the way out of this isolation. Not only were bilateral relations further developed, but Moscow served as Hanoi's major supporter in the drive against Washington—for the cause of UN membership first (Vietnam was finally admitted in September 1977), and then for U.S. reconstruction aid for Vietnam (on which no progress was made). The Soviet Union also was diplomatically valuable to Vietnam in the effort to keep China at arm's length. Historical antagonism with the Chinese has taught Hanoi the value of an ally who is both powerful and distant. Moscow's support for Hanoi's claims to the Paracel and Spratly island groups was particularly significant.

Given Vietnam's history of independent behavior—not only in its resistance to French and then American domination but also in its neutrality in the Sino-Soviet dispute—one might well expect the Vietnamese leadership to be less than satisfied with this degree of dependence on the Soviet Union. Indeed, from 1975 to 1978 there was growing evidence of subtle but significant changes in the relationship. During this time Hanoi undertook accelerated efforts to diversify its sources of economic and technological assistance. Significant successes were obtained in negotiations with the International Monetary Fund, with France, and with Japan.

In the political arena, too, Vietnam had some success in emerging from its isolation. In Southeast Asia, Vietnam's perception of ASEAN began to change after that organization's summit in August 1977. Hanoi perceived several developments there as being positive—including the offers of goodwill to the nations of Indochina and the refusal of the leaders to convert ASEAN into a military alliance—and responded publicly to them.[42] The evolution of Vietnamese policy was even more significant in bilateral relations. Political, economic, and goodwill missions from Hanoi began to circulate through the region, the most notable being those of Deputy Foreign Minister Phan Hien in July 1976 and Foreign Minister Nguyen Duy Trinh in December 1977. During the visit of a U.S. delegation to Hanoi in March 1977, the Vietnamese took a further step to respond to lingering regional suspicions by enunciating a four point foreign policy toward Southeast Asia: Point one—respect for each other's independence, sovereignty, territorial integrity; nonaggression and noninterference; equality, mutual benefit, and peaceful coexistence; two—denial to any country of the use of one's territory as a base for direct or indirect aggression; three—establishment of good-neighborly relations, economic cooperation and cultural exchange and settlement of disputes through negotiations; four—development of cooperation among the countries of the region for the prosperity of each and for the sake of genuine independence, peace and neutrality in Southeast Asia.[43] By the beginning of 1978, Hanoi had at least reasonably positive relations with all the ASEAN capitals.[44] Although ties with the United States were not forthcoming, Vietnam was accepted at the Nonaligned Summit in Colombo, Sri Lanka in 1976 and began to build relations with Japan. Most importantly, the Sino-Vietnamese relationship underwent gradual improvement. Visits increased, the tempo of China's aid program accelerated, and Communist Party leader Le Duan even thanked the PRC—by name—at the 1977 Bolshevik Revolution celebration in Moscow. Differences between Moscow and Hanoi also became more visible. These were manifested in an unwillingness to endorse the collective security idea for Asia, a subtler and more flexible approach toward ASEAN; and there were similar differences in dealing with China.

Thus, developments between 1975 and 1978 indicate that Vietnam was increasingly seeking to strengthen its own independence and autonomy and, still relying on close ties to the Soviet Union, to differentiate its own interests from those of its Soviet benefactors. Whereas both Hanoi and Moscow seek a reduced role for the United States in the region, the underlying goal of enhancing Vietnam's role in Southeast Asia is a much more operational, immediate, and complex one for the Vietnamese themselves than it is for the Soviets. Unless Vietnam chooses to take the revolutionary and ideological bath which it has thus far eschewed, it must attain economic development and stronger economic and political ties within the area in order to play a prominent regional role. Hanoi cannot afford to bear the degree of apprehension, let alone hostility, toward ASEAN that Moscow does, for it would be counterproductive in two ways. First, it would jeopardize relations with these states, and second, it would hamper Hanoi in obtaining the kind of economic and technological assistance needed from Japan and the West—needs which well may be unavailable from the Soviet Union in sufficient quantity, quality, or sophistication. Moreover, the ASEAN states have repeatedly stressed their wish for the United States and Japan not to undertake large-scale aid programs to Vietnam. Presumably, as the ASEAN perceptions of a Vietnamese threat recede, the opposition to such aid for the SRV will likewise diminish.

A similar situation involves the goal of containing the growing Chinese role in Southeast Asia. There is an agreement on opposition to China between Vietnam and the Soviet Union, and this has motivated a good deal of cooperation between the two. But there are also differences and the main one is that, roughly speaking, Moscow's operational motivation is anti-China while Hanoi's is pro-Vietnam. In order to enhance its own role, Vietnam has to recognize geographical realities and avoid alienating China gratuitously. For this reason, and for the purpose of asserting its own independent nationalism, the country also needs to continue its historical role of independence in the Sino-Soviet dispute. Finally, if relations with China become too strained, Hanoi runs the risk of being isolated in the region. Chinese diplomatic activity in the 1970s, which has included significantly improved bilateral relations with each state except Indonesia, strong support for ASEAN, and mediation efforts in such problems as the Thai-Cambodian border dispute, had to be worrisome to the Vietnamese. Thus, Hanoi has needed at least "normalized" relations with the PRC for a variety of reasons, while Moscow has operated with far fewer constraints.

This is not the place to take up the details of the escalating border war between Vietnam and Cambodia during 1978, the blitzkrieg Vietnamese invasion which overran Cambodia in December and January, or the Chinese invasion of Vietnam which followed a month later in February 1979. Certainly these developments have altered the situation in Indochina and the USSR role there. And it should be noted that, as in the other areas of the Soviet Union's Asian interests, Moscow was not the major actor in these events. Both the Vietnamese-Cambodian and the Sino-Vietnamese conflicts have roots deep in history: ancient nationalist antagonisms which have only been further aggravated by new politics, ideologies, and foreign policies.[45] Although Moscow and Beijing have both been drawn in further, neither conflict has been a Sino-Soviet "proxy war" (as Zbigniew Brzezinski described the Vietnamese-Cambodian struggle in early 1978).

The framework of Vietnamese and Soviet goals and policies in the region we have set forth argues that there would be real costs to Hanoi and, to a lesser extent, Moscow in an agressive policy toward Cambodia. Among other things, Vietnam's carefully derived conciliatory image in the region as well as its economic development plans would be dealt a damaging blow. Chances of progress in relations with Washington would be set back, and the growing normalization with the PRC also would be disrupted. Finally, the SRV's effort to strengthen its independence from Moscow would then have to be set aside. For the Soviet Union and China carefully developed "respectability" in the eyes of non-Communist Southeast Asian states would be damaged. That Hanoi undertook its invasion of Cambodia, and Beijing initiated its action against Vietnam, in spite of these costs and further risks, testifies to the crucial importance of these situations to the leaders in Vietnam and China. The situation in Cambodia was intolerable to the Vietnamese, and the Chinese found it unthinkable to allow Vietnam to "get away with" its invasion of China's ally.

The interweaving of developments in the region itself and with external powers from mid-1978 on is exceedingly complex. Much in the way of factual information, not to mention data on motivations, is lacking. Nevertheless, a tentative scenario of interactions can be presented. For Vietnam, economic problems were worsening. The five-year plan was substantially behind schedule. In the southern part of the country particularly, the economic problems were becoming increasingly serious. Vietnam's response was twofold; first, it was to seek further outside assistance, and this included new overtures to the United States—Hanoi in the summer of 1978 dropped its previous demand for reparations as a precondition for diplomatic ties; and second, to undertake internal reforms to further the building of socialism and economic development, especially in the south. The second aspect hit Chinese residents of Vietnam particularly hard. About this time also, the Chinese leadership appears to have chosen a new, less restrained, higher pressure line vis-á-vis Vietnam. Growing Chinese hostility toward Vietnamese positions on Cambodia and the long-standing Sino-Vietnamese border issue was escalated by the overseas Chinese issue. Beijing had begun early in 1978 to be more sympathetic to these Chinese for China's own economic reasons, and these developments in Vietnam were the first opportunity to demonstrate the new approach.[46] These growing tensions with China and pressing economic needs—to which the West and particularly the United States was not responsive—led Hanoi to appeal to Moscow for membership in the Council for Mutual Economic Assistance (COMECON). In late June at the COMECON Council's thirty-second session in Bucharest, Romania, Vietnam became the organization's tenth member much to the surprise of most observers.[47] The political advantage for the Soviet Union of tying the SRV closer to Soviet interests may well be offset by the substantial economic drain that will be put on Moscow and the organization to meet Vietnam's needs. In any case, China's subsequent response of terminating all its economic and technical assistance to Vietnam only added to Hanoi's economic dependence.

Vietnam was finding the Cambodian situation only the less tolerable at this very time. After making the decision to topple the Pol Pot regime in the summer or early fall, Hanoi moved to cut the costs and risks of such a move. Efforts continued to be made into the fall to court the United States, perhaps in hopes that Washington could keep Beijing from becoming too involved. This effort failed and, indeed, the United States sided more with China—and Cambodia—in the growing conflict. (It may be of interest to note that the hardening of the Chinese approach to Vietnam coincided with the ending of Dr. Brzezinski's visit to China in May 1978.) In October, Vietnamese Prime Minister Pham Van Dong toured Southeast Asia in an attempt to strengthen Hanoi's conciliatory image there in the face of the impending invasion. Finally, and most significantly, Le Duan and Pham led a party-government delegation to Moscow in November. Faced with escalating Chinese hostility and making no progress in relations with the United States, the Vietnamese leaders saw no alternative to a closer relationship with Moscow. The two states signed a 25-year Treaty of Friendship and Cooperation. Closely resembling other such Soviet-sponsored treaties, the one with India, for example, this treaty's main significance is symbolic: Soviet defense of Vietnam if the latter is attacked.[48] In late December the Vietnamese invasion began. In mid-February, subsequent to Deng Xiaoping's threatened retaliation while touring the United States in January, China launched its invasion "to teach Vietnam a lesson." The Soviet Union issued warnings and threats to China and supported Vietnam in the United Nations but stayed out of the conflict. Although we are unlikely ever to know how close the USSR came to intervening militarily, the Chinese withdrawal removed Moscow from what surely was the difficult dilemma of needing to defend its ally while wanting to avoid a major conflict over Vietnam with China.

What all of these recent developments mean for Soviet interests is still not clear. Politically, the Russians have gained insofar as Vietnam is a closer ally by virtue of COMECON membership, the treaty, and the thoroughly hostile Sino-Vietnamese relationship. Moreover, the obnoxious Pol Pot regime is gone and China's own respectability has been tarnished by its aggression against a smaller neighbor.[49] Soviet costs are a loss of credibility for Vietnam and itself in Southeast Asia—especially given the USSR veto of the ASEAN-backed resolution in the Security Council—and the increased economic drain brought on by its Vietnamese ally's enormous needs. For Hanoi, its "juggling act" between the West and the Communist world and between the Soviet Union and China indeed "seems to have gone all thumbs" as developments raced beyond Hanoi's control.[50] Given the value of such a "juggling act" to Vietnam's interests and Hanoi's past skill in performing it, however, one ought to expect this stage of such close Soviet-Vietnamese relations to be only temporary. That is, the framework presented earlier will be indicative, when this phase of Sino-Vietnamese tension abates, of Vietnamese behavior and Soviet-Vietnamese relations. Perhaps one shorthand key to the degree of influence Moscow will wield in the immediate future will lie in whether the Soviets are granted base facilities at Cam Ranh Bay or elsewhere along Vietnam's coast. Although there were reports in May 1979 of Soviet warships at Cam Ranh, it was doubtful that an actual base had been established. The granting of such a base to the Soviet Union would run counter to a number of Vietnamese interests vis-à-vis the United States, ASEAN, and their own long-term opposition to military bases on foreign soil. Again, however, the degree of Soviet influence is likely to depend not only on Soviet behavior but also, and significantly, on Chinese and U.S. policies.[51]

NORTHEAST ASIA: SOVIET AMBIVALENCE

In the 1970s new trends began to develop in the potentially (and historically) volatile area of Northeast Asia. In particular, an old arena of great power competition between Russia and China became a new and vital focus: Japan. Economic and political strains in the previously close U.S.-Japanese relationship, compounded by the "shock" of the Nixon visit to China, have made Japan something of a new actor in Asian, if not world, politics. Moscow was quick to seek an advantage in these strains between Tokyo and Washington and to try to prevent a significant rapprochement between Tokyo and Beijing. In the first visit of the Soviet Foreign Minister in five years, Mr. Gromyko, along with a top Soviet expert on China, was dispatched to Japan in January 1972— that is, prior to Nixon's summit conference in Beijing—in an effort to counter these new U.S.-China ties. Soviet anxiety about the possibility of a Sino-Japanese axis of sorts in Asia was evidenced by the efforts of Gromyko, and of his government afterward to offer Japan a peace treaty as well as a variety of significant economic inducements (for the tapping of the vast resources in Siberia and the Soviet Far East). That Moscow's initiatives at least had an impact on Beijing, if not Tokyo, is apparent from the fact that soon afterward the Chinese began putting out feelers to the Japanese. In September 1972 new Japanese Premier Tanaka journeyed to China. Diplomatic ties were established, relations were gradually normalized, and trade and economic exchanges rapidly increased.

Clearly the Russians and the Chinese have sought to utilize their new relations with Japan against each other. Beijing has been worried about the strategic implications of possible Japanese assistance for Soviet projects near the Chinese border, while the Soviets have denounced Chinese attempts to drive a wedge between Japan and the Soviet Union. Given the value to Moscow of closer Soviet-Japanese relations, relations which would thus minimize the threat of a United States-China-Japan united front, it is surprising that these Soviet efforts of the early 1970s have gradually decreased in intensity and had little effect in strengthening the relationship between Moscow and Tokyo. The crux for the Soviets is simply that the price demanded by the Japanese has been too high. In any case, it seems that by the end of the 1970s, Beijing in building new relations with Tokyo, and Washington in maintaining its ties there, had done better than Moscow had done in its efforts to ingratiate itself with the Japanese.

In addition to historical enmity, Soviet-Japanese relations have been beset by significant bilateral differences. One of these has been over fishing rights and zones. During 1977 the two sides struggled through 73 days of extremely tough negotiations with the final agreement being, on balance, disadvantageous to the Japanese side. Another area of friction has developed in the economic sphere. Despite great promise, Soviet-Japanese economic relations have still not matched initial expectations. Early aspirations were centered in the prospect that Japanese capital and ingenuity would develop the abundant raw material resources in Siberia. Although a number of important projects are under way, others have been scrapped, and the extent of Japanese participation remains smaller than anticipated. This state of affairs is most likely due to a mixture of factors, including Japanese doubts about project profitability, Soviet proposal changes in midstream, unacceptable terms set by the Soviet Union, and—perhaps most importantly— the growing attractiveness for Japan of the Chinese market and investments in the PRC.

The main stumbling block to improved Soviet-Japanese relations has been the territorial issue.[52] Japan contends that the four "northern islands" (three islands and a small archipelago actually) which the Soviet Union occupied at the close of World War II represent an unresolved dispute. In 1956 the USSR agreed to return the southernmost two islands (including the archipelago) upon the signing of a peace treaty (from World War II). However, since that time the Soviets have gradually hardened their position and now contend that there is no unresolved issue. Strident Chinese support for the Japanese on this issue, support which dates from Mao's linking in 1964 of China's and Japan's territorial grievances against the Soviet Union with those of other states, some in Eastern Europe, increase Soviet fears of opening a

Pandora's box by their returning any of the islands. The Soviet Union clearly is apprehensive of potential irredentist claims that could be presented around the entirety of the country's border.

The overriding area of concern for Moscow is Japanese foreign policy. A major fear is the growth of cooperation among the United States, Japan, and China that would work to the detriment of Soviet interests in Asia. The Pacific Doctrine of 1975 pointed toward precisely that eventuality. Since that time, the Soviets have seen new developments which are bringing this apprehension closer to reality. For one thing, and this is a major factor in Moscow's outlook on Asia, the Soviets believe that Washington is gradually developing Japan to be its proxy in Asia. The United States envisions a division of labor whereby a newly militarized Japan takes on a major responsibility to provide the region's security. Japan's economic diplomacy will be a primary facet of this. The Russians are, of course, quick to point out that the Mutual Security Treaty between Washington and Tokyo remains in force.[53]

The other development which is making the Washington-Beijing-Tokyo triangle[54] a reality to the Soviet Union is the Sino-Japanese Treaty of Peace and Friendship signed in August 1978. The Soviets have fruitlessly broached such a treaty of their own with the Japanese, but the latter have refused to sign an agreement without a resolution of the territorial issue. The Soviets in turn devoted their attention to seeking to prevent Tokyo and Beijing from concluding the agreement. Most Soviet efforts were concentrated on warning the Japanese of the unfavorable reaction such an agreement would create in the Soviet Union, in Soviet-Japanese relations, and in terms of peace and stability in Asia. What particularly bothered Moscow was China's intention to include an anti-hegemony clause in the agreement. Moscow reportedly went so far as to rush Gromyko to Tokyo in early 1976 "with an offer to return two of the four northern islands in exchange for a firm pledge that Japan would not be party to an antihegemony clause."[55] Tokyo rejected this as interference in their policy. Despite delays and Japanese efforts to reach a compromise with the PRC regarding the clause, the agreement which was finally signed included the antihegemony clause. Since then, the development of Sino-Japanese relations, political and economic, have continued apace, and have far outstripped Soviet-Japanese ties.

By the end of the 1970s, then, Moscow seemed to be coping unsuccessfully with the changing environment of Northeast Asia. Even in Korea there were no developments which were to the Soviet Union's advantage. Not only did the North Korean leadership under Kim Il-sung lean slightly toward China (and Chinese Premier Hua Guofeng visited in May 1978 to strengthen this) but the constraints on Soviet policy were so great as to straitjacket Moscow's behavior: the Soviet Union cannot risk a conflict given its more important relations with the United States and cannot advocate a peaceful settlement—other than on Pyongyang's terms—given its competition with China for North Korea's allegiance.[56] A maintenance of a quiet status quo is the most Moscow can hope for. Japan may be less potentially explosive than Korea, but in the long run the former is far more critical for Soviet interests in Asia. Here, too, *immobilisme* seems to be the dominant theme in Soviet policy. In Arnold Horelick's words,

> What is surprising is not the activation of Soviet diplomacy toward Japan, which did follow immediately on the heels of the 1971 'Nixon shocks,' but its faltering and vacillating course, and the failure of Soviet diplomacy to seize fresh opportunities.[57]

It may well be that the Kremlin is gripped by a basic ambivalence as to how to deal with an emerging Japan. In any case, the stalemate in Moscow-Tokyo relations that Horelick observed in 1976 is still true at the end of the decade and thus all the more remarkable given the importance of Japan to Soviet interests in Asia.[58]

CONCLUSION: WHERE DOES MOSCOW GO FROM HERE?

This chapter has attempted to construct a framework through which Soviet behavior in Asia might be understood. The hope is that this framework will serve as a means of interpreting specific Soviet actions and daily events and for dealing with the unresolved questions about Soviet motivations and policies. This framework provides a context for understanding the past, current, and, not least, future particulars of Soviet interests and policies in Asia. Soviet foreign policy in Asia in the 1980s will be affected and constrained by the same kinds of factors as operated in the 1970s. The analysis in this chapter thus provides a basis for assessing the future of Soviet Asian behavior.

The diversity and complexity of Asia make simple and sweeping conclusions dangerous and potentially misleading. Among those statements that can be made, perhaps the most important is that while the Soviet Union may not have vital interests in Asia—other than its direct confrontation with China—the region is of immense importance to it. This is so for a number of reasons. The areas of Asia border the Soviet Union. It is in Asia that the interests of all the major powers meet. It was in Asia that the United States once tried to build a wall of containment around the Soviet Union. It is, finally, a region where the Sino-Soviet rivalry is the most active and the most intense.

There is abundant evidence that Moscow sees its rivalry with Beijing as a zero-sum game. In this case, the results are not very positive or encouraging for the Soviets. This is especially true in Northeast Asia, non-Communist Southeast Asia, and in an overall sense in regard to the collective security idea. In Indochina the Soviets have a definite plus, and in South Asia they are also the winners. Yet even in these two cases, there are definite limits to the Soviet Union's success. The real winners appear to be those smaller states seeking greater independence and maneuverability in world affairs. This desire for independence—which will continue to assert itself even in Vietnam—constitutes a major obstacle to the expansion of Soviet influence. The desire of most of these states to avoid being caught in the middle of the Sino-Soviet dispute is another. The competition between the Soviet "outsider"—especially valid in the ASEAN area but no longer so in South Asia or Indochina—and the "natural" Pacific powers of China, Japan, and the United States is still another. A final one is the limited means Moscow can bring to bear in Asia other than military clout; for example, the economic aid Moscow can offer is on too small a scale to cope with the massive needs in many countries.[59]

Questions abound regarding the future of Asia's international relations. These concern particularly India's nonalignment, Indonesia's role, Vietnam's independence, Japan's world and regional role, and the United States' future involvement. Although Moscow has not been overly successful in general, there is no evidence that Moscow is giving up the game. As one analyst stated after a review of Soviet commentary on the subject:

> The overall impression . . . is that they recognize the need for a patient, long-term Soviet effort to attract the Asian states to a Soviet-focussed collective security system as an alternative to the dissolving US-built or sponsored alliance system or their replacement with Chinese and Japanese dominance.[60]

Thus, while Moscow is likely to continue its efforts to contain the influence of others while expanding its own, Soviet frustration is also likely to become apparent. A recent example can be seen in a Soviet analysis which was castigating Beijing's "hegemony-seeking" in Asia. Referring to "peace-loving nations" of Asia, the writer concluded his article by saying that these states

> will have to show greater vigilance in respect of the Peking militarists' dangerous plans in the Far East and Pacific if they are to frustrate these expansionist plans and strengthen peace and international cooperation.[61]

Yet, the Soviet Union's interests are too deeply tied into Asia for Moscow to allow itself the luxury of much more explicit criticism. The prognosis is for a continuation of Soviet efforts toward the same goals and via the same means. Whether the Soviets will be any more successful than thus far depends primarily on developments that are largely beyond their control.

NOTES

1. I am using the term "influence" in a specific way: the ability to affect the behavior of another state in the manner desired. For an excellent analysis of the concept, and for insightful case studies which apply it, see Alvin Z. Rubinstein, ed., *Soviet and Chinese Influence in the Third World* (New York: Praeger, 1975).

2. Roger E. Kanet, "Soviet Attitudes toward Developing Nations Since Stalin," in *The Soviet Union and the Developing Nations*, ed. Roger E. Kanet (Baltimore: The Johns Hopkins University Press, 1974), p. 50.

3. A good discussion of the Soviet approach to Asia can be found in Thomas P. Thornton, "The USSR and Asia," in *Asia and the International System*, ed. Wayne Wilcox, Leo E. Rose, and Gavin Boyd (Cambridge, Mass.: Winthrop, 1972), pp. 273–303.

4. Much of the framework for the discussion in this section is based on the author's "Sino-Soviet Relations in an Era of Détente," *Asian Affairs* (May-June 1976): 287–304.

5. All military figures are taken from the annual issues of *The Military Balance* (London: International Institute of Strategic Studies).

6. See ibid. for 1978–79.

7. For analysis of the negotiations, and the linkage of the negotiations with broader issues, see the excellent study by Kenneth G. Lieberthal, "Sino-Soviet Conflict in the 1970s: Its Evolution and Implications for the Strategic Triangle" (Rand Publication R-2342-NA, July 1978). Through mid-May 1979, there had been no talks since April-June 1978 session.

8. For a detailed analysis of Soviet and Chinese policies from the time of Mao's death until the summer of 1977, see Robert C. Horn, "China and Russia in 1977: Maoism without Mao," *Asian Survey* (October 1977): 919–30.

9. Sino-Soviet interactions at the Bolshevik Revolution anniversary celebrations in Moscow are interesting to observe as a "barometer" of relations. In November 1976, Soviet remarks about China were so mild that the Chinese delegate did not feel compelled to walk out, which he had done every year since at least 1970. In 1977, the Chinese even attended the Soviet reception, the first time in more than a decade that that had happened. In 1978, however, Moscow returned to the attack and Chinese diplomats once again walked out in protest.

10. Even Albania has become alienated from Beijing. In fact, Tirana has now become the center of loyalty for those "radical" splinter parties who oppose détente and relations with the West.

11. *New Times*, no. 14 (April 1972): 38–9.

12. *Soviet News*, June 11, 1973.

13. *Christian Science Monitor*, December 18, 1978. See also *New Times*, no. 49 (December 1978): 10–11.

14. For an example, see the *Renmin Ribao* editorial, "A New Move in the Kremlin's Global Strategy," in *Beijing Review (Peking Review)*, no. 39 (September 29, 1978): 12–15.

15. Dmitry Volsky, "Harking Back," *New Times*, no. 52 (December 1975): 10–11. See also *Izvestia*, December 16, 1975.

16. I. I. Kovalenko, *Sovetskii Soiuz v bor'be za mir i Kollektivniu bezopasnost' v Azii* [The Soviet Union in the Struggle for Peace and Collective Security in Asia] (Moscow: Nauka, 1976). The following discussion is based on the analysis of this book in Lilita Dzirkals, *Soviet Perceptions of Security in East Asia: A Survey of Soviet Comment*, (Rand Publication, P-6038, November 1977), pp. 5–10.

17. *NCNA*, December 29, 1978.

18. For a detailed analysis of changes in these interrelationships during 1969, see Robert C. Horn, "Indian-Soviet Relations in 1969: A Watershed Year?" *ORBIS* (Winter 1976): 1539–63.

19. For this argument, see ibid.

20. The title of William Barnds' chapter in Rubinstein, *Soviet and Chinese Influence*, pp. 23–50.

21. V. Volodin, "Peking Manoeuvres in South Asia," *International Affairs*, no. 11 (November 1978): 22.

22. Ibid.

23. Ibid.

24. A. G. Noorani, "Foreign Policy of the Janata Party Government," *Asian Affairs* (March-April 1978): 225. Many of the points which follow are insightfully discussed in this article.

25. See *Overseas Hindustan Times*, March 8, 1979.

26. Soviet commentators have picked up this and other themes as well. See, for example, V. Tretyakov's dispatch from New Delhi, significantly entitled "Visit Wrecked," in *New Times*, no. 10 (March 1979): 24. The "timing of the aggression," wrote this correspondent, "once again demonstrated to the world the duplicity of the Chinese leaders and their utter disregard for India's prestige."

27. See, for example, Leonid Teplinsky, "The People Defend their Revolution," *New Times*, no. 14 (April 1979): 10–11.

28. See, for example, Dmitry Volsky, "A Strategy without a Future," *New Times*, no. 33, (August 1978): 4–5. See also Dzirkals, *Soviet Perceptions of Security*, pp. 50–68.

29. For a good discussion, see S. P. Seth, "The Indian Ocean and Indo-American Relations," *Asian Survey* (August 1975): 645–55. The Soviets have not endorsed the proposal to make the Indian Ocean a nuclear free zone, a proposal the Indians have also opposed (which is hardly surprising given New Delhi's nuclear capability).

30. Volodin, "Peking Manoeuvres in South Asia," p. 26.

31. See *Pravda*, January 18, 1978.

32. For detailed analysis, see Robert C. Horn, "Moscow's Southeast Asian Offensive," *Asian Affairs* (March-April 1975): 217–40, and "Moscow and Peking in Post-Indochina Southeast Asia," Asian Affairs, September-October 1976, pp. 14–40.

33. See the interview with Suharto in *Asian Wall Street Journal*, February 21, 1979.

34. Paval Mezentsev, "Cooperation in Many Fields," *New Times*, no. 14 (April 1979): 8–9. See also "The Prime Minister of Thailand to Visit the Soviet Union," *Radio Liberty Research* RL 96/79 (March 21, 1979).

35. A. Usvatov, "Soviet-Singapore Relations," *New Times*, no. 17 (April 1976): 16.

36. Mezentsev, "Cooperation in Many Fields," p. 9. Emphasis added. The dissolution of SEATO led to similar assessments: see, e. g., A. Usvatov, "SEATO is Dead—Is it ASEAN Now?" *New Times*, no. 28 (July 1977): 8–9.

37. See Justus M. van der Kroef, "ASEAN Security and Development: Some Paradoxes and Symbols," *Asian Affairs* (June 1978): 143–60. For other recent and useful analyses of Southeast Asian security issues, see Sheldon W. Simon, "The ASEAN States: Obstacles to Security Cooperation," *ORBIS* (Summer 1978): 415–34; Jusuf Wanandi, "Security in the Asia-Pacific Region: An Indonesian Observation," *Asian Survey*, (Decem-

ber 1978): 1209–20; and Donald E. Weatherbee, "US Policy and the Two Southeast Asias," *Asian Survey* (April 1978): 408–21.

38. *Pravda*, February 25, 1976. The Chinese did not overlook this omission either: "Confronted by growing obstacles which have created difficulties for them, the peddlers are now trying to sell old wine in a new bottle;" *Peking Review*, no. 14, (April 2, 1976): 20, 24.

39. Mezentsev, "Cooperation in Many Fields," p. 9. Emphasis added. A major obstacle in Moscow's view to the establishment of such a zone is the existence of foreign military bases in ASEAN countries.

40. See Bernard K. Gordon, "Loose Cannon on a Rolling Deck? Japan's Changing Security Policies," *ORBIS* (Winter 1979): 967.

41. The discussion in this section is largely drawn from that in Robert C. Horn, "Soviet-Vietnamese Relations and the Future of Southeast Asia," *Pacific Affairs* (Winter 1978–79): pp 585–605. Laos is not treated separately here due to lack of space. Moreover, since 1975 Laos has been largely dominated by Vietnam. Thus, the Soviet role is substantial and Sino-Laotian relations have been strained. The Laotians sent a token force to aid Vietnam in Cambodia, have reportedly allowed the Russians to install military and information gathering equipment on its border with China and have declared China to be the "number one enemy"; see, e. g., *Los Angeles Times*, May 20, 1979. Beijing has responded by castigating Moscow and Hanoi for being "criminally responsible for the deterioration of Sino-Lao relations;" see "Disruption of Sino-Lao Friendship is Deplorable," *Beijing Review*, no. 11 (March 16, 1979): 21–3.

42. See Denzil Peiris, "Sympathy from the Hanoi Communists," *Far Eastern Economic Review FEER*, August 26, 1977, pp. 40–1.

43. Ibid., May 20, 1977, p. 12.

44. For a further argument to the effect that Hanoi's "conciliatory posture" has "eased regional anxieties about Vietnam's intentions," see Franklin B. Weinstein, "US-Vietnam Relations and the Security of Southeast Asia," *Foreign Affairs* (July 1978): 842–56.

45. Among the good discussions of this context of the Vietnamese-Cambodian conflict, see Tai Sung An, "Turmoil in Indochina: The Vietnam-Cambodia Conflict," *Asian Affairs* (March-April 1978): 245–56; Marian Kirsch Leighton, "Perspectives on the Vietnam-Cambodia Border Conflict," *Asian Survey* (May 1978): 448–57; and Joseph J. Zasloff and MacAlister Brown, "The Passion of Kampuchea," *Problems of Communism* (January-February 1979): 28–44.

46. See *FEER*, June 16, 1978, pp. 17–24. Moscow has, of course, taken every opportunity to attack Beijing's ties to the Overseas Chinese and has pointed out the latter's potential role as a "fifth column"; see, e. g., Yori Plekhanov, "Peking's Double Game," *New Times*, no. 22 (May 1978): 23–5. China's strident defense of the Chinese in Vietnam has undoubtedly increased the worries of those states in Southeast Asia with significant minorities.

47. See J. L. Kerr, "The 32nd Session of the COMECON Council," *Radio Free Europe Research* RAD Background Report 154, July 7, 1978. See H. G. Trend, "COMECON Economic Aid to Vietnam," RAD Background Report 225, October 11, 1978, for more on Vietnam's economic needs.

48. The text can be found in *New Times*, no. 46 (November 1978): 5–6. Article 6, which calls for consultations if either is attacked and for "effective measures" to remove any threat and to ensure peace and security, is almost identical to Article 9 in the treaty with India.

49. See the editorial, "Lesson for Whom?" in *New Times*, no. 12 (March 1979): 1.

50. Barry Kramer in the *Wall Street Journal*, July 7, 1978.

51. For arguments in favor of U.S. recognition of Vietnam and a discussion of the

reasons why, see Weinstein, "US-Vietnam Relations," and Horn, "Soviet-Vietnamese Relations." For opposing arguments, see Bernard K. Gordon, "Japan, the United States, and Southeast Asia," *Foreign Affairs* (April 1978): 579–600.

52. See Peggy L. Falkenheim, "Some Determining Factors in Soviet-Japanese Relations," *Pacific Affairs* (Winter 1977–78): 604–24; and Joseph M. Ha, "Moscow's Policy Toward Japan," *Problems of Communism*, September-October 1977): 61–72.

53. See e. g., D. Petrov, "Japan's Place in US Asian Policy," *International Affairs* (October 1978): 52–9.

54. Ibid., p. 58.

55. Ha, "Moscow's Policy Toward Japan," p. 65.

56. These dilemmas for Soviet policy are well described in Donald S. Zagoria, "Korea's Future: Moscow's Perspective," *Asian Survey* (November 1977): 1103–12; and Young C. Kim, "Pyongyang, Moscow, and Peking," *Problems of Communism* (November-December 1978): 54–8.

57. Arnold Horelick, *Soviet Policy Dilemmas in Asia* (Rand Publication P-5774, December 1976), p. 10.

58. Indeed, the Soviet military buildup on two of the disputed islands early in 1979 provoked a strong protest from Tokyo including a statement by Prime Minister Ohira that Japan would have to strengthen its military defenses to counter the USSR's Asian buildup.

59. A good discussion of Soviet problems in Asia can be found in Donald S. Zagoria, "The Soviet Quandary in Asia," *Foreign Affairs* (January 1978): 306–23.

60. Dzirkals, *Soviet Perceptions of Security*, p. 96.

61. V. Borisov, "Hegemony in the Far East—the Peking Policy," *International Affairs* (October 1978): 43. For another recent attack on China's Asian policy, see Y. Semyonov, "Beijing's Policy Constitutes a Military Threat," International Affairs (April 1979): 64–74.

· 4 ·

JAPAN AND ASIAN SECURITY
Martin E. Weinstein

I t is reasonably simple to describe Japan's role in the security arrangements of East Asia from the end of the 1940s to the early 1970s.
Japan's role was membership in the free world, built around close,
cooperative security and economic relations with the United States.
Japan was a lightly armed trading state, with its energies concentrated
first on economic recovery from the disastrous Pacific war, and then on
spectacular economic growth, which by the end of the 1960s made
Japan the third largest industrial economy in the world. During that
period, the United States guaranteed Japan's external security and
backed its guarantee with nuclear and conventional forces, which held
unchallenged predominance in the Western Pacific to the very coast of
Asia. Moreover, for most of these years, the United States was also the
single most important source of Japan's imports, including essential raw
materials such as food, coal, mineral ores, scrap metals, and lumber, as
well as the largest foreign market for Japan's manufactured exports.[1]

Japan's relations with the non-Communist states of Asia were
clearly secondary to the U.S. tie. Although the cold war might have
been expected to generate a degree of cohesion among Japan, South
Korea, Nationalist China, and the Southeast Asian states, in fact, the
bitterness left behind from Japan's military aggression greatly retarded
this process. Through the 1950s, and even into the 1960s, U.S. encouragement and good offices were necessary in reestablishing economic/dip-
lomatic relations between Japan and its free world Asian neighbors. In
the case of South Korea, diplomatic relations were actually not established until 1965.

Although diplomatic relations between Japan and the Soviet Union were restored by the normalization agreement of 1956, the territorial dispute over the northern islands blocked the conclusion of a peace treaty and kept Soviet-Japanese relations cool. Moreover, considering the size of their economies and their apparent complementarity (Japanese technology and capital, undeveloped resources in the Soviet Far East), it may now seem surprising how limited Soviet-Japanese economic relations have been. During the period under discussion, they accounted for approximately 2 percent of Japan's foreign trade. The marked improvement in Sino-Japanese relations in recent years may lead us to forget that during the 1950s and 1960s, Tokyo and Peking had no diplomatic ties, and that the relations between them were frequently more strained than those between Tokyo and Moscow.

In brief, Japan's role in Asian security arrangements from 1948, when the American occupation shifted from a policy of weakening to one of rebuilding Japan, until roughly 1971-72, when U.S. China policy was suddenly reversed (without consulting Japan), was in most respects a classical cold war role. The United States was Japan's principal ally and protector. Japan, with U.S. help, slowly cultivated diplomatic and economic links with its non-Communist neighbors. The 38th parallel, the Taiwan Straits, and the Sea of Japan were the political, strategic, and economic demarcation lines of Japan's world. Beyond these lines lived the Communist enemies with whom Japan talked and traded but little. If the Japanese made a virtue of cold war necessities, however, they were also most deeply concerned that the cold war not turn hot. It is important to note that the Japanese government generally took a decidedly less rigidly antagonistic stance toward the Soviets, the Communist Chinese, and the North Koreans than did the United States. The Japanese government's policy aimed at, and contributed substantially to, making the U.S.-Japan alliance a defensive, unprovocative, stabilizing element in East Asia.

Japanese policy during the Vietnam War partly illustrates this point and also demonstrates the limits of Japanese influence over U.S. policy. Japan was a source of logistical support for U.S. military operations in Vietnam, but the Japanese government refrained from publicly endorsing or supporting U.S. policy in Indochina and frequently irritated American officials by expressing reservations and doubts over their policy in that region. The Sato and Tanaka governments, of course, were well aware that the Vietnam War was unpopular in Japan and that their own electoral positions would not be strengthened by speaking out in favor of the war. Beyond this domestic political consideration, however, Japanese officials were also deeply concerned that the U.S. obsession with Vietnam was diverting U.S. attention and resources from Northeast Asia. They also worried over the possibility that U.S. failure in Vietnam would weaken the entire American military position in Asia, including the U.S. security commitment to Japan. Consequently, the Japanese government was unhappy over the escalation of the war from 1965 to 1968; was relieved when the United States began to extricate itself in 1968–69, and was dismayed by the collapse of the Paris peace agreements between 1973 and 1975.

SHIFTING ALIGNMENTS: BEFORE AND SINCE 1972

Allusions to the cold war and lines of demarcation notwithstanding, the period of the 1950s and 1960s has receded rapidly in our memories, and it would be well to note briefly just what the Asian distribution of power and the regional security arrangements were before the Shanghai Communique of 1972. To begin with, the end of the Pacific war found the United States with an overwhelming, seemingly unchallengeable military predominance in the Western Pacific and along the maritime fringes of East Asia. The huge naval and air forces that the United States had built to defeat Japan, held sway from the Japanese Archipelago through South Korea, on south to the waters around Taiwan, Indo-china, and the Malay Peninsula. The only other significant military power in Asia at the end of World War II was the Soviet Union. As a consequence of the numerical weakness and the short range of Soviet Pacific naval and air forces as well as the serious problems that the Soviets then had in supplying their forces in Asia, they were, in 1945, in a clearly inferior, defensive military position. Nevertheless, motivated perhaps by concern over the safety of their expansive, resource-rich but lightly populated and lightly defended Maritime Provinces, the Soviets acted energetically to assert themselves as an Asian power.

Although Stalin was not successful in his bid, in 1945, to establish a Soviet occupation zone in northern Hokkaido,[2] Soviet forces, in the closing days of the war, did capture all of Sakhalin, the entire Kurile Island chain, and the disputed northern islands. Moreover, Soviet forces pushed on through Manchuria and set up a zone of occupation in Korea, north of the 38th parallel. Following the Communist takeover of China in 1949, the conclusion of the Sino-Soviet pact, and the surprisingly vigorous Communist Chinese military performance in the Korean War (1950–53), it appeared that the Soviets, by means of a successful alliance policy, had assumed the leadership of an aggressive, disciplined Sino-Soviet (North Korean) bloc. This bloc not only seemed to balance U.S. military superiority offshore, but taking advantage of the economic and political instability then prevailing in East Asia, threatened by the use of subversion, if not direct aggression, to extend its control over the non-Communist states of the region.

By the end of the Korean War, then, East Asia had become a major theater in the cold war. The demarcation lines at the 38th parallel and in the Taiwan Straits remained intact through the 1950s and 1960s despite clear evidence that the Sino-Soviet block had been transformed into a bitter, occasionally violent Sino-Soviet dispute and despite U.S. failures and frustrations in Vietnam. It was not until the signing of the Shanghai Communique in February 1972 that the line in the Taiwan Straits was blurred over, and the Sino-Soviet confrontation finally broke down the bipolar Asian security arrangements that had been put in place during the Korean War. The 38th parallel, however, continues to be a sharp line. As anyone knows who has been to the demilitarized zone in Korea in recent years, the tension and hostility of the cold war persist there, as though detente and rapprochement had never come about.

When one tries to understand why the 38th parallel remains a line of dangerous confrontation, despite the improvement in Sino-American and Sino-Japanese ties, it becomes apparent that in the course of the 1970s, Asian international politics and security arrangements have lost their earlier, bipolar, cold war simplicity. Following the Damansky Island fighting between Soviet and Chinese troops in 1969, and during the rapid buildup of the Soviet army in Eastern Siberia (from 23 divisions in 1969 to 44 by 1972), China's leaders seem to have concluded that the Soviets were a more dangerous threat than the U.S. capitalist-imperialists. Survival required China to cooperate (to what extent is still not clear) with the lesser enemy against the greater enemy. The United States government, then in the midst of its painful extrication from Vietnam and seeking a dramatic foreign policy initiative, was quick and eager to exploit the new Chinese position. A U.S. ping-pong team was invited to the Canton tournament in the spring of 1971. In July of 1971, Dr. Kissinger made his secret visit to Peking, and in February 1972, President Nixon placed his stamp on the United States-China rapprochement by his visit to China and his signing of the hopeful, but vaguely worded Shanghai Communique.

Although it is generally agreed that the United States and China are no longer the bitter, hostile cold war adversaries that they were from the Korean War until 1971, it is not clear how cooperative and durable their current rapprochement will be. Moreover, the breakdown of the Cold war alignments has not been followed by the emergence of a well-defined new system. Seven years after the Shanghai Communique, and despite the normalization of U.S.-Chinese diplomatic relations, the Taiwan issue remains unresolved. North Korea, though it has serious economic problems, has been engaged in an impressive arms buildup since the early 1970s. South Korea, alarmed by the prospect of having all U.S. ground forces withdrawn by 1982, is now also engaged in a rapid and expensive military buildup. Peking and Moscow continue to compete for influence in Pyongyang. Despite recent evidence that North Korea is drawing closer to Peking, the tense confrontation between North and South Korea persists and threatens to be further aggravated by the arms race that is now underway on the peninsula.

Finally, it should be noted that U.S. naval combat tonnage in the Pacific declined from 900,000 tons in 1965 to 600,000 tons in 1975, while the number of U.S. combat aircraft in the region dropped from 920 to 500. During the same period, the Soviet Pacific fleet increased from 700,000 tons to 1.2 million tons, while the number of Soviet combat aircraft went up from 1,430 to more than 2,000.[3] Although these figures suggest that a fundamental shift has taken place in the distribution of military power in East Asia, the issue is shrouded in controversy. Does the Sino-Soviet dispute and the U.S.-China rapprochement compensate for U.S. military decline and the Soviet augmentation? What will the United States, the Soviet Union, and China do in the event hostilities break out again in Korea? The fact that one cannot answer these questions with any confidence reflects the murkiness of the present strategic situation in East Asia.

Given the pace and scope of the changes that have been going on around Japan during this decade, it is astonishing how little Japan's foreign and defense policies and its role in regional security have changed. Although the reliability of the U.S. security guarantee was shaken by the defeat in Vietnam, and further eroded by the apparent reversal of the U.S.-Soviet military balance, Japan has continued to rely on the Mutual Security Treaty and on U.S. forces for its defense. Despite periodic announcements in the media that Japan is rearming or planning to rearm, the evidence at the end of 1978 is that no more than 1 percent of Japan's GNP will be spent for defense. The planned procurement of F-15 fighter-interceptors and PC-3 antisubmarine aircraft during the next 3–5 years will only maintain Japan's extremely weak military position relative to that of the Soviets, the Chinese, and even the North and South Koreans.[4]

Japan has become the major economic power in Southeast Asia, but it plays only a minor political role in the region, and none at all in military-strategic terms. Following the establishment of diplomatic relations with China in the fall of 1972, Japan moved very cautiously, and it was not until 1978 that a major trade agreement and finally the long-awaited Treaty of Peace and Friendship were concluded between

Tokyo and Peking. The major obstacle in the conclusion of the Peace and Friendship Treaty was Chinese insistence that the treaty include a denunciation of hegemony, which seems perfectly harmless, except that in Peking's lexicon "hegemony" means Soviet foreign policy. The Japanese government did not want to conclude a treaty directed against the Soviet Union as this would almost certainly further chill relations with Moscow. After several years of haggling, a compromise was reached in the summer of 1978, in which hegemony was denounced in the treaty preamble while Article 4 of the text declares that the treaty is not directed against any third power. Theoretically, this solved the impasse. In practice, however, it appears that Soviet, Chinese and U.S. officials have all ignored Japanese disclaimers, and have publicly interpreted the treaty as an anti-Soviet document.

While recognizing that Japan has become China's largest trading partner, it is well to keep in mind that the PRC trade accounts for only about 4 percent of Japan's foreign trade, and that despite (or more accurately because of) Japan's apparent tilt toward China in 1978, the Japanese Government is being extremely careful not to further aggravate its cool relations with Moscow. In fact, although it has received far less publicity than the agreements with China, the Japanese government, early in 1978, authorized the building and export to the Soviet Union of a huge 80,000 ton dry dock, which will be used at Vladivostock to service the Soviet Pacific fleet, including the new Kiev-class aircraft carriers which the Soviets are preparing to deploy in the Pacific.[5] This dry dock, scheduled for delivery in early 1979, will significantly increase Soviet naval and air capabilities in the Western Pacific and along the Chinese coast. It will probably do more to strengthen Soviet military capabilities over the next 5–10 years, than the economic and diplomatic agreements with China will increase Chinese military strength. Moreover, the Japanese government's willingness to sell the Soviets this much needed dry dock suggests that the Peace and Friendship Treaty concluded with Peking is not drawing Japan into a U.S.-Chinese coalition against the Soviets in Asia.

In brief, although the events of the 1970s have led Japan to modify its earlier role in regional security, that role remains in several essential respects unchanged. Japan is still a lightly armed trading state. Although the U.S.-Japanese economic link has been attenuated by the decline of the United States as a supplier of coal, metal ores, and lumber to Japan, the United States remains Japan's largest foreign market. Moreover, despite the diversification of Japan's overseas economic activity, the alliance with the United States continues to be the centerpiece of Japan's foreign and defense policies. Although the Japanese have been quick to use the U.S. rapprochement with China to expand their own trade with that nation, they have been very cautious about being drawn into the political-strategic arrangements that led to that rapprochement.

Thus, despite all the changes that have occurred around Japan, Japan remains a militarily weak, politically subordinate actor in East Asia. Given the opportunities and dangers that have developed in the international environment, and the energy, discipline, and organizational skills of the Japanese, it may be difficult to understand why Japan has persisted in its low posture foreign policy, and why there is so little evidence that Japan is planning to change its role. While analyses of recent policy can help explain this seeming paradox, it is most useful to look back to the Japanese historical experience in foreign affairs. For the lessons and the perspective which the Japanese, including the ruling Conservatives, the Opposition, and most of the voters, derived from this historical experience continues to define the options and the basic direction of Japanese policy.

JAPAN'S DILEMMA

For Americans, who are accustomed to believing that they can define for themselves the nature of international relations and the level of their involvement in these affairs, it is difficult to comprehend the harsh, narrow necessities of Japan's international position. The Japanese have not been able to indulge themselves in the luxurious range of choices that have been open to the United States. Since they were forced to give up their rigid isolation in the middle of the nineteenth century, their options have been severely circumscribed by the requirements imposed by industrialization and by Japan's geography. In a fundamental sense, Japan's present international position has its roots in the beginnings of its industrialization in the late nineteenth century, and it is reasonable to anticipate that the essentials of this position will persist as long as Japan is an industrial society.

The leaders of Japan during the reign of the Emperor Meiji (1868–1911), in common with their counterparts in much of the non-Western world, perceived that the superior weapons and military forces which enabled Europe and the United States to dominate much of the world, were a product of industrial, machine society. They quickly concluded that the way to survive in the Western-dominated world was for Japan to have its own factories, arsenals, and shipyards in which to build its own weapons. Unlike most of the non-Western world, the Japanese rapidly and thoroughly accomplished these goals. Before the Meiji period ended, Japan was making its own war ships and artillery, and had fought successful wars against China (1894–95) and Russia (1904–05). As a result of these wars, Japan acquired an empire that included Southern Sakhalin, Korea and Taiwan. Moreover, Japan had entered the world economy as a manufacturer—an importer of raw materials and an exporter of industrial products.

Contrary to the initial expectation of the Meiji leaders, however, industrialization and modern weaponry, while they did lead to wealth and power, did not provide Japan with a high degree of independence and security. By the 1920s if not earlier, Japanese leaders such as Prime Minister Hara Kei, Foreign Minister Shidehara Kijuro, and Admiral Kato Tomosaburo saw that industrialization and economic growth were also leading Japan into a position of chronic economic and strategic vulnerability.

The explanation of this anomaly is simple. The Japanese islands are extremely poor in mineral resources, so that virtually all of the fuel and raw materials necessary for industry must be imported. The greater Japan's industrial production, therefore, the greater its dependence on imported fuels and raw materials. This was true in the 1920s, and it is true today, even though the value of foreign trade and imports has been a dwindling proportion of Japan's gross national product. For what this dwindling proportion means is that the Japanese have been adding greater value to their finished product and consuming more of it themselves. *Yet the energy and material necessary to fashion the finished product remain indispensable.* Moreover, as Japanese industry has grown, the absolute quantities of imported fuels and raw materials have also grown. Japan now imports more petroleum than any other country in the world. As a result of this process, Japan has had to extend its search for resources far beyond East Asia, to North America, India, the Middle East, and Latin America.

The essence of Japan's international position, then, is that its survival as an industrial state is contingent upon its access to a worldwide network of fuels and raw materials. The unavoidable task of Japan's foreign policy is to maintain that access.

The fundamental foreign policy options for Japan, therefore, derive from the question of whether and how Japan can maintain this access. Japan must either be able to buy from those who control the sources of energy and raw materials; control the sources itself; or face the prospect of industrial stagnation and decline.

In the years before the Pacific war, when Japan's energy and raw material requirements were only a fraction of what they are now and could conceivably have been satisfied within the Asian-Pacific region, Japanese foreign policy makers were conscious of these three options. The decision in 1941 to make war against the United States and Great

Britain, was taken in the belief that: the first option, peaceful trade, had become unworkable in the international environment of protectionism and violence of the 1930s; the United States was pushing Japan toward the third option of industrial stagnation and decline by means of its embargoes on Japan's vital imports of petroleum and scrap iron; the second option, the creation of a Greater East Asian coprosperity sphere, could only be realized if the United States and Great Britain were driven out of the region by military force.

The Pacific war, of course, proved to be the greatest disaster in Japan's history, leading as it did to economic collapse, total military defeat, and the loss of empire. For Japanese of all political persuasions, the lesson taught by the war is that Japan cannot hope by military means to win control of a sphere of influence within which it can enjoy economic and military security. This lesson has been reinforced by Japan's phenomenal postwar economic growth, which has rendered the notion of regional autarky hopelessly obsolete by extending Japan's economic lifeline far beyond East Asia and the Western Pacific. More-over, the development of nuclear missiles has made narrow, densely populated, intensively industrialized Japan into one of the most mili-tarily vulnerable of the developed countries. In short, a traumatic military defeat, economic growth, and developments in military tech-nology have combined to eliminate the second option as a rational choice.

Therefore, in the minds of most Japanese of whatever political persuasion, there is at present no rational military option for Japan and no active military role in Asian security arrangements. The unspoken assumption behind most of the thinking and writing on foreign policy in Japan is that Japan must either prosper or decline as a peaceful trading state. In this frame of mind, a serious threat to Japan's military security, if and when it should appear, would probably evoke an attempt first to defend Japan by alliance with a militarily strong protector, and then, if that does not suffice, an attempt to come to terms with the attacker, assuming that his demands will be reasonable. The possibility that Japan could ever again be engaged in a large-scale, protracted war simply does not cross the minds of most Japanese, with the exception of the small group of defense community intellectuals who support the "requisite capability" and "autonomous defense" theses which are explained later in this essay.

Against the background of this broad historical and strategic analysis of Japan's international position, one can begin to understand why Japan's foreign policy makers have not seen the much publicized end of the cold war as an opportunity to strike out on a new, bold, independent course. The conservative, prudent men who have been guiding Japan in international politics since World War II do not see the security and prosperity they achieved in the 1950s and 1960s as a spring-board from which to project Japan as an independent strategic actor in global or regional politics. They realistically perceive that Japan's industrial development and prosperity are more a source of vulnerability and weakness than of strength. They are keenly aware of how limited their foreign policy options are. They can only hope that U.S. détente with the Soviet Union and rapprochement with China will not become euphemisms for a world of cutthroat economic nationalism and political and military instability. For Japan is ill equipped to cope with such a world.

JAPANESE SECURITY: RECENT DEVELOPMENTS

From 1945 until 1964, there was no sustained general public discussion in Japan of security and defense issues.* While particular incidents, such as the American effort in 1955 to deploy Honest John missiles to Japan or the Diet ratification of the revised Security Treaty in 1960, generated public demonstrations and severe media criticism of the Government's foreign policy, there was no dispassionate public examination of defense questions until 1964. Then, prompted largely by China's first atomic tests, the intellectual journals, the newspapers and television networks, and the publishers, began to carry articles, programs, and books on Japan's security policy and the changing international environment.

Since 1964, the security debate has waxed and waned in magnitude and intensity, but it has never fallen silent. The arguments over the reversion of Okinawa in 1967–69, the publication of the government's first White Paper on Defense in 1971, and the Middle East War and oil embargo in 1973–74, all heightened Japanese awareness of and interest in security questions and were occasions for an outpouring of writing and broadcasts on defense issues. In each instance, the Japanese and foreign media were prone to conclude that the new security debate indicated that Japanese pacifism had faded away, and that rearmament and a basic change in Japan's defense policy was implicit in the debate and imminent. The fact that no such change has yet come about should caution us against drawing similar dramatic conclusions from the current debate.

The current debate was to a large extent generated by President

---

*For much of the material in this section, the author is indebted to an unpublished paper by Taketsugu Tsurutami, "Security Debate in Japan."

Carter's announced plans in 1976–77 to withdraw all U.S. ground forces from South Korea by 1982. The planned U.S. withdrawal announced against the background of the defeat in Vietnam, a general U.S. military decline in Asia, and the growth of Soviet capabilities in Asia, have provoked a vigorous public discussion on every aspect of Japan's security policy. The present agenda includes debate on the reliability of the U.S. guarantee, the significance of the Soviet buildup, the prospects of closer relations with China, the future of Korea; as well as issues closer to home, such as the legal authority of uniformed officers to order their men into action in the event of an attack against Japan, and the extent to which Japanese and U.S. forces would coordinate their actions in the event of a military emergency.

The four alternative defense postures that emerge from the current security debate in Japan are as follows: the permanent limits thesis, the basic defense policy, the requisite capability thesis, and the autonomous defense thesis. They share large areas of mutual convergence, thus making it difficult to delineate clearly where one ends and another begins as well as to ascertain where a participant in the debate stands in a given moment.

Four Alternative Defense Postures

The Permanent Limit Thesis

Variously referred to as "the fundamental spirit thesis" (*kihon teki seishin ron*) and "the 'bounds' thesis" ('*waku' ron*), this represents an approach to national defense that underlays the past government policy and still is most consistent with the pacifist inclination of the general public as well as most of the "progressive" opposition. It represents not so much a realistic concern about external military security as a captious wariness of the domestic consequences of an activist defense policy. The limits (or bounds) its proponents refer to are five: the spirit of the peace constitution, the principle of civilian control of the military, the exclusively defensive character of the Self-Defense Force (SDF), the three anti-nuclear principles, and the ceiling of 1 percent of the GNP for defense appropriations.

The issue of the SDF's constitutionality was once highly emotional, but the inevitable generational change in the population (over half of the population was born after August 15, 1945) plus a series of definitive court rulings (for example, Sunakawa and Hyakuri) eventually led to a popular acceptance of the constitutional legitimacy of the SDF.[6] There remains, nevertheless, a quite strong feeling that the peace constitution is a unique national document. Thus, the proponents of the permanent limits thesis insist that the nation must remain faithful to its pacifist spirit (fundamental spirit), for it is this spirit, they argue, that makes Japan unique among nations.

The principle of civilian control of the military assumes a great psychological magnitude because of the character and consequences of the prewar history of civil-military relations. There is an understandable apprehension on the part of many Japanese about the danger of resurgence of military influence in government and politics. As if to keep this apprehension alive, there appear from time to time inside stories about the pattern of interaction and relations between the uniformed and the civilian sectors of the Japanese Defense Agency (JDA), alleging the dominance of the former over the latter and the latter's unquestioned deference to the former's "professional expertise."[7] There is also suspicion, which MPs themselves confirm, that most of the politicians remain indifferent to what is going on inside the JDA and to civil-military relations, thus in effect leaving issues of security and defense to military officers in the JDA and a handful of promilitary defense specialists within the ruling Liberal Democratic Party (LDP).[8] Permanent-limits advocates fear that any activist defense policy would run the risk of increasing the power of the military in government.

The "exclusively defensive posture" principle is the empirical correlate of the fundamental spirit. It dictates that the nation make judicious efforts to avoid even appearing to increase its military power lest it cause fear and anxiety among neighbors. The government in the past went so far as to strip the F-4s (the current mainstays of the Air Self-Defense Force acquired at enormous costs) of its key operational features (bombing and midair refueling capabilities) in order to keep them exclusively defensive.

The three antinuclear principles (so-called *Hikaku san gensoku*) were enunciated in 1967 by the then prime minister, in response to pacifist opposition and popular demands precipitated by China's nuclear explosions and the war in Vietnam. The prime minister pledged that Japan, as a matter of deliberate policy, would neither produce nor obtain nor permit the deployment of nuclear weapons. The principles have since been adhered to by the successive governments, although it should be noted that no LDP government has ever accepted that nuclear weapons are proscribed by the constitution.

The fifth limit or bound is the long-standing budgetary practice of limiting the defense appropriations to the maximum of 1 percent of the GNP. This limit came about by a happenstance of earlier budgets quite unrelated to security requirements as such. The first year for which the SDF budget went below 1 percent of the GNP was 1959 when Japan had just launched a massive economic growth program. There is no evidence that the first below 1 percent defense appropriations were deliberate. In any event, the mere fact that the rate of annual economic growth in the 1960s generally exceeded 10 percent insured that 1 percent or less of the GNP for defense was sufficient to generate consistent increases in the SDF budget. That it was so, however, was purely a matter of statistical accident and not related at all to serious and comprehensive planning of national security requirements. In any event, the "1 percent limit" eventually became an operating rule for the nation's budgetary process, a rule to which all other sectors of government bureaucracy, their lateral policy counterparts within the ruling LDP, and their respective client groups and institutions in society became committed for their self interests. Its supporters argue, moreover, that 1 percent of the GNP is the maximum of what the public would tolerate for defense expenditure. In fact, in 1976 the cabinet officially accepted this argument, on the proposition that the annual rate of real growth in the GNP would average 6 percent into the mid-1980s.[9]

The Basic Defense Policy

Called *Kiban teki boeiryoku koso* (literally, the fundamental defense capability plan), this constitutes the current defense policy of Japan. What is meant by "basic" is that the SDF, and not the U.S. military, would be the basis of national defense and that the security arrangement with the United States would "supplement" them.[10] This is meant to contrast with the earlier government proposition that the SDF were to play a role "supplementary" to U.S. forces in case of serious military contingencies. Thus, under the current policy, Japan would prepare herself to cope, on her own, with an indirect aggression and a small-scale limited aggression, while repelling a large-scale aggression in cooperation with the United States.[11]

The basic defense policy rests, much as does its predecessor (that is, the permanent limits thesis), on the basic reliability of the United States and the unlikelihood of a major war involving the nation's security. Its proponents thus point to the East-West détente, the Sino-American normalization, and the trend toward multipolarity and greater economic and political interdependence in the world. The policy is also based on the proposition that the nation's military capability should be strictly defensive in posture.

Regarding the nation's domestic condition, the policy rests on the contention that "however powerful the SDF may become and no matter what sophisticated weaponry they may acquire, they could not constitute a genuinely effective defense capability unless it enjoyed the people's understanding, support, and cooperation."[12] The policy regards the SDF as quantitatively adequate but needing qualitative improvement. Such improvement involves, in part, the replacement of the F-4s with the F-15s as the mainstays of the Air Self-Defense Force (ASDF) and the acquisition of P-3C anti-submarine reconnaissance planes and helicopter carriers for the Maritime Self-Defense Force (MSDF). It must, however, be done with great circumspection and sensitivity toward neighboring states. A major proponent of the basic defense policy argued:

> If Japan's peace-time defense capability is too large, it would arouse fear and alarm among our neighbors. On the other hand, if it were too small, it might create a vacuum in the Far East, thus causing instability in the region. We should therefore take care to limit our basic defense capability to the minimum necessary level as peace-time defense capability.[13]

The policy also emphasizes what one JDA official calls "a proper balance between the SDF capability and the 'home front system' (*koho shien taisei*)."[14]

The basic thrust that makes the current policy distinct from its predecessor is that it purports to assume a greater share of national defense by preparing the SDF to deal with small-scale limited war contingencies with the security treaty with the United States as complementary to the task. To this extent, some analysts are tempted to regard the basic defense policy as moving away from total dependence upon U.S. forces, hence as demonstrating "an unprecedented realism and rationality in Japan's defense thinking."[15]

The Requisite Capability Thesis

This option is a loose distillation of various demands for a militant defense posture, such as the "as-required defense forces thesis" (*shoyo boeiryoku ron*) and the "activist defense thesis" (*sekkyoku boei ron*) that go as far back as the establishment of the SDF. Put simply, its various proponents argue that the level of Japan's military capability is woefully insufficient and that it should be determined not according to the constitution or to the public opinion but by the magnitude of potential external contingencies and the extent of actual or potential adversaries' capabilities. This "definition by situational contingencies" approach is presumably rendered increasingly plausible by a number of external developments in the present decade, such as the rise of petropolitics (not only of the Arab states but, more recently, of China and the Soviet Union); the lowering of America's politicomilitary posture in Asia and the Pacific; the expansion of the Soviet Asiatic Fleet and the consequent exposure of Japan's vital life line to Soviet naval threat; the continuing instability of Southeast Asian nations through whose narrow waters Japan's life line extends; and the possibility of another violent outbreak on the Korean peninsula with the completion of U.S. troop withdrawal. Moreover, proponents of the requisite capability thesis argue that the level of SDF capability conceived twenty years ago and more or less adhered to since then was based on calculations of trade requirements and military technology that have long ceased to be realistic.[16] In short, circumstances have long changed in the direction of requiring a greatly expanded defense capability for the nation.

Some proponents of this requisite capability option stress the necessity of acquiring deterrent as well as counterattack capabilities, and they speak even of engaging in a preventive attack, albeit in a circumlocutory fashion. Thus, one pro-requisite capability LDP leader anticipates a contingency that would call for SDF forces to operate "hundreds of miles away [from Japan] in order to protect the merchant fleet or . . . to prevent intrusion into Japanese air space by hostile aircraft."[17] Early this year, the JDA director general exhorted SDF officers that their capability should be such that potential adversaries would fear them, for a nation whose defense forces could not be feared would be unable to deter aggression.[18] And the chairman of the Joint Staff Council in a widely debated article argued that only offensive capabilities would ultimately insure the nation's security.[19]

As mentioned earlier, the requisite capability thesis is not new. What is new about it is the candor and aggressiveness with which its proponents now promote it. During the 1950s and 1960s, the thesis (or any of its variations) was consciously downplayed in public. There were occasions when requisite capability utterances were made by government officials, but they were made more by way of an aside or something akin to the slip of the tongue and were quickly qualified or explained away almost as soon as they were made. Officials were quite sensitive to what might be termed an anti-military allergy of the public and opposition parties. Thus, while the government never accepted the argument that a radical expansion of the SDF would be in violation of the constitution, it was always careful to point out the distinction it saw between what was constitutionally permissible (military expansion) on the one hand and what was politically desirable (nonexpansion) on the other and to stress the latter over the former as its criterion of policy. For example, in 1959, the then JDA director general observed: "It is not the intention of the Constitution that we acquire weapons that would threaten other nations." In 1967, the Prime Minister noted: "The self-defense capability of our nation ought not to be such as to pose an aggressive threat to other nations."[20] Early in the current decade, the government decided to strip the F-4s of their bombing and midair refueling capacities on the grounds that it was "desirable" in view of the spirit of the constitution not to have an ability to bomb other nations. Until recently, therefore, any statement smacking of the requisite capability thesis was commonly hedged with the qualifier of "not posing an aggressive or offensive threat." That constraint, however, seems to have gone out the window. And one commentator speaks of Japan's basic defense posture evolving from an exclusively defensive one to one of tactical offense.[21]

The Autonomous Defense Thesis

The so-called *jishu boei ron* alternative, on the surface at least, arises from any combination of three motives: national pride, the nation's responsibility commensurate with its capability, and mistrust of the United States. The general thesis itself is even older than the requisite capability thesis, dating back to early postwar years. Originally promoted by former Imperial military officers, the nationalist motive of the thesis has it that an independent national defense capability is an indispensable mark of a sovereign state.[22] Many influential members of the defense community argue that Japan is not a full-fledged nation but remains a semination so long as her security is underwritten by "tax payers of the United States and South Korea."[23]

While, prior to the decade of the 1960s, the nationalist craving for independent military forces was not matched by the recovering nation's economic capability, it was whetted as the nation entered the period of rapid growth, providing an additional argument that the nation should assume a defense responsibility that is commensurate with its growing economic power. The "commensurate responsibility" argument need not be recounted here, for it is self-explanatory, except to note that it is compatible with the frequently expressed U.S. desire for Japan to increase her defense capability, and that it inevitably promotes the idea of self-sufficiency in arms research, development, and also production.

A third putative motivation underlying the autonomous defense thesis is an allegedly increasing doubt about the U.S. resolve and will to come to Japan's aid in case of serious military contingencies. The lowering of the U.S. politicomilitary profile in Asia through the Nixon doctrine, the end of the Vietnam War, and the decision to withdraw U.S. ground combat troops from Korea has strengthened the misgivings about the ultimate reliability of the United States as a security partner. Some within Japan's defense community contend that the relevant events of the past several years suggest that the United States is reverting back to the "Europe first" policy.[24] Moreover, in their eyes, events within the United States in the past decade or so indicate a serious decline in the discipline and political will of that country. Under these circumstances, Japan has no alternative to building sufficient military forces of her own to defend herself from external threat and aggression.

In one sense, the autonomous defense thesis is consistent with the apparent intent as well as the letter of a number of key official documents and authoritative statements of the past regarding the role of the SDF. As early as 1955, the JDA announced that its efforts were "directed at establishing a proper and appropriate self-defense system *necessary for an independent nation*.[25] The Basic Policy of National Defense formulated by the National Defense Council and approved by the cabinet in 1957 stipulated a gradual increase of the nation's effective defense potential *"in keeping with the national strength and national conditions* within the limits necessary for self-defense."[26] The revised Japan-U.S. security treaty of 1960 in its third article provided: "The Parties, individually and in cooperation with each other, *by means of continuous and effective self-help* and mutual aid will maintain and develop . . . their capacities to resist armed attack." In 1970, the Prime Minister told the Diet: "We will build up our defense capability and will rely on the security treaty *to supplement* whatever is lacking."[27] Thus, proponents of the autonomous defense could contend that the implementation of their approach is warranted not only by the changed and changing external environment but also by the promise contained in the past government policies and the security treaty with the United States.

Although the current security debate has not brought about any significant changes in either Japan's relative military strength or in the policy of relying on the United States for Japan's external defense, there is a significant new element in the current discussion. Until the middle of this decade, the pro-U.S. politically conservative Japanese who staunchly supported the security treaty, were concerned that U.S. military predominance in the Western Pacific, combined with anticommunist fervor and Yankee toughness could lead to an unnecessary war with the Soviets and Chinese—one in which Japan would unavoidably be involved. The thrust of Japanese policy then was to keep the shield of the security treaty intact while seeing to it that the American sword stayed safely and unprovocatively in its sheath. This was the purpose of the Prior Consultation Notes appended to the 1960 security treaty by the Kishi cabinet.

Now the questions in the minds of Japan's ruling conservatives are of an entirely different order. They are still pro-U.S., and they still support the security treaty, but now they wonder whether the treaty and the U.S. forces which stand behind it are adequate for Japan's defense. Given the changes that occurred as a result of Vietnam and

Watergate in the U.S. world outlook, in Congressional and bureaucratic attitudes toward overseas military interventions, and perhaps most importantly, in the shrinking of U.S. military strength in the Western Pacific, Japanese now wonder what the Mutual Security Treaty means to the United States, and what it will mean in the 1980s. Does it represent an unequivocal commitment to fight in Japan's defense, or does it mean something less? If so, how much less? Are the Seventh Fleet and the Fifth Air Force an effective deterrent against the Soviet Pacific Fleet and air forces? If deterrence fails, will the U.S. naval and air forces be able to keep open the lines of communication to Japan and the Western Pacific? What can Japan do?

The most significant change that has occurred in Japanese foreign and defense policy is that moderate, cautious Japanese conservatives are now asking themselves these questions, not in a panicky or even an urgent way, but deliberately and seriously. Ten or 20 years ago they did not. They then took American military predominance, nuclear and conventional, in the air and on the seas, as an unshakeable premise upon which Japanese policy could be built. Now, they do not. No one in Japan has yet proposed clear, convincing answers to these questions. And in view of the demonstrated success and enormous inertia of existing policies, dramatic departures in Japanese foreign and defense policy do not appear imminent. Nevertheless, we should realize that fundamental changes have occurred in Japanese *perceptions* and that these *perceptual* changes are opening the possibility of substantial changes in Japanese policy in the 1980s.

NOTES

1. For a more detailed discussion see Donald Hellman, *Japan and East Asia: The New International Order* (New York: Praeger, 1972); and Martin E. Weinstein, *Japan's Postwar Defense Policy, 1947–1968* (New York and London: Columbia University Press, 1971).

2. Harry S. Truman, *Memoirs, Vol. I. Year of Decisions* (Garden City: Doubleday, 1955) pp. 430–32; and Ministry of Foreign Affairs of the U.S.S.R., *Stalin's Correspondence with Roosevelt and Truman, 1941–1945* (New York: Capricorn, 1965), p. 226.

3. Japan Defense Agency, *Defense of Japan, 1976*, p. 15. Diagram 3. Outline of Changes in Military Deployments In and Around Japan.

4. *JPE Aviation Report*, Jan. 25, 1978, pp. 1–6.

5. *Yomiuri Shimbun*, September 28, 1978, p. 1.

6. Over 80 percent of the public view the SDF as legitimate. See, for example, *Asahi Shimbun*, January 1, 1978, p. 9.

7. See, for example, Osamu Kaihara, *Nihon Boei Taisei no Uchimaku* (Tokyo: Jiji Tsushin Sha, 1977), passim but esp. pp. 211–21. Kaihara speaks of "collective hypnosis" of civilian officials by the military brass and the rubber-stamping role they allegedly play in the agency's decision making.

8. See Sankei Shimbun, *Nihon no Anzen* (Tokyo: Sankei Shimbun Sha, 1976), vol. 1,

p. 181; "Ronso: Nihon o mamoru towa doyu kotoka," *Chuokoron*, January 1978, p. 84; and Mainichi Shimbun, ed., *Kokumin to Jieitai* (Tokyo: Mainichi Shimbun Sha, 1969), p. 56.

9. *Asahi Shimbun*, October 10, 1977, p. 2; and Sankei Shimbun, *Nihon no Anzen*, vol. 2, pp. 156-9.

10. See, for example, Prime Minister Fukuda's statement in the House of Representatives Budget Committee on February 6, 1978 in *Asahi Shimbun*, February 17, 1978, p. 2.

11. *Boei Nenkan 1978* (Tokyo: Boei Nenkan Kanko Kai, 1978), p. 603.

12. Ibid., p. 281.

13. Michita Sakata as quoted in Sankei Shimbun, *Nihon no Anzen*, vol. 2, p. 156.

14. Statement by the director of the Defense Bureau of the JDA at the House of Representatives Budget Committee, February 17, 1978, as reprinted in *Boei Nenkan 1978*, pp. 104-5.

15. Makoto Momoi, "Basic Trends in Japanese Security Policies" in Scalapino, ed., *The Foreign Policy of Modern Japan*, Berkeley: University of California Press, p. 359.

16. For this argument, see, for example, Tadao Kusumi, "Japan's Defense and Peace in Asia," *Pacific Community* 4 (April 1973): 431-32.

17. Yasuhiro Nakasone as quoted in Robert Osgood, *The Weary and the Wary: U.S. and Japanese Security Policies in Transition* (Baltimore and London: The Johns Hopkins University Press, 1972), p. 54.

18. Taro Akasaka, "Boei Rongi no kuruizaki," *Bungei Shunju*, March 1978, p. 164.

19. *Asahi Shimbun*, January 25, 1978, p. 2.

20. Both quoted in *Sekai*, April 1978, p. 116.

21. Kaoru Murakami, *Nihon Boei no Koso* (Tokyo: Simul, 1976), pp. 150-52.

22. For example, one former Imperial admiral lamented that "it is disheartening to place deterrent power in the hands of another country, even though it is an allied power": Former Vice Admiral Fukudome as quoted in John Endicott, *Japan's Nuclear Option: Political, Technological, and Strategic Factors* (New York: Praeger, 1975), p. 63.

23. Murakami, *Nihon Boei no Koso*, p. 142.

24. Masamichi Irie, "Shin joseika de Nihon gaiko o kangaeru," *Jiyu* (May 1978): 31.

25. Quoted in Momoi, "Japanese Security Policies," p. 345. Emphasis added.

26. Kusumi, "Japan's Defense and Peace in Asia," p. 421. Emphasis added.

27. Ibid. Emphasis added.

· 5 ·

THE UNITED STATES
AND THE SECURITY OF ASIA
Norman D. Palmer

For at least the fourth time since the end of World War II, the United States is attempting to reshape its policies toward Asia. In every case this has been necessitated by changing conditions in Asia and by a variety of false assumptions and basic mistakes on the part of the United States.

In the late 1940s and 1950s, U.S. plans and hopes for a new order in Asia that would both be compatible with U.S. interests and create a peaceful environment in Asia were anchored in a friendly and effective nationalist government in China and a reemerging Japan under U.S. tutelage, but were shattered by the Communist victory in China and by the Korean war and its aftermath. In the 1960s, as the divisions created by the events of the previous fifteen years seemed to be becoming less serious, the deepening American involvement in Vietnam gradually distorted almost all aspects of U.S.-Asian relationships and created deep divides not only between the United States and many Asian countries but also within American society. The psychological wounds created by the Vietnam experience have by no means been completely healed, and there remain numerous problems, not least security, begotten for the United States as well as many Asian countries by the outcome of the Vietnam struggles—for these struggles have continued in a different form even after the U.S. withdrawal. Yet other matters concerning Asia have been given a higher priority, and the United States has had an opportunity to make further efforts to reshape its Asian policies in the light of changing circumstances and national interests.

In the 1970s, the Nixon and Ford administrations made further efforts to reshape policies toward Asia. The emphasis was placed, as President Nixon stated in his fourth report to the Congress on U.S. Foreign Policy for the 1970's (submitted in May 1973), on ending conflicts (mainly in Vietnam), strengthening partnerships (especially with Japan), and building new relationships (referring to the opening to China).[1] These efforts had some success, but they did not add up to a coherent or consistent policy. Moreover, they had inherent difficulties and inconsistencies, which were complicated by some of the diplomatic mistakes of the U.S. administrations and by the adverse reaction of Japan, America's major ally in Asia, to such moves as the "Nixon shocks" of 1971. The United States did not give Asian relations and problems the kind of priority in its overall foreign policies that many Asian leaders felt was essential, and the "withdrawal mood" in the United States increased Asian doubts about U.S. credibility, capabilities, and will. Watergate and its aftermath led to virtual paralysis in the final months of the Nixon administration; and Nixon's successor, President Ford, was never able to give adequate attention to Asia or do much more than begin to assuage Asian doubts and hurt feelings.

The Carter administration is making a fourth effort to reshape U.S. policies toward Asia. It is attempting to improve the image and the credibility of the United States in Asia and to reassure Asians that the United States has no intention of withdrawing from Asia (except in a limited military sense), and also that it recognizes the new realities, changing circumstances, and growing importance of Asia.

THE GROWING DIMENSIONS OF SECURITY

For a major power like the United States, Asian policies must obviously be developed within the framework of global priorities and objectives. It is understandable that U.S. foreign policy has continued to be rather Eurocentric; but at the same time it largely revolves around interactions with three other states, the Soviet Union, Japan, and the People's Republic of China—the three major Asian powers. U.S. relations with these states in particular and with Asia in general are therefore a part of its global, not just Asian, policies. This is a striking reminder that in this era of interdependence, at least for the major states, virtually all major aspects of foreign policy are essentially aspects of global, and not just of bilateral, regional, or even continental, relationships. Thus, for example, the course of the Sino-Soviet conflict, the evolving relations between Japan and the People's Republic of China, between the Soviet Union and Japan, and between the United

States and the other three powers are not only central factors in Asian international relations and in U.S.-Asian relations, but in contemporary international relations generally. And the security of Asia as well as the question of the proper role of the United States in that security are aspects of the even larger problem of security in an increasingly interdependent world in the nuclear age.

U.S. military withdrawal from the Asian mainland, (with the exception of the decreasing presence in South Korea) presumably does not signify that interest in Asian security is declining in the United States. In fact, one could argue that it signifies quite the opposite: a belated recognition of the limits of military power and of direct military intervention in Asian affairs as well as of the necessity of basing Asian security on broader foundations. Hopefully, it may also be interpreted as a recognition of "the growing dimensions of security," which were aptly described in a report of a working group on security of the Atlantic Council of the United States late in 1977:

> In the nuclear age, in an increasingly crowded and interdependent world, security is not a matter merely of military strength. Security also involves a combination of many other factors, including domestic as well as foreign ones: political, economic, social and psychological. It is the combination of these factors which Communist doctrine calls the "correlation of forces." The West cannot afford a narrower view. Nor can security be limited to any specific geographic area. Its ramifications are global.[2]

THE FOURTH EFFORT: PROS AND CONS

Critics at home and abroad seem to believe that the fourth effort of the United States to reshape its Asian policies has been no more successful than the previous efforts. The Carter administration, some critics maintain, is dangerously inexperienced in dealing with Asia, and the wages of inexperience are high. This administration began by trying to base its entire foreign policy, not just its Asian policies, on "demilitarization and reconciliation with communism," and this helped create an image of a weak and indecisive United States led by a weak and indecisive President. Several disparate objectives were sought: trilateralism, human rights, normalization of relations with all communist states, and tactical withdrawal from regions such as Korea.[3] The United States alienated its major Asian allies, notably Japan, and seemed to be more interested in moving forward at all costs in normalizing its relations with the People's Republic of China and improving its relations with nonaligned states, such as India and Indonesia, than in supporting and working with its allies. It has given a rather low priority to Asia generally, and especially to the "non-influential" states of that vast area, meaning the majority of Asian states. The United States has not been sufficiently aware of the consequences of its military and psychological withdrawal from Asia upon the Asian balance. It has remained largely insensitive to Asian nationalism, even though its spokesmen have shown a greater recognition of the strength and changing nature of that nationalism. The Carter administration has, in short, failed to develop adequate policies, not to mention an overall policy or policy framework where Asia is concerned.

Spokesmen of the Carter administration present a very different interpretation of recent U.S. policies toward Asia. One of the clearest and most comprehensive overall reviews was presented by Secretary of State Cyrus Vance in late June 1977 in an address on the "United States and Asia" before the Asia Society in New York. His opening remarks are worth quoting at some length:

> I should like to advance the basic proposition that our prospects for sustaining and developing effective relationships with the countries of East Asia are more promising than at any time since World War II. The fundamental challenges facing the Administration are to consolidate the positive developments of the past few years—the emergence of an even closer partnership with Japan, a promising "opening" with China, the growing prosperity of the Pacific Basin economy, the emerging cohesion of the ASEAN grouping—and to prevent or mitigate adverse trends which could strain the presently favorable regional environment. High stakes hang on our ability to meet this challenge, for our interests in Asia are enduring and they are substantial.
>
> I hope to leave you with these understandings:
>
> First, the United States is and will remain an Asian and Pacific power.
>
> Second, the United States will continue to play its key role in contributing to peace and stability in Asia and the Pacific.
>
> Third, the United States seeks normal and friendly relations with the countries in the area on the basis of reciprocity and mutual respect.
>
> Fourth, the United States will pursue mutual expansion of trade and investment across the Pacific, recognizing the growing interdependence of the economies of the United States and the region. And
>
> Fifth, we will use our influence to improve the human condition of the peoples of Asia.
>
> In all of this, there can be no doubt of the enduring vitality of our country's relationships with the peoples of Asia and the Pacific.
>
> To the people of Asia I say tonight without qualification that our

nation has recovered its self-confidence at home. And we have not abandoned our interest in Asia.

We are and will remain a Pacific nation, by virtue of our geography, our history, our commerce, and our interests. . . . Our tasks are to help consolidate the emerging peaceful balance in Asia and to promote economic growth that offers promise to its people.

The United States recognizes the importance of its continuing contribution to Asian security. We will maintain a strong military presence in the area.[4]

A more concise, but less balanced, summing up of U.S. policy toward Asia was given by the other top foreign affairs adviser to President Carter, Dr. Zbigniew Brzezinski in a long and generally impressive interview with James Reston of *New York Times* in late December 1978:

We are now fully out of the Asian mainland; and we have a stable relationship with Asia based on two points of anchorage—Korea and, if you will, Thailand and Malaya-Singapore; offshore allies; and our increasingly friendly relationship with China—in addition to Japan as our closest friend.[5]

Read in the full context of Dr. Brzezinski's analysis, these comments on U.S. policy toward Asia seem less unbalanced and enigmatic than they do when isolated. In the isolated form, they do not add up to an accurate overview of U.S. objectives and policies in Asia, and they could easily be misunderstood. Surely Dr. Brzezinski did not mean his statement, "we are now fully out of the Asian mainland," to be taken literally. The United States is out of the Asian mainland only in the limited sense that it no longer has substantial armed forces anywhere in that continent (and this does not include "offshore allies" like Japan and the Philippines). It is difficult to accept the interpretation that "we have a stable relationship with Asia" at a time when U.S. foreign policies toward Asia as well as conditions in, and relations between, the various countries and regions of that vast continent are undergoing many changes in many uncertain directions. The identification of Thailand and Malaya-Singapore as the "two points of anchorage" for America's "stable relationship" with Asia is very curious indeed. Surely the United States has stronger anchors in Asia. It is withdrawing troops from Korea, and its continuing support of South Korea is tempered by its declining military presence and its distaste for the regime of Park Chung Hee. Its relations with Thailand are much more limited and distant then they were in previous years; and its relations with Malaya (Malaysia) and Singapore, while generally satisfactory, are not really central to its overall Asian policies. The reference to "offshore allies" is an ambiguous one. One would assume that Brzezinski was referring primarily to Japan, but this seems unlikely in view of his specific reference to Japan at the end of his summary sentence. He could hardly be referring to Taiwan or the Philippines—which are or have been offshore allies—because his interview was given a few days before the withdrawal of official recognition of the Republic of China on Taiwan became effective, because relations with the Philippines under Marcos have become rather strained, and because the future of American air and naval bases in that island nation is uncertain. Hence he may have been referring to Australia and New Zealand, and perhaps to even more distant offshore allies, which again are only peripheral factors in the overall U.S. relationship with Asia. The references to the new relationship with the People's Republic of China and the continuing relationship with Japan are much more obvious. One only wonders why they were made at the end of an otherwise curious sentence.

EAST ASIA

East Asia is obviously an area of major concern to the United States. It has been called "perhaps the most critical geopolitical region in the world."[6] It is clearly a major theater on which the international drama in future years will be played. Hence it has global as well as regional status and significance. It is a central theater of the five power world of Mr. Nixon and Dr. Kissinger, and one of the three power centers with which the Trilateral Commission (where President Carter is supposed to have received some "basic training" in world affairs) is primarily concerned.

For the United States, in spite of the continuing Eurocentrism of its foreign policy, East Asia is becoming an area of almost equal importance to Europe. Indeed, some Americans would argue that it has already achieved this status and that the United States should recognize this fact and its implications. Dr. William R. Kintner, former U.S. Ambassador to Thailand, for example, has asserted unequivocally that "U.S. foreign and security policy must accord East Asia a status equivalent to that which we have habitually assigned to Western Europe."[7] For East Asia is not only the area that contains one fourth of the world's population and two of its major nations—one the second most economically productive and the other the most populous. It is also where the major powers interact perhaps most directly and most conspicuously. Thus for the United States as well as the Soviet Union (which can be considered an Asian state, but only peripherally an East Asian state), and even for Japan and China, the area is a focal point of the international system as well as a major international region. As a report of a conference on "Pacific Asia and U.S. Policies," sponsored by the Pacific Forum in Honolulu in 1978, stated:

> the most critical challenge to U.S. leadership continues to be the interaction among the major powers—the United States, Japan, the People's Republic of China and the USSR. The political security and economic interests of all four nations converge in East Asia.[8]

It is the geopolitical significance, the interactions—and often the rivalries—of the major powers, as well as the convergence of interests between regional and external states that should be borne in mind when more specific aspects of East Asian domestic or international developments are discussed. Viewed in this context, it is obviously impossible for the United States to withdraw from East Asia, except in a limited military sense. Hence the United States must give a high priority to the East Asian area. This means that it must become more familiar with the area, with its history, its culture, the aspirations of its people, as well as with the character of leadership in the various political entities and the prevailing and probable future trends in foreign and domestic policies. From this perspective U.S. contacts with East Asia are woefully inadequate and superficial, and U.S. policies toward the states of the area are sadly lacking in coherence and conceptual framework.

With all of the states of East Asia, the United States has had extensive and changing relationships. This is dramatized by developments and problems that make headlines in American newspapers: the normalization of relations with the People's Republic of China; the withdrawal of recognition from Taiwan; the abrogation of the mutual assistance treaty with the derecognized government; the still unanswered question of the U.S. reaction to a possible PRC siege on Taiwan. Further, we have the question of U.S. troop withdrawals from South Korea; debates over the problem of reconciling President Carter's iterated priority on human rights with developing our relations with regimes that openly violate such rights; the continuing tensions in Sino-Soviet relations and to a lesser degree Soviet-Japanese relations; differences between the United States and Japan over trade and other economic issues, and over broader questions of regional, Asian, and international security and responsibilities.

Japan

Most American specialists on East Asian affairs would probably agree with Edward Neilan that "American policy in Northeast Asia should be fundamentally based on a strong partnership with Japan and even-handed relations with every other nation in the region." They would probably also subscribe to Neilan's view that "for the rest of the century—and perhaps beyond—our relationship with Japan will be fundamental to our interests in the region and more significant than ties with China."[9] A strong partnership with Japan is deemed essential for the promotion of American interests on a global scale as well as in Asia and more specifically East Asia. As Robert Shaplen noted in December, 1976, "The American-Japanese alliance remains the linchpin of our Asian policy, and, in trilateral terms, of our Euro-Asian policy."[10]

The Carter administration has continued to emphasize the central importance of its relations with Japan. It has stessed its willingness to adhere to the commitments of the security treaty, to assist Japan in other ways in meeting its security needs, as well as to welcome Japan's increasingly influential role in world affairs generally and work closely with that nation in seeking mutually acceptable solutions to a wide range of problems in bilateral and multilateral economic relationships.

The significance of the U.S.-Japanese security treaty and of the general relations between these countries have been affirmed continually by almost all leading U.S. and Japanese foreign policy spokesmen in recent years. In his address to the Asia Society in New York on July 29, 1977, Secretary of State Cyrus Vance said: "Of our allies and old friends, none is more important that Japan. Our mutual security treaty is a cornerstone of peace in East Asia."[11] But there is a growing recognition in both the United States and Japan that the American-Japanese connection cannot be taken for granted, and that there is some possibility of growing estrangement in future years. The differences between the two countries are many and they seem to be increasing. The Japanese have not yet recovered from the "Nixon shocks" of 1971, the initiation of the American opening to China in 1971 caught the Japanese by surprise and made them rather disgruntled and uneasy. It seemed incredible to many Japanese that their U.S. ally would begin a new demarche toward China, Japan's giant neighbor in East Asia, without consulting or at least informing Japan. Nixon's economic announcement of August 1971 was almost as unexpected and unwelcome, and again the Japanese, an increasingly important agent in the international economy, were caught by surprise. In their judgment they were adversely affected by decisions of their U.S. ally which changed the nature of the international economic and monetary system.

In wide areas of trade and investment the United States and Japan are both partners and rivals. The extensive trade between the two countries is so unbalanced that the huge trade deficit with Japan is a major part of the U.S. overall unfavorable balance of trade. Under American pressure, Japan has undertaken a series of "voluntary" steps to reduce its exports to the United States, but many members of Congress and influential spokesman and lobbyists for U.S. business and financial interests favor more tariffs and other protective measures. Americans are concerned over heavy Japanese investments in the United States and with the success of Japanese competition with U.S. products in U.S. markets in areas as important as automobiles, television sets, and electronics. U.S. business and financial interests have long complained that the policies of the Japanese government make it difficult for them to do business in Japan (Japanese and U.S. business concerns compete in many parts of the world.) On the other hand, the two countries work closely together in a number of international and regional economic organizations, such as the World Bank, the International Development Association, the Organization for Economic Cooperation and Development (OECD), the Asian Development Bank, and a number of aid consortia. Japan and the United States are two of the three major centers of economic and financial power in the non-Communist world, and they work together and with the countries of Western Europe in many areas of mutual interest, both officially and unofficially (for example, through the Trilateral Commission).

Political relations are generally good, but here too it is not difficult to find areas of divergence and doubt. Many Japanese feel that their country is still too heavily dominated by the United States. There is growing evidence that Japan is working for a more independent position in international affairs. This is most obvious in its own region, East Asia, and increasingly in Southeast Asia and in other parts of the Asian continent. The Treaty of Peace and Friendship between Japan and the People's Republic of China (signed in Peking on August 12, 1978) will undoubtedly have a profound effect on the balance of power in East Asia and on Japan's relations with both the United States and the Soviet Union.

As Ralph Clough has observed, "The U.S. link with Japan . . . is the crucial U.S. security interest in East Asia."[12] He might have added that it is also "the crucial U.S. security interest" in all of Asia, unless a major confrontation develops in Asia between the United States and the Soviet Union, or the United States and China, or the United States and both Communist giants. The core of the security relationship of the United States and Japan is the security treaty to which both countries still attach major importance. But as Ernest Lefever has pointed out, in Japan there is a "growing apprehension about the instability of the American security commitment."[13] There is also a continuing internal opposition to the security treaty, and to the heavy dependence on the

United States for the security of the country. Major opposition parties are on record with pledges that if they come to power they will insist on substantial modifications, or perhaps even the revocation, of the treaty. Japan is still obviously reluctant to devote substantially increased funds to defense or to face the prospect of looking after its own security as a nonnuclear power. But clearly there is a new security consciousness in Japan, as was illustrated in the 260-page Annual Defense White Paper issued in July 1978.[14]

The United States would like to have Japan assume a greater part of the burden for its own defense and a greater role in regional and international security arrangements, without terminating its existing security ties with the United States. On the whole, the United States would like to maintain the rough equilibrium of power existent in East Asia, with the four major powers most concerned—Japan, China, the United States, and the Soviet Union—all having some significant role.

The People's Republic of China

The fundamental change in the U.S. approach to the People's Republic of China in the 1970s, which led to the establishment of full diplomatic relations on January 1, 1979, has profoundly affected the whole spectrum of U.S. Asian policies, the balance of power in East Asia and other parts of Asia, and indeed in the entire world. The change was initiated in the early 1970s, as symbolized by Dr. Kissinger's secret visit to Peking in July 1971 and President Nixon's visit in the following February. The bases of the new relationship were laid down in the Shanghai communique, which was issued at the end of President Nixon's visit. In the succeeding years President Ford visited China, as did Dr. Kissinger and other high-level American officials, and even Mr. Nixon made a return visit as a private citizen; while there were no reciprocal visits from high-level Chinese officials until the offical one of Chinese Vice Premier Teng Hsiao-ping and a sizable party in January 1979. Hundreds of Americans have visited China, and a few Chinese have come to the United States. Some trade began to develop between the two countries. A U.S. liaison office was established in Peking, and a similar Chinese office was opened in Washington, D.C. Hence, a kind of informal international relations was carried on long before the establishment of full diplomatic relations and the evaluation of the liaison offices to embassies.

Even though relations with the PRC have been normalized, these relations will certainly remain essentially abnormal, limited, and difficult for the foreseeable future. Communist China and the United States are far apart in many basic respects and they have many differences in outlook and objectives. But they also have many mutual interests. The absurdity of the absence of recognition and significant relations between the most powerful nation of the free world and the most populous nation in the world had long been apparent to both sides. Presumably the mutual interests include an interest in the preservation of peace in East Asia based in the equilibrium existent there and in the containment of expanding Soviet power and influence in the Asian area and elsewhere. But the United States must not become too directly involved in the Sino-Soviet conflict, and it is probably unwise for it to exploit this conflict—since this might well boomerang—or to identify itself too closely with any of the Communist states in their rivalry with each other.

Ralph Clough has aptly summarized the short and long-range concerns of the United States with regard to the People's Republic of China:

> The long-term U.S. concern with China is comparable to that with India: both nations contain enormous and growing numbers of people who must somehow be provided an opportunity to emerge from poverty and join the modern world if they are not to become a perpetual source of trouble, discord and danger. The short-time U.S. concern with China is more like that with the Soviet Union: the problem is to reduce the danger of large-scale war and little by little to develop ways of cooperating continuously.[15]

Taiwan

A major stumbling block in the development of official relations between the United States and the PRC has been the issue of Taiwan. The Shanghai communique of February 1972 contained a frank recognition of the differing approaches on this issue, although it also included an American acceptance of the view, shared by both the Communist and Nationalist Chinese, that there is only one China. As a price for the establishment of formal diplomatic relations with the PRC, the United States was compelled to agree to withdraw its recognition of, and to declare its intent to terminate its security treaty with, the Republic of China on Taiwan. This action was described in Taiwan and in some circles in the United States as a betrayal of a faithful ally and as a unilateral abrogation of a long-standing security commitment to Taiwan; it was taken not only as evidence of American bad faith and weakness but as a step that would inevitably have a dangerously destabilizing effect on all of East Asia and perhaps in larger areas as well. The United States did not yield to the insistence of the Chinese Communist leaders that it must end most of its multifarious contacts with Taiwan. Extensive economic and cultural contacts will presumably continue, and the formal agreements incorporated in more than 80 economic, commercial, cultural, and other understandings will be reviewed and presumably largely maintained. The U.S. negotiators were unable to obtain a pledge from the PRC that it would seek a resolution of the Taiwan issue only by peaceful means; but they made it clear that the use of forceful methods here would create major complications in U.S.-China relations and dangerously destabilize the power balance in East Asia and elsewhere.

South Korea

An American move that in the view of many East Asians including South Koreans, Japanese, and even Chinese Communists, will have destabilizing effects in East Asia and only add to the security problems there is the effort to implement Jimmy Carter's campaign pledge of withdrawing U.S. ground forces from South Korea. These apprehensions have been mitigated somewhat, but not removed, by the more extended timetable for the withdrawal of American ground troops (a period of four to five years) and by the pledge to maintain U.S. air, naval, and other supporting elements in South Korea as well as help it improve its own defense capabilities.

The United States supported the abortive negotiations between South and North Korea on eventual unification of the peninsula. It also favors the admission of both North and South Korea into the United Nations, "without prejudice to ultimate reunification." It has proposed negotiations "to replace the existing armistice with more permanent arrangements" that would involve representatives of South Korea, North Korea, and the PRC, "the parties most immediately concerned," and perhaps lead to a larger conference "with Korea's other neighbors, including the Soviet Union." As Secretary of State Vance stated in a major address in late June, 1977, "We are prepared to move toward improved relations with North Korea, provided North Korea's allies take steps to improve relations with South Korea." In deference to South Korean sensitivities, he was careful to assure that "we will enter any negotiations over the future of the peninsula only with the participation of the Republic of Korea."[16]

While South Koreans are uneasy about possible U.S. contacts with and support of the Kim Il Sung regime in North Korea, they are much more uneasy with the decision of President Carter to withdraw U.S. ground troops. They feel uncertain of the precise nature of the U.S. commitments to their security and development, for to their view the United States has given an undeservedly low priority to Korea's situation. They also resent the apparent linkage of U.S. policies toward South Korea with those toward Japan. President Park Chung Hee is unhappy over continuing criticism in the United States of his rather repressive regime, especially on issues of political democracy and human rights. Many Americans, in turn, including many members of the Congress, seem to favor decreasing military and other support to the Park regime. Allegations, some with considerable substantiation, of payments to members of the American Congress by Koreans have added new strains in U.S.-South Korean relations.

In spite of all of these problems, relations between the United States and South Korea are still close, in economic, political, cultural, and other areas including military cooperation. But the question of the extent and reliability of the American commitment to the defense of South Korea is today a worrisome one, in the United States as well as in East Asia.

SOUTHEAST ASIA

The situation in Southeast Asia, as well as the American involvement in that region, has changed fundamentally as a result of the following: the Vietnam war and its aftermath; the dissolution of the Southeast Asia Treaty Organization (SEATO); the growing concern of many Southeast Asian nations about their internal and external security and about the activities and objectives of the major powers in the area; the increasing emphasis on regional cooperation, especially through the Association for Southeast Asian Nations (ASEAN); and changing patterns of internal politics and external relations. Even during the Ford administration, there were some indications that the United States was prepared to recognize the new realities in Vietnam, even to the extent of establishing formal diplomatic relations with the ruling Communist regime. But this issue seems to be in suspension because the United States and Vietnam have been unable to work out agreements on specific points, in particular a system for identifying and returning the remains of Americans missing in action in Vietnam; and because of U.S. concern about the conflictual involvement of China and the Soviet Union in the Indochina area, and then, too, U.S. disapproval of the Vietnamese military takeover of Cambodia in late 1978. The problem of the care and resettlement of many thousands of refugees from the Indochinese states has added further complications.

With the ASEAN nations U.S. relations have undergone some rather marked changes. In general, relations with the two ASEAN states with which the United States had had close and special ties, namely the Philippines and Thailand, have become more distant and also difficult, while on the other hand, relations with the remaining members of ASEAN—Indonesia, Singapore, and Malaysia—have become more extensive and significant.

Thailand

Thailand was a major SEATO ally of the United States, and it permitted large U.S. bases in the country and large-scale U.S. military operations to use its territory during the Vietnam war. Since the U.S. withdrawal from Vietnam, it has no longer permitted American bases and troops to remain. It has experienced internal political changes that have been viewed with some doubt in the United States. It has tried to develop a more detached position in its external relations, even verging on nonalignment. The Thais, no doubt, would argue that their new external orientation is simply another example of their well-known realism and pragmatism. Now that a U.S. military presence no longer exists on the mainland of Southeast Asia, and now that a mood of withdrawal seems to prevail in the United States, and this at a time when the Soviet and Chinese activity in Southeast Asia seems to be increasing—along with an increasing Japanese economic if not political or military involvement—Thais point out that they must readjust their policies to the new realities. U.S. relations with their country, however, continue to be friendly if less close or committed than they were once.

The Philippines

Stresses and strains in U.S.-Philippine relations have been developing for some time, especially since President Marcos came to power in December 1965. Unofficial (and to some extent even official) opinion in the United States has been quite critical of some of the more repressive policies of the Marcos regime, and the latter in turn has reacted strongly and indignantly against these criticisms. Toward the end of the Vietnam war the Marcos government was increasingly critical of U.S. actions there, and increasingly noncooperative. Relations are now so uncertain that even the future of the American bases in the Philippines seems to be in question and this is a matter of high concern to the United States. The naval base at Subic Bay and the air base at Clark Field are the main fulcrums of American strategic and tactical power in the entire region of the southwestern Pacific and Indian Oceans. A new agreement regarding these bases has been under negotiation for several years, but has not yet been reached. President Marcos has occasionally threatened to force the United States to abandon the bases altogether, while other times he has insisted on extraordinarily heavy payments as a condition for the extension of the agreement on the bases. His ambivalence and demands on this issue are viewed in some quarters in the United States as marking a strategy to use the bases issue for financial blackmail, and to try to mute criticism of his regime; and further, to convince other Asian states that the Philippines is genuinely interested in developing more "independent" foreign policies and in emphasizing its "Asianness" and its ties with its fellow Asian states, especially with the other members of ASEAN.

ASEAN

When ASEAN was first formed, the United States seemed to regard it with some suspicion, particularly as ASEAN seemed desirous of ignoring the security needs of its members and of turning the region into a "zone of peace, freedom and neutrality." The ASEAN nations themselves seemed to look with suspicion on the United States as being one of the major powers seeking too conspicuous a presence in the area. Now these views have changed considerably. The United States is now strongly supportive of greater regional cooperation in Southeast Asia, which is most manifest in ASEAN, and the ASEAN states now seem more apprehensive of U.S. neglect of the region than of excessive U.S. involvement.

In August 1978, the first formal high-level consultation between the United States and ASEAN took place in Washington, D.C., at the foreign minister level. Apparently, security considerations were not directly discussed, as ASEAN seems to eschew this subject, but they were clearly present in the minds of all the participants. This was indicated in one report of the meeting:

> The purpose why the U.S. staged this high-level meeting, the first of its kind . . . was to demonstrate the American commitment to the region from which it was thought to be pulling out because of the Vietnam trauma. Both sides confined themselves in their formal statement, however, to bread and butter issues on the formal agenda. This was in conformity with the ASEAN claim that its concerns are purely economic. But it is quite clear that the discussions took note of the political and security environment in which ASEAN is pursuing its plans for economic development.[17]

Future U.S. Policies

Professor Robert Scalapino has outlined a broad and suggestive perspective of probable trends in Southeast Asia and of desirable U.S. policies relating to the area in the post-Vietnam era:

> Actual developments in Southeast Asia over the next few years will be highly complex, representing various combinations of compromise political settlements and military "solutions," with correspondingly different impacts on American policies. In whatever event, the region will put American foreign policy capabilities to the test in several respects. . . . in few regions is there such a high premium on the ability to act, and coordinate action, at several levels simultaneously. Certain bilateral relations pertaining to Southeast Asia will continue to be important in the years ahead. Special bilateral relations with Indonesia, Thailand, Malaysia, and Singapore will probably have meaning for the foreseeable future. And in each case, some differentiation in treatment may be required. At the same time, every encouragement should be given to an indigenous regionalism that can be self-generating and begin to cope with political and security problems. . . . Beyond this, it is now clear that truly international undertakings involving powers external to the region are essential if there is to be any comprehensive approach to current needs. Both informally and through existing institutions—or new ones, if required—the United States should seek to strengthen interaction with the PRC, the USSR, and Japan of the type lending itself to a shift from war to peaceful coexistence and mutual aid.
>
> The United States should be able to support the so-called neutralization of Southeast Asia without qualms. . . . Few regions in the world are so positioned and so structured internally as to provide a better test of the feasibility of "neutralization" supported by multipower guarantees and assistance.[18]

SOUTH ASIA

In the total context of its global concerns and overall foreign policies South Asia is a relatively neglected area. From a security point of view the United States has never been as involved in this region as in East Asia and (at least during the heyday of the Vietnam war) Southeast Asia. From this perspective, its main concerns in South Asia have related to the activities of the Soviet Union and Communist China in the area and to the possible spillover effects of internal weaknesses or disturbances or interregional conflicts. For example, the United States was most concerned when the Indo-Pakistan war in 1971 led to the breakup of Pakistan, the emergence of India as an even more dominant regional power, and closer relations between India and the Soviet Union. This put the United States for the time being on a curious parallel track with China.

Since the United States sought to have amicable relations with both India and Pakistan, the strained relations between these two South Asian states greatly complicated U.S. objectives and associations in the region. The United States was careful not to allow its military assistance to Pakistan, its bilateral mutual security arrangements with that country, and its multilateral security relations with Pakistan in SEATO (and to a limited extent in CENTO as well) to be interpreted as a commitment to support Pakistan in its continuing conflicts with India; but obviously Pakistan, and to some extent India as well, were inclined to give these arrangements a more regional interpretation. The alleged pro-Pakistan biases in official U.S. policy seemed to be confirmed by the "tilt toward Pakistan" during the 1971 crisis in South Asia.

The Carter administration has given more continuous attention to South Asia than has almost any previous U.S. government, with the possible exception of the short-lived Kennedy administration in 1961-63 and the Nixon administration during the 1971 South Asian crisis. Since the governmental changes in India as well as the United States in 1977, U.S. relations with India have substantially improved, although basic problems and differences remain. Relations with Bangladesh and Sri Lanka and Nepal have been generally good, if rather limited. Only with Pakistan have relations failed to improve and have in fact deteriorated in some respects.

U.S. interests and concerns diverge markedly from those of India and Pakistan on a wide variety of economic, political, and security issues, including nuclear issues. India is critical of the military policies of the United States, of its huge military establishment, its military aid and arms sales policies and programs, and its alleged failures to move rapidly enough toward the reduction of international tensions and of nuclear and conventional armaments. India refuses to adhere to the nuclear nonproliferation treaty until the superpowers make substantial reductions in their own nuclear arsenals and are willing to associate with other countries in the NPT on a basis of equality. India is especially upset by the failure of the United States to adhere to the schedule agreed upon in 1963 to provide enriched uranium for the nuclear power plant at Tarapur, near Bombay. Pakistan is upset by the efforts of the United States to coerce France into cancelling the agreement that would provide Pakistan with a nuclear reprocessing plant—efforts that the French seemed to be resisting quite firmly until 1978, when they suggested modifications in the agreement with Pakistan tantamount to a withdrawal of its commitment. Pakistan is also unhappy at the refusal of the United States to provide modern fighter planes and other military equipment.

On the official level, however, in spite of certain areas of disagreement and tension, relations between the United States and both India and Pakistan have continued to be quite good, if not really close. The same observation can be made about U.S. relations with the other states of South Asia. Even with Bangladesh, where the problem of satisfactory relations seemed to be complicated by the U.S. "tilt toward Pakistan"— and therefore against the former East Pakistanis who were brutalized in 1971—quite satisfactory, if limited, relations have developed.

Except in extreme crisis periods, as in 1971, or in relation to global rivalries and priorities, the United States has given little attention to South Asia. But the Carter administration, from the beginning, has shown an awareness of the region's importance in the international system; and unlike most previous American administrations, it has also shown an awareness that its approaches and policies toward Asia must extend at least to the Khyber Pass, with due consideration to the impact on Asia of developments elsewhere.[19]

In a broader perspective, the United States must be concerned with the course of events in South Asia, a region that contains nearly one fifth of the human race and three of the four most populous Muslim states, a region that is in turn the most populous of the Third—or "Fourth"—World as well as a center of the nonaligned world. The United States must be concerned with the activities and objectives of other major states in the region, notably the Soviet Union and Communist China.

A new subject of deep concern has arisen more recently from the conjunction of greater political instability in the major states in the area, notably Pakistan and the alarming changes that have occurred in the neighboring countries of Afghanistan and Iran. The dangers of spillover effects of internal instabilities in South Asia and the neighboring countries to the east and of possible external intervention to take advantage of these changes are all too obvious. In a broader geopolitical and geostrategic sense South Asia must now be considered a part of the "crescent of crisis" that extends from Bangladesh to the Horn of Africa and includes the volatile and conflict-ridden, but strategically, politically, and economically vital Middle East.[20] Hence the United States must review its security and political commitments and its political and geopolitical assessments in this entire "crescent of crisis," in relation to similar interests and commitments elsewhere and to its evolving relations with the Soviet Union and China.

STRATEGIC ALTERNATIVES

Ernest Lefever has suggested that from the military-strategic point of view "four courses are possible" for the United States in the Pacific region "in the remaining two decades of the century." They are as follows: "strengthening U.S. security commitments"; "maintaining approximate present levels of support"; "decreasing significantly U.S. support and commitment"; and "withdrawing completely from the Western Pacific." Lefever believes that "The second course of action seems most probable in the immediate future—with ups and downs in the level of support." He points out that "Much will depend on external developments—particularly the perception of threat." He also argues that "Any significant diminution of the U.S. commitment in the Pacific would have an adverse impact on the security of the area and on Washington's reputation for and capacity to support its allies elsewhere in the world."[21]

Since the United States, in the post-Vietnam era, has already greatly reduced its military presence on the Asian mainland (and further reduction is almost certain for South Korea and likely for Japan and the Philippines), the maintainance of approximate present levels of support in the Western Pacific will in itself be a considerable reduction of past levels of support, and may in fact be associated with a fairly significant withdrawal (in the military-security and psychological sense) from mainland Asia and even the entire Western Pacific region. Some analysts argue that, while this is a result mainly of circumstances that the United States could not control and compulsions which it could not resist, it may prove a good thing for the countries of Asia and for the United States. It would lessen the danger that the United States might become further involved in the Asian "quagmire"—to use a word that Daniel Ellsberg applied to Vietnam—and it would provide an incentive to Asians to take more responsibility for dealing with their own security and other affairs.

From this point of view, a policy of detachment and not of involvement would be in the best interests of the Asian states and the United States. Detachment, in the opinion of Selig S. Harrison, a seasoned observer of the changing Asian scene,

> would be the most valuable contribution that the United States could make to the evolution of an intra-Asian balance reinforced by a structure of arms control agreements. The capacity of the United States to affect the indigenous momentum of Asian events is relatively limited . . . but its capacity for distortion through artificial power inputs is infinite.[22]

In a paper entitled "Competitive Strategic Perceptions Underlying U.S. Policy in Asia" (prepared for a conference on "Pacific Asia and U.S. Policies" sponsored by the Pacific Forum in Honolulu and a number of other organizations), Professor Robert A. Scalapino suggested that the Administration has not yet been able to choose between, or combine important elements of, competing alternative strategies. He labeled these alternatives the 'withdrawal' strategy, the 'united front' strategy, and the "equilibrium" strategy. The conference report summarized these three strategies, based on Professor Scalapino's analysis, and considered briefly their implications for U.S. policy:

> The "withdrawal strategy," in essence, calls for the relinquishment by the United States of any significant role in Asia by completing the military withdrawal from the so-called exposed areas of South Korea and Taiwan and subsequently from other Asian states, and by dismantling the security treaty structure of the 1950s. At the same time it calls for retaining economic and political links in the area. . . . An alternative to the withdrawal strategy is that of a "united front" in which the United States, Japan, the PRC and some smaller Asian states would coalesce against the Soviet threat. . . . The third suggested strategy is the "equilibrium" strategy. It is based on the argument that, under present world conditions, a strong element of balance of power politics among nations, however unfortunate, is inevitable. . . . Therefore, the United States should maintain its defense commitments. At the same time, the United States should encourage greater Asian self-reliance and regional cooperation through such organizations as ASEAN. . . . Elements of each of these strategies can be found in U.S. policy in the Asian/Pacific area. While there is nothing necessarily wrong with this . . . the resulting composite policy . . . does not form a conscious and coherent design. Therefore, U.S. policy appeared to be neither predictable nor wholly credible.[23]

From a military-strategic point of view, as J. L. S. Girling has noted,

> The United States, in practice, has adopted a fallback strategy. It relies on aid and naval mobility from bases along the Pacific Rim, extending from Japan and Okinawa, to Guam, the Philippines (subject to negotiation) and Australia.[24]

This may be the most desirable strategy under present and probable future circumstances, and it may in fact be the only realistic one; but it may accurately be described as more a policy of "decreasing significantly U.S. support and commitment," at least in Asia and the Western Pacific, than one of "maintaining approximate present levels of support"—although, as has been noted, the "present levels of support" are in effect a significant decrease from past levels. Moreover, the United States may not be well prepared to maintain even "a fallback strategy," unless the withdrawal mood in the country gives way to a more positive attitude and unless the military—especially the naval—capabilities of the United States are maintained at strengths appropriate to the missions assigned them. This consideration particularly troubles some of the top naval commanders, past and present. In a recent article in a major journal published in Japan, Admirals Elmo Zumwalt and Worth H. Bagley write:

> In contrast to its more rational and objective policies toward Europe, Washington is caught in the grip of an emotional and blurred vision of its interests in Asia. Intent on adjusting its strategic power in Asia to accommodate domestic concerns, the U.S. is touching the vital interests of other countries in a way that may disrupt regional stability. . . . Our power at sea in the Western Pacific is not being structured in ways that reflect the actual or potential dependence which U.S. policy is giving to it. . . . From the vantage point of the strategist, U.S. policies in the Pacific are placing sole security reliance on American sea power that is already over-committed. . . . it is certain that a further downgrading of the American strategic position and power in the Pacific promises to have a critical effect on American influence and stability not just in Asia but in all parts of the world.[25]

Obviously, U.S. military-security policies, as well as overall foreign policy, will be greatly affected by any major changes in the Asian or world environment, and our cognizance of this might well prompt a careful reassessment of American policies and interests. At present there seems to be a kind of power equilibrium in East Asia and the Western Pacific, and the situation in South and Southeast Asia, while rather fluid and uncertain, does not seem to pose immediate security problems of great magnitude, either for the countries of the area or for the United States. But this generally favorable strategic picture could change drastically, and the United States must be in a position to make a reasonably accurate assessment of existing and probable future trends and their implications for U.S. policy.

> In view of the Soviets' active policy in the Asian/Pacific area, shifting regional balances, and an American policy that was described as lacking credibility and coherence, Asia's relative quietude may represent only a passing phase.[26]

TOWARD A MORE CREDIBLE AND COHERENT ASIAN POLICY

Some observers believe that the Carter administration is well aware of the lack of "credibility and coherence" in its policies regarding the Asian/Pacific region, and is giving a higher priority to this region. In May 1978, James Reston wrote in the New York *Times*: "The Carter Administration is making a conscious effort to emphasize and improve its relations with the countries of Asia." Reston seemed to feel that this effort was due both to immediate and to long-run considerations. "The main thing is that Asia is clearly critical to the establishment of a world order, and after a period of neglect, Washington is beginning to give it a proper place in planning for the last quarter of the century."[27]

In attempting to develop a more "credible" and "coherent" policy toward Asia, the United States is handicapped by some aspects of its past record in Asia, by the confusing nature of the changing Asian scene, conflicting objectives, other priorities and concerns, as well as an abyssmal lack of understanding or even interest in the peoples, cultures, and states of Asia. A constructively critical analysis of some of the major faults in the whole American approach to Asia is presented by Selig Harrison in his book bearing the suggestive and disturbing title, *The Widening Gulf: Asian Nationalism and American Policy:*

> While thinking of itself as the defender of nationalism, the United States has in actuality misunderstood what nationalism is in the Asian context and has more often than not been its enemy. Similarly, while historically dedicated to maintaining a balance of power in Asia, the United States has inadvertently warped and distorted the evolution of power relationships in Asia since the end of World War II, strengthening power imbalances and posing the unprecedented danger of a regional consolidation hostile to American interests. Having thrown history temporarily out of joint, as it were, the United States now faces the difficult task of reassessing the Asian landscape with more finely sensitized antennae.[28]

In spite of some evidences that the Carter administration is in fact as well as in rhetoric giving more attention to Asia, the results of this new approach cannot yet be assessed; and there is little basis for believing that the United States is really gearing itself for "the difficult task of reassessing the Asian landscape with more finely sensitized antennae." In fact, there are some trends in the opposite direction. American priorities and concerns are elsewhere, either on problems within the American society or parts of the world outside Asia. In general, programs of Asian studies in the United States are receiving less rather than more support, and those that are flourishing are often concentrating on rather esoteric aspects of Asian culture or philosophy. What are needed are sophisticated studies of the relationship between basic cultural and philosophical values and experience and contemporary trends and developments in Asia.

Some sympathetic observers seem to feel that the United States is paying even less attention to Asia than in the past, when it should be doing the opposite. In an address given at a conference of Cultural Affairs Officers from U.S. Embassies and representatives from Binational Exchange Commissions in the East Asian and Pacific areas, in February, 1976, Dr. Soedjatmoko, a perceptive scholar-diplomat from Indonesia, observed that America was not listening enough to Asia, and that "It is now listening even less than before. . . . The almost total self-absorption that now occurs as a result of the self-examination in the United States, has in a sense increased the U.S. insensitivity to the world," and especially to Asia. "Both in the United States and in Asia," he pointed out, "the trends are not favorable to better listening to each other."[29]

It seems obvious, therefore, that in addition to developing a more "credible" and "coherent" policy toward Asia and the Pacific region, one that will give adequate attention to Asian realities and sensitivities as well as to overall American political, economic, and security interests, "A much greater American public awareness and understanding of Asia, and its importance to the future strategic and economic security of the United States, needs to be fostered."[30] After all, as a report issued by the Pacific Forum of Honolulu in 1978 emphasized, "In the next decade the Pacific Basin, with thirty-seven independent countries and territories and more than half the world's population, will be the scene of the greatest economic growth, the greatest interaction of peoples, and the greatest increase in trade in the world."[31]

In the affairs of this vast region, and in all of Asia, the United States will inevitably play a major role, with increasing involvement in many respects and decreasing involvement in others. This challenging and rather frightening task must be given a much higher place on the American agenda in the coming decades.

NOTES

1. *U.S. Foreign Policy for the 1970s: Shaping a Durable Peace*, A Report to the Congress by Richard Nixon, President of the United States, May 3, 1973 (Washington, D.C.: U.S. Government Printing Office, 1973).

2. *The Growing Dimensions of Security*, A Report by the Atlantic Council's Working Group on Security (Washington, D.C.: The Atlantic Council of the United States, November, 1977), p. 1.

3. *Pacific Asia and U.S. Policies: A Political-Economic-Strategic Assessment* (Honolulu: Pacific Forum, 1978), p. 2.

4. The text of this important address is available as a release of the Bureau of Public Affairs of the Department of State.

5. "The World According to Brzezinski," *New York Times Magazine*, Dec. 31, 1978.

6. Edward Neilan, "American Policy and Northeast Asia," *Policy Review*, no. 6 (Fall 1978): 105.

7. William R. Kintner, "Trip Report: A Visit to East Asia" (Philadelphia: Foreign Policy Research Institute, 1978).

8. *Pacific Asia and U.S. Policies*, p. v.

9. Neilan, "American Policy and Northeast Asia," pp. 117, 106.

10. Robert Shaplen, "Three Areas of Asia Concern for Carter," *Philadelphia Inquirer*, Dec. 5, 1976.

11. Cyrus Vance, "United States and Asia," address before the Asia Society in New York, June 29, 1977.

12. Ralph N. Clough, *East Asia and U.S. Security* (Washington, D.C.: The Brookings Institution, 1975), p. 43.

13. Ernest W. Lefever, "United States, Japan, and the Defense of the Pacific," *Policy Review*, no. 6 (Fall 1978): 99.

14. Ibid., p. 100.

15. Clough, *East Asia and U.S. Security*, p. 31.

16. Address before the Asia Society in New York, June 29, 1977.

17. Dilip Mukerjee, "U.S. Reassures ASEAN Members," *The Times of India*, Aug. 29, 1978.

18. Robert A. Scalapino, *Asia and the Road Ahead: Issues for the Major Powers* (Berkeley: University of California Press, 1975), pp. 269–270.

19. See Norman D. Palmer, "The United States and South Asia," *Current History* 76 (April 1979).

20. See "The Crescent of Crisis," *Time*, Jan. 15, 1979.

21. Lefever, "United States, Japan," pp. 98, 103.

22. Selig S. Harrison, *The Widening Gulf: Asian Nationalism and American Policy* (New York: The Free Press, 1978), p. 387.

23. *Pacific Asia and U.S. Policies*, pp. 4–5. This is a summary of a paper entitled "Competitive Strategic Perceptions Underlying U.S. Policy in Asia," which Professor Scalapino prepared for a conference sponsored by the Pacific Forum, Honolulu, Hawaii, on "Pacific Asia and U.S. Policies."

24. J. L. S. Girling, "Southeast Asia and the Great Powers," *Pacific Community* 9 (January 1978): 201.

25. Elmo Zumwalt and Worth H. Bagley, "Strategic Deterioration in the Pacific: The Dilemma for the U.S. and Japan," *Pacific Community* 9 (January, 1978), pp. 115, 118, 127–28.

26. *Pacific Asia and U.S. Policies*, p. 2.

27. James Reston, "Why Carter Is Turning to Asia," *The Mirror* (Singapore), May 29, 1978, p. 3. This is a reprint of a column by Reston that appeared originally in the New York *Times*.

28. Harrison, *The Widening Gulf*, p. 36.

29. Soedjatmoko, "Is America Listening Enough to Asia?" *The Asian Student*, Feb. 12, 1977. This is the text of Dr. Soedjatmoko's address.

30. *Pacific Asia and U.S. Policies*, p. 31.

31. Ibid., p. 1.

· 6 ·

SOUTH ASIA:
SECURITY AND STABILITY
UNDER CHALLENGE
Sudershan Chawla

Security and stability in South Asia are primarily dictated by the state of relations among India, Pakistan, and Bangladesh. In addition they are dependent upon the interests and actions of China and the two superpowers, the United States and the Soviet Union, in this region and the surrounding areas. This is not to suggest that regional states such as Nepal and Sri Lanka have no role to play. The other states in the area are relatively weak; their activities in the last three decades have neither caused wars nor upheavals that shook the subcontinent. Furthermore, the scope of this article being limited, it does not address itself to relations among all the states of South Asia.

In general the subcontinent has been relatively quiet since the 1971 war, but events in the neighboring regions in the recent past have had an unsettling effect. Furthermore, relations between India and China and India and Pakistan are far from being cordial or fully normal. The three wars (1962, 1965, and 1971) and subsequent negotiations have not settled all the outstanding disputes. The leadership of the major powers (China, the United States, the Soviet Union) and the states of South Asia in preparing for future possibilities has taken actions that set the dimensions of security and stability in the area. The dual task of uplifting an underdeveloped economy and providing a viable defense

India, Pakistan, and Bangladesh alone are the focus of this article. They have been and will continue to be the major participants in activities which impact the security and stability of the region.

continues to strain the energies of the peoples of the region. It is fraught with problems which exacerbate the threats to peace in the area.

INDIA AND CHINA

Relations between the People's Republic of China and India did not begin on a friendly note, even though India was one of the first nations to recognize the Communist regime on the mainland as the legitimate government of China. October 1949, when the Communist Party of India was engaged in intensive terroristic activities, Mao Tse-tung sent a message to Ranadive, the Secretary of the Party, wishing the Indian Communists speed in their attempts to liberate India and expressing the hope that India would one day go the Chinese way. Similarly, prior to the Chinese attack on Tibet in 1950, the *New China News Agency* reported that the "Anglo-American imperialists and their running dog," Pandit Nehru, were plotting a coup in Lhasa for the annexation of Tibet.

In March 1950, Nehru expressed a desire before the Indian Parliament to sign a treaty of friendship with the new regime on mainland China. There was no response of any sort from Peking. When, in December 1952, India advanced certain proposals for a Korean truce, they were denounced by Peking in rather strong language.

The picture suddenly changed in 1953. The Peking regime agreed to a settlement in Korea in March 1953 that was based mainly on the proposal submitted in 1952. In his opening speech before the Geneva Conference in April 1954, Chou En-lai expressed regret that an important Asian country like India, devoted to world peace, could not be present at the conference. On his return from Geneva, the Chinese prime minister paid a three day visit to New Delhi. Only a few months later, Nehru returned the courtesy of the Chinese premier by journeying to Peking for a visit that lasted 12 days. What was even more significant was that on April 29, 1954, the governments of India and China signed an "agreement on trade and intercourse between the Tibet region of China and India." The preamble stated that the agreement was based on the principles of mutual respect for each other's territorial integrity and sovereignty, mutual nonaggression, mutual noninterference in each other's internal affairs, equality and mutual benefit, and peaceful coexistence. These five principles formed the most notable feature of the agreement, as Nehru himself said before the Indian parliament, and later became the landmark of India's foreign policy under the name of Panchsheel.

The year 1955 saw India and China closer to each other than ever before. Cultural exchanges between the two countries and missions of goodwill surpassed all previous records. At the Bandung Conference, India took great pains to establish that India and China could share the leadership of the Asian-African world. In the United Nations, India worked relentlessly for recognition of the mainland regime as the legitimate government of China, even though the United States opposed this vehemently. This was the period when the popular slogan in Peking and New Delhi was: "Hindi Chini, Bhai Bhai."[1]

Two developments in 1959 completely overshadowed this period of goodwill, a condition that may never return. The Tibetan problem erupted with renewed fury. The sporadic fighting between the Tibetans and the occupying Chinese forces that had raged over a period of some three years mushroomed into a major Tibetan revolt on March 10, 1959. The Dalai Lama, leader of the Tibetans, fled Lhasa and was granted political asylum in India. Prime Minister Nehru let it be known that the Tibetan leader would not be surrendered to the Chinese government under any circumstances. China resented this, and it reacted by imposing strict restrictions on the movements of Indian nationals as well as the Indian representatives in Tibet.

The news that Nehru brought to the Indian Parliament on August 28, 1959, was even more alarming. During the preceding two or three years there had been incidents of intrusion on India's northern border by Chinese troops. While the prime minister described most of these incidents as being of a minor nature, it soon became clear that India and China were involved in a serious boundary dispute that covered the entire 2,500 mile-long border between the two countries.[2]

The period between October 1959 and October 1962 was marked by a series of diplomatic moves. Prime Minister Chou En-lai made a personal visit to New Delhi in 1960. But there were no results. While both nations exchanged some sharp remarks, each professed no intention of resort to arms to solve the boundary dispute that had assumed an ugly character. Then on October 20, 1962, like a bolt from the blue, a better trained, better supplied, better organized, more disciplined, and numerically superior Chinese army marched across the northern border into Indian territory. The campaign which lasted for about a month was a one-sided affair. The Indian army was completely routed. Chinese troops made deep thrusts into India on several fronts.

Just as suddenly as the initial attack, on November 21, 1962, China declared a unilateral cease fire along the entire Sino-Indian frontier. She also announced that starting on December 1, 1962, the Chinese frontier guard would withdraw to positions 20 kilometers behind the line of actual control which existed between China and India on November 7, 1959. India had no choice but to accept an outcome that China had imposed at the point of a gun.

Whether China was provoked by India into taking this action or whether it was a calculated Chinese move punitive in character is a controversial point not relevant for discussion here.[3] What is important to stress at this point is that China's expedition against India had wide implications for the security and stability of the subcontinent—its aftereffects continue to influence the policies of South Asian states.

Without doubt China established her military superiority on the Asian scene. She destroyed the image of India as an Asian power. It was manifest that China would now figure in any major move that nations of the region might contemplate in relations with each other. But also, China with this action established herself as a major threat to any nation in the area that dared to defy her will.[4]

While India, after this humiliating experience, rushed to build her military strength in the coming years, something which had been sorely neglected until then, the Sino-Indian conflict produced an incentive for Pakistan to befriend China, for the two countries now shared a common enemy in India.

This was an interesting development in view of the fact that in 1954 the United States and Pakistan had signed a security pact which sought to bolster Pakistan militarily in order to enable her to fight communist expansionism. But this held no significance for Pakistan in the new context. Having failed to influence India to accede to her demands in Kashmir through the medium of the military treaty with the United States, Pakistan now turned toward China with the hope that she would prove a more effective ally where Pakistani interests were concerned. A situation had thus arisen where India faced two antagonists both with designs on territory that India claimed as hers. Based on what had already transpired, the two could very well contemplate a joint military action against India in the future. India hastened to prepare an effective defense. Events in succeeding years not only forced India to qualify her policy of nonalignment; they made it clear that the nature of the challenge India faced warranted that she too look for allies to ensure future security.

India and Pakistan went to war for the second time in 1965. India was apprehensive that China would use the occasion to strike again. China did issue an ultimatum of sorts to the Indian government but failed to carry out the threat when Britain and the United States warned that intervention could have serious consequences for China.

Between March and December 1971, relations between two wings of Pakistan, West and East, deteriorated steadily and led to a civil war. India supported the aspirations of East Pakistanis for independent status and creation of the state of Bangladesh. China came out firmly in support of Pakistani President Yahya Khan's action in suppressing the revolt. She condemned the free Bangladesh movement, accused India of expansionist tendencies, and charged her with intentions of breaking up Pakistan.

Prospects of another war between India and Pakistan as a consequence of the above developments loomed large. Once again the big question was whether China would intervene. Indian calculations were that the possibility was greater this time than on previous occasions. The restraint imposed by the Western powers in 1965 was missing. The United States involved in an effort to make a complete break with the past and start an era of normal relations with China, informed India that if China intervened, no response to that move would come from the United States.[5] While India's military strength in 1971 was far superior to what it had been in 1962, she was still no match for China, a nuclear weapons state since 1964. A security treaty with the Soviet Union appeared as the only alternative open to India at this juncture.

Relations between the two Communist giants, China and the Soviet Union, had soured in 1959. But how deep the split was, and how intense the rivalry, did not become evident until 1968. After that, the bond of communist ideology was no bar to open hostility between the two. No wonder then that while China was maneuvering to mend fences with the United States, as a check against the Soviet Union, that nation itself was encouraging security alliances in Southeast Asia and South Asia apparently with China in mind as the future threat in these areas.

Checking China, therefore, became a common goal for India and the Soviet Union at this point, although for different reasons. New Delhi sought an assurance against Chinese intervention in the Bangladesh affair, while Moscow sought an ally in opposing Chinese "hegemonism." And so India and the Soviet Union signed a security pact in August 1971; a pact which is labeled as a treaty of friendship and cooperation but is indeed defense oriented.

The Indo-Pakistani war of December 1971 resulted in the dismemberment of Pakistan and the birth of a new nation, i.e., Bangladesh. China refrained from involvement in the war. It was widely believed that the Indo-Soviet treaty had discouraged China from taking any action in behalf of Pakistan. However, China showed her disapproval of the new developments on the subcontinent by not recognizing the state of Bangladesh. She also vetoed UN membership for the new nation.*

In late 1974, possibly emboldened by her new relationship with the Soviet Union, India incorporated the Himalayan kingdom of Sikkim into an Indian state when the domestic situation within the kingdom became

---

*Diplomatic relations between China and Bangladesh were established on October 4, 1975. China also withdrew her objection to Bangladesh's UN membership at that time.

highly unstable. While this was unacceptable to China, she accused India of expansionism but went no further.

ATTEMPTS TO IMPROVE RELATIONS

In 1976, after the death of Premier Chou En-lai, India judged the time as ripe to test if Chinese foreign policy was changing direction. She announced in April that an ambassador would be assigned to Peking in the coming months. While the Chinese did not respond with a similar announcement at the time, before the end of 1976 diplomatic relations between India and China, which had been lowered to the chargé d' affaires level in 1962, were restored to the ambassadorial level. No further progress was made, however, until the new government of Morarji Desai came to power in India. The leadership in Peking and in New Delhi made repeated statements expressing interest in taking steps toward normalization of relations between the two countries. Finally, China invited India's foreign minister to visit Peking in October 1978, with a view toward exploring the possibilities to improve mutual relations.

Both sides welcomed the development. But both sides approached the event with great caution. That China now considered the Soviet Union as the biggest threat to her security as well as to world peace was well known in every quarter. India was aware that in this context the Indo-Soviet treaty made India a tool of the Soviets in their hegemonist designs where Peking was concerned; and that, therefore, China would use the occasion to probe whether India could be weaned away from this position with an offer of concessions on the boundary issue. Furthermore, in earlier statements the Chinese leadership had made it clear that it continued to support the Pakistani stand in Kashmir. But the new regime in India was eager to manifest that the Soviet tie did not compromise India's freedom of diplomatic maneuver. India also desired to strike rapprochement with China in order to secure relief from the increasing burden of defense. Also, if the boundary dispute could be resolved, there would be little reason for the two giant Asian neighbors to nurse feelings of fear and suspicion. This would enhance India's chances for organizing a structure of stability and security in the region, with no interference from outside.

The two parties were conscious of these underlying currents. They were nonetheless intent on seizing the opportunity which held prospects for a change. Ironically, what unfolded thereafter left the situation in a state of uncertainty even worse than before.

The official visit of India's Foreign Minister Atal Behari Vajpayee, initially scheduled for October 1978, did not materialize until February 1979. Even though the foreign minister did fall ill during this period, that did not halt speculation that the delay was politically motivated, What gave substance to such speculation was rising tensions between China and Vietnam in the background.[6] Matters had reached a point where the possibility of a war between the two loomed large. Because of a security pact between Vietnam and the Soviet Union, one similar to that between India and the Soviet Union, there were fears that such a war could expand to include the Soviet Union and then others beyond that. Given the cordial relations between India and Vietnam, the occasion would necessitate a proper Indian response. Could it be that India was, therefore, in doubt at the last moment whether this was an appropriate time for high level negotiations between India and China to search for normalization of relations? All this notwithstanding, Foreign Minister Vajpayee arrived in Peking on February 12, 1979, for an eight-day stay in China.

India's external affairs minister was well received. He had extensive conversations with China's Foreign Minister Huang Hua. He also met with Prime Minister Hua Kuo-feng and Vice-Premier Teng Hsiao-ping. In public statements issued by the leaders of the two countries, they emphasized that no specific problems were discussed because the objective of this meeting, the first high level meeting since Chou En-lai's visit to India in 1960, had been to permit a general exchange of views on a number of international problems in addition to problems directly affecting bilateral relations. As China's foreign minister said at a banquet in honor of the visitor:

> During his stay here, we had the pleasure of having a sincere and candid exchange of views with His Excellency on the international situation and issues in our bilateral relations. . . . Our two sides also exchanged views extensively on ways to increase contacts and cooper-ation in the trade, cultural, scientific and technological and other fields . . . The current visit of His Excellency the External Minister, Mr. Vajpayee to China is a significant event in our bilateral relations and a good beginning for further developing the friendly relations between our two countries and solving unsettled bilateral questions.[7]

In reporting to the Indian parliament on his return Vajpayee said that it was neither his own nor China's expectation that his visit could solve the difficult problem of approximately 50,000 square miles of territory in contention between the two states. He added that the preliminary contacts "have at least unfrozen the Sino-Indian border issue." He stated that the Chinese leadership recognized the importance of a satisfactory solution of this issue; also he had made it clear to them that "if relations of mutual confidence are to be established between India and China," the boundary question must be settled.[8]

The foreign minister told the lower house that he was informed by the Chinese leaders that they no longer gave support to the rebels in Nagaland, Mizoram, and Manipur—Indian territories in the Northeast Frontier area.

On the question of the Dalai Lama and Tibetans in India, Vajpayee assured the Chinese that in case the spiritual leader and his followers judged conditions in Tibet stable enough for their return and desired to do so, India would have no objection to this. The question of surrendering them did not arise.

Referring to the Kashmir question, India's foreign minister said:

I informed the Chinese leaders that under the Simla agreement, to which both countries are parties, we are committed to the final settlement of the Kashmir question through bilateral relations. It has been the considered view of the government and all sections of the people in India, that unlike the stand taken by the Chinese in the 1950s, the attitude adopted by the People's Republic of China in the last decade and a half had been an additional and unnecessary complication to the prospects of Sino-Indian relations. In this connection, I also reiterated our concern at the construction of the Karakoram highway across the territory which formed part of the state of Jammu and Kashmir[9]

Other statements made by Vajpayee indicated that the Indian side chose not to discuss the superpower rivalry with China; they also did not discuss relations between India and other nations which had no bearing on Sino-Indian relations.

If the visit of India's foreign minister had concluded after these exchanges with no additional dimensions, one could have held out hope for drastic reduction of tension in South Asia. The final outcome, however, was distinctly different.

On February 17, 1979, the Chinese armies marched into Vietnam. At no time during their conversations did the Chinese deem it necessary or proper to alert India's envoy about this contemplated move. He learned of the attack in a telephone call from New Delhi and was advised to cut his visit short and return to India. Because of the abruptness with which the sojourn ended, there were no statements of mutual gratification or communiques issued when Vajpayee left China.

The visit which had been heralded as the dawn of a new era in bilateral ties went sour. That the attack should have taken place while the Foreign Minister was in China was seen as indication that the host country held India in low esteem and was unconcerned about her reaction.

REPERCUSSIONS

India on her part manifested her protest and anger against China's move in statements made by the leaders subsequent to Vajpayee's return. In a statement issued after the Vietnamese ambassador in New Delhi called on him, Prime Minister Morarji Desai said that he was shocked and distressed at China's attack that created a situation endangering world peace. He emphasized that China must withdraw its troops from Vietnam immediately.[10]

Desai condemned the action in much stronger terms in a TV interview with the press on February 27. Answering a question on the subject, he said:

> We do not want to improve relations by saying wrong things. We have to say what is right, we will continue to say it and at the same time will try to improve relations. What China has done against Vietnam will have to be called as [sic] aggression. We have to say what is right.[11]

In a debate in the lower house of the Indian parliament on the Chinese attack on Vietnam, Foreign Minister Vajpayee said: "All countries have to put pressure on China to withdraw. An aggressor cannot be allowed to enjoy the fruits of aggression."[12]

Clearly India sided with Vietnam in the Sino-Vietnam conflict. This posture reinforced the Chinese belief that India is in the Soviet camp, India's denials notwithstanding. Soviet Premier Alexei Kosygin's visit to India during the second week of March and his statements while in India further encouraged this belief.

Kosygin began his official visit to India on March 9. Sensitive to the fact that this visit came on the heels of Sino-Vietnam conflict and the Indian foreign minister's visit to China, Prime Minister Desai informed the press that the Soviet leader's visit had been arranged a year earlier. Kosygin, however, made maximum use of the occasion to denounce China in the strongest terms.

On the very first day of his visit, the Soviet prime minister condemned China for its agression on Vietnam in two separate speeches. But in his address to the Indian parliament he launched a diatribe against Chinese conduct in the conflict. He said:

> What punishment a criminal deserves who has encroached on the life of an entire nation and who seeks to assume the right to use arms against other peoples and decide their fate as he pleases, burns their houses, kills their women and children.[13]

Kosygin urged the members of the Indian parliament to join in an effort to "check the policy of hegemonism and expansion which is no less dangerous for peace." The Indian government, even if embarrassed by some of these developments, did assure the Soviet representative that they were in accord with the Soviet Union in their assessment of the Sino-Vietnam confrontation. India refrained from equating Vietnam's activities in Cambodia in January, which resulted in the overthrow of the Pol Pot regime, with China's conduct vis à vis Vietnam. And Prime Minister Desai conveyed to Kosygin that Indian efforts to normalize relations with China would not affect the close relationship between their two countries. Desai also commended the Soviet Union for the "restraint which your great country exercises."[14]

Before Kosygin left he signed several agreements which committed the Soviet Union to cooperate with India in economic and scientific fields over a period of some 15 years. But he also left behind a burdensome task for India which was to explain to China that Indo-Soviet friendship need not be a barrier to close relations between China and India. A reading of the events reveals that this may not be possible.

For India, China's attack on Vietnam brought back memories of 1962. If one examines the reasons for Chinese action in 1962 as opposed to 1979, it is apparent that there are dissimilarities, but the similarities in the two situations are too significant to ignore. In both cases China's attack was short lived and punitive in character.[15] The Chinese made this clear by unilateral withdrawal on each occasion after being satisfied that due punishment had been executed and the adversaries taught a lesson. Foreign Minister Huang Hua put this bluntly at a press conference in Peking on March 16, when he said that the Chinese had "attained all their goals." The armed forces of China, he maintained, had dealt "devastating blows to the (Vietnamese) armed forces . . . deflating the arrogance of the Vietnamese aggressors and exploding the myth of their invincibility."[16]

In 1962 the Chinese proved that India had no credentials to claim leadership in Asia. In 1979 they proved that nations of South and Southeast Asia would have to reckon with China were they to take independent action in regional political situations which was unpalatable to China.

The Chinese did not intervene in the Indo-Pakistani war of 1971. That the Indo-Soviet treaty restrained them is widely accepted. Why then was China able to punish Vietnam for its actions in Cambodia when Vietnam also had a security treaty with the Soviet Union? Quite clearly in 1979 China could take greater risks emboldened by its new relationship with the United States, which she calculated would inhibit the Soviet Union from taking any precipitous action against her. There is then the obvious implication that China is now relatively free to intervene in the affairs of bordering regions. Bent upon demonstrating that she is undaunted by fear of Soviet counter attack, China has proved herself capable of limited military action against an Asian state defiant of her will—given that the danger of a prolonged full scale war appears remote.

It has been revealed that the Soviets advised the Indian government against a China visit by the foreign minister at the time because of strong suspicion that an attack on Vietnam was in the offing.[17] Unprepared to believe the Soviets because of the intense Sino-Soviet hostility toward each other; eager to demonstrate to China that India was not shackled by her ties with the Soviet Union; anxious to strike a new relationship with China to resolve some tension-creating problems, India took a calculated risk. She was nursing an old dream that the politics of the subcontinent could be left to the three main contenders— India, Pakistan, and Bangladesh. Once again the reality of international politics was forced upon India by China. Even if the Vajpayee visit had not taken place, except for the fact that the bitterness caused by the experience would have been missing, the resultant situation would be the same. South Asia would never be free from the impact of major power actions and reactions.

Sino-Indian relations are at a standstill. China's foreign minister did inform his Indian counterpart that China had stopped aiding the rebels on India's northeastern frontier. Outside of that, the issues which have caused conflict and concern in the past remain unresolved.

Vajpayee's visit might have "unfrozen" the boundary issue. But some 17,000 square miles of territory in the west and approximately 33,000 square miles of territory in the east is still in China's hands. The Aksai Chin road, built to link the Aksai Chin area of China with Tibet, passes over land under dispute. The Karakoram road recently constructed for direct access between Pakistan and China passes over territory India claims to be a part of the Indian state of Jammu and Kashmir. In a statement made in April 1978 before the Rajya Sabha, the upper house of the parliament, Prime Minister Desai declared that "till the question of Indian territory in Chinese possession was decided, there could be no question of 'full friendship' between the two countries."[18] In October he told a public meeting that "India was firm on getting back occupied land from China." Addressing a news conference in Colombo on a visit to Sri Lanka in February 1979, he reiterated India's stand, saying that the road built by China at the Karakoram range was built "on our legal territory," and better relations with China could come about "only if the question of occupation was resolved."[19]

While China has stated that she would welcome resolution of Indo-Pakistani disputes through bilateral negotiations between them, not long before the anticipated visit of the Indian envoy, China declared her support of Pakistan on the Kashmir issue. By building the Karakoram highway which opened in 1978, China is committed to protect Pakistan's hold on that land.

There is no immediate threat that these disputes will erupt into open conflict. But as long as they remain alive, they are a source of tension and possible warfare for which the nations of the subcontinent must be prepared. For India, continued reliance on the Indo-Soviet treaty is part of the preparedness to meet such a challenge. This is no comfort for China who now sees the Soviet Union as enemy number one.

In recent years the Asian scene has experienced rapid changes. There have been radical shifts in relationships among nations. One cannot deny, then, that there is room for Sino-Indian rapprochement— the dialogue rudely interrupted by recent events could start again. But as one commentator says one cannot overlook the

> unpleasant implications of the Chinese aggression on Vietnam. In spite of the friendly Chinese commentary on the Vajpayee visit, how can anyone in this country [India] place any faith in Peking's professions about its desire to find a peaceful settlement of the boundary question? And has not the Chinese arrogance in action made utter nonsense of the repeated Chinese stress on equality between the two sides round the conference table? [20]

INDIA AND PAKISTAN

It is no exaggeration to say that peace and tranquility left the Indian subcontinent the day it was partitioned into independent states of India and Pakistan. Even if the division did solve some problems, it gave birth to hostilities of a wide variety which have been the source of three wars, dismemberment of the original state of Pakistan, great power manipulation, and the promise of continued unrest in the area.

Reasons for prolonged friction between India and Pakistan range from the religious and ethnic to the economic and psychological. But it can be said that war over Kashmir in 1948 put the two on a collision course from which they have departed only for short intervals to this day. [21]

The background to the Kashmir conflict is a complex one. Suffice it to say that when the two failed to find a mutually satisfactory solution, militarily weak Pakistan, in order to deal with India from a position of strength, looked for outside sources to bolster her power. She found the United States ready and willing to give her the military and economic assistance she sought in return for bases which the United States could use for intelligence gathering.[22] India resented this, and she turned down a similar offer from the United States. New Delhi wanted to keep cold war tensions away from South Asia; interference in South Asian affairs by great powers was anathema to India. But she failed to reckon with the fact that her neighbors felt no obligation to join the nonalignment crusade when their interests in contest with more powerful states remained unsatisfied.

Pakistan and the United States signed a military pact in 1954. Pakistan also joined the military alliances of Southeast Asia Treaty Organization (SEATO) and Central Treaty Organization (CENTO). India reacted by refusing to negotiate the Kashmir issue on a basis earlier agreed upon. Thus the problem remained unresolved, and relations between India and Pakistan began a gradual decline.

A skirmish over another piece of territory in dispute, namely the Rann of Kutch, snowballed into the second war over Kashmir in September 1965. The three week fighting ceased when the United States and Britain halted all military and economic aid to the countries at war. Also the United States, Britain, and the Soviet Union joined together in sponsoring a UN resolution calling for ceasefire.

Subsequent to the ceasefire, all efforts by the UN to untangle the situation failed. Eventually Soviet Prime Minister Alexei Kosygin invited Prime Minister Shastri of India and President Ayub of Pakistan to Tashkent, in the Soviet Union, on Janaury 3, 1966, in an attempt to resolve the thorny issue. While the Tashkent Declaration of Janaury 10, 1966, resulted in withdrawal of troops to lines held prior to August 1965, it did not go much beyond the agreement that the two sides would continue to meet to resolve the dispute peacefully. The goodwill generated by the Tashkent conference failed to settle the Kashmir issue—relations between India and Pakistan remained tense.

The incident, however, highlighted the fact that the security problems of the subcontinent had asumed a complex character. In the early 1960s, there was a thaw in cold war tensions. The United States and the Soviet Union started on the road to détente with the conclusion of the Nuclear Test Ban Treaty in 1963. But during this period Sino-Soviet relations began their decline. Relations between China and the United States were still quite bitter. Thus the interests of the United States and the Soviet Union coincided at this point where both opposed any increase in China's influence on the Indian subcontinent. Based on this the United States came to India's aid subsequent to the Chinese attack in 1962 in spite of Pakistan's objections. And as Pakistan warmed up to China, seeing in her a natural ally against India, the Soviet Union moved to discourage this trend. It was in this context that the Indo-Pakistani war of 1965 ended with developments such as the following: the United States stopped all military aid not only to India but also Pakistan, a U.S. ally in several anticommunist security pacts; during the conflict China threatened to intervene in behalf of Pakistan but was restrained by warnings from Britain and the United States that this could result in serious consequences for China; and the Soviet Union, long hostile to Pakistan over her membership in SEATO and CENTO and pursuing a neutral course here, invited India and Pakistan to come to the Soviet Union to settle their differences.[23]

As for the main parties in the 1965 conflict, Pakistan discovered that the defense treaty with the United States could not be activated to settle scores with India. Henceforth Pakistan turned toward China for military assistance. India discovered that the U.S. friendship carried severe limits; the United States could not be a major source of modern military weapons for India at the cost of totally alienating Pakistan.[24] And since in the presence of two hostile neighbors, China and Pakistan, India could ill afford to neglect the building of adequate defense against future threats, she launched a diplomatic offensive to puncture Soviet neutrality and rebuild close friendship between the two countries. In time the Soviet Union became the main source of economic and military assistance for India.

By no means did the twisting and turning of events and relationships on the subcontinent end at this juncture. India and Pakistan were at war again in 1971. In March, political developments in the two wings of Pakistan culminated in a civil war between East and West Pakistan. As the situation escalated into a full-scale war between Pakistani troops and Mukti Bahini—the Bengali freedom force—millions of terror stricken East Pakistanis fled to the neighboring state of West Bengal in India. The Indian government was subjected to tremendous domestic pressure for recognition of a free government of Bangladesh and intervention by the Indian army on behalf of forces of liberation. And this took place when on December 3, President Yahya Khan of Pakistan declared war on India.

It is not relevant to debate here as to who was the aggressor. The fact is that the political situation in Pakistan had been unstable since 1969 when President Ayub Khan, unable to cope with country's problems, handed over the presidency to General Yahya Khan. He too was unable to find a solution acceptable to leadership in both wings of Pakistan. When General Yahya Khan attempted to suppress the opposition in the East, he was faced with a rebellion which he could not control.

No amount of discussion and debate can absolve the leadership in

West Pakistan of the major responsibility for permitting the differences between the Eastern and the Western wings to rise to the civil war level. No amount of explanation can justify the failure of President Nixon to exert sufficient pressure on General Yahya Khan to relent from brutal suppression of the people in Bangladesh or work out a feasible solution to the issue. And looking at the background of Indo-Pakistani relations, it should come as no surprise that at a certain point in the course of events India felt compelled to intervene in the interests of her security.

The 14-day war ended on December 16, 1971, when the Pakistani army surrendered unconditionally in Bangladesh. This engagement placed Indo-Pakistani relations in an entirely new context. It changed the map of the subcontinent. That this occurred without direct involvement of any of the major powers needs explanation.

In the wake of the 1969 border conflicts between China and the Soviet Union, the United States began probing the possibilities of a dialogue between itself and China that could lead to normalization of relations between the two. Since it was an attempt to wipe out a legacy of harsh relations that had prevailed from the day the communists took over power on the China mainland, and since domestic forces opposing such a move on the American scene were formidable, this sensitive issue was handled with the utmost secrecy. The party that did the probing in behalf of the United States was General Yahya Khan, the president of Pakistan. The efforts did not bear fruit until 1971. Therefore, just at the time that the most serious conflict hung over the subcontinent, the United States and China were about to announce a major breakthrough in their attempts to normalize relations. The mediator Pakistan was thus not only left alone to handle the situation in its eastern wing; it could count on the full support of both the United States and China.

President Nixon warned India that his government would not approve of any intervention by India in a Pakistani affair that was strictly internal. Henry Kissinger, then national security aide to the President, stopped in New Delhi prior to his secret trip to Peking. He informed the Indian government that "if China entered the fray between India and Pakistan, India must not expect any help from the United States."25 Prime Minister Indira Gandhi, who read the events as dictating a course which would lead to Indian intervention, took an unprecedented step to protect her country's interests. In August 1971, India and the Soviet Union signed a treaty of friendship and cooperation that for all practical purposes is a mutual security pact. On the eve of the third Indo-Pakistani war, then, the United States and China stood behind Pakistan. The Soviet Union backed India. This prevented direct external intervention on behalf of either party, but it did not stop a war that ended in the dismemberment of Pakistan.[26]

MOVES TOWARD RECONCILIATION

When the hostilities ceased, India insisted that any permanent settlement of outstanding issues must be a result of bilateral talks between the two countries. Mrs. Gandhi initiated the first summit meeting with Pakistan's new president, Zulfikar Ali Bhutto, in Simla, India, in June–July 1972 to discuss and resolve outstanding issues.

The Simla Agreement, signed by Prime Minister Gandhi and President Bhutto on July 3, 1972, was the beginning of an attempt by the two long-standing antagonists to put their relationship on a new footing in the aftermath of the 14-day war. Both sides agreed "that the basic issues and causes of conflict which have bedeviled the relations between these countries for the last 25 years shall be resolved by peaceful means." It was also agreed that differences would be settled through bilateral negotiations without any involvement of an outside power.

In the succeeding years India and Pakistan made some progress towards normalization of relations. Diplomatic ties severed in 1971 were fully restored in 1976; air and railroad traffic suspended in 1965 was resumed; there was talk of establishing active economic relations. But if some believed that despite the highly traumatic consequences of the war, where Pakistan lost nearly half of her territory and a major source of economic support, the new leadership in that country was prepared to accept the transformed power realities of the subcontinent and pave the way for an era of stability, such thoughts proved to be wishful thinking. The Kashmir issue was not touched by the war, but surfaced repeatedly as a manifestation of ever present hostile feelings between the two neighbors. In 1974 India's explosion of a nuclear device became a further source of friction between the two. Internal political upheavals have generated new sources of tension. And to make the picture even more gloomy, political developments in Iran and Afghanistan have cast their dark shadow on the subcontinent, only to stress that the goal of security and stability is nowhere in sight for this region.

Speaking before the Lok Sabha—the lower house of the Indian parliament—in December 1978 Foreign Minister Vajpayee said that the "bogey of India's intentions and the issue of self determination in Jammu and Kashmir were stridently raised in Pakistan whenever the rulers there found the internal situation getting out of hand." He warned the Pakistani rulers not to contemplate "misadventures," for it was this type of conduct in the past that led to the establishment of an independent Bangladesh. Reaffirming that Jammu and Kashmir is an integral part of India, he said that the question yet to be settled was the "continued illegal occupation by Pakistan of two fifths of Jammu and Kashmir territory."[27]

That Pakistan would never accept what is suggested by the Indian side is no secret. Pakistan President General Mohammad Zia-ul-Haq, found an opportunity to convey this when China's vice-premier visited Islamabad in January 1979. Speaking to the press during his visit, Vice-Premier Li Hsien-mien stated that he was there to discuss problems of mutual concern to China and Pakistan. Confirming that the Kashmir issue had come up, he proceeded to say that China fully supported President Zia's stand that the only way to settle that problem is to apply the self-determination principle in Jammu and Kashmir.[28]

Closely related with the Kashmir issue is the arms race between Pakistan and India. Ever since the first confrontation over Kashmir in 1948, Pakistan has sought to assure itself that India will not be able to impose a military solution in this regard. India on her part has believed that a major goal of Pakistan's foreign policy has been to search for sources of modern military weapons in order to force India to relinquish her hold on Kashmir. How else could Pakistan justify membership in various military pacts, ask the Indians? And to prove that Pakistan is the aggressive party, India cites that the initiative in all cases of military action over Kashmir was taken by Pakistan. Besides other consequences of the point-counterpoint in this case, one result is quite apparent—an arms race. Even the 1971 war did not bring this to an end.

Zulfikar Ali Bhutto, who assumed power after the Indo-Pakistani war, paid a visit to the United States in February 1975. It is reported that during his visit, he sought to persuade the U.S. government that it must resume the arms sales to Pakistan that were suspended in 1973. In justifying his request, he maintained that Indian expansionism did not stop with the creation of Bangladesh. He was concerned that India intended to further dismember Pakistan and impose a Kashmir settlement by force. He cited India's nuclear explosion and its incorporation of Sikkim[29] as an associate state of the Indian Union in 1974 as testimony of added strength and desire for expansion on the part of India.[30]

Apparently Bhutto was successful. Not heeding the strong protest of India's then Foreign Minister Y. B. Chavan who wrote a personal note to Secretary of State Henry Kissinger, the United States announced its decision to resume the sale of arms to Pakistan soon after Bhutto's visit.[31]

The United States in defending its position, and in an attempt to put Indo-United States relations on a new course in the late 1970s, has repeatedly assured India that weapons sold to Pakistan are neither offensive nor massive in character. But reports that subsequent to the November 1978 visit to Pakistan by Lucy Benson, U.S. undersecretary of state for security, technology, and science, the United States sold a few destroyers and a number of Angusta submarines to Pakistan, brought a quick reaction from India. Answering questions on Indian TV, Foreign Minister Vajpayee said that the futility of arms aid to Pakistan had been conveyed to the United States. And that if "huge stocks of arms could not save the Shah of Iran," they could do little for Pakistan whose problems were economic and internal and had nothing to do with security threats from India, since such a threat was nonexistent.[32]

From the Indian point of view, any arms aid exacerbates the conflict between India and Pakistan. From the Pakistani point of view, absence of a military parity would turn Pakistan into an appendage of India. U.S. reaction to developments in Iran and Afghanistan could result in military benefits for Pakistan, notwithstanding India's serious concern that such an action would be a replay of the drama of the 1950s. As one Indian commentator has said:

> From the Indian point of view the most ominous development in this connection has been the return by the US to its original reflex of pumping arms into Pakistan ... But then the turmoil in Iran may not be the only reason for the US decision to resume arms supplies to Pakistan.
>
> The consolidation of the Taraki government in Afghanistan and the undoubted increase in the Soviet influence there has come in handy to all those who have a vested interest in a reversion by the US to the policy of militarily building up Pakistan as a counterweight to India. It is no secret that Pakistani diplomats in Washington have been harping on the theme that just as the Indo-Soviet threat led to the creation of Bangladesh and the Soviet-Vietnamese treaty to the overthrow of the Pol Pot regime in Kampuchea, the Afghan-Soviet treaty cannot but mean serious trouble in Baluchistan and the NWFP provinces of Pakistan unless effective deterrent measures are taken in advance.[33]

Will the United States continue to arm Pakistan in the light of recent reports that Pakistan could possess a nuclear weapon in the next few years? Ever since India detonated a nuclear device in May 1974, Pakistani leaders have made it known that they will not rest until Pakistan too possesses a nuclear weapon capability. On hearing about the Indian nuclear explosion, the then Prime Minister Bhutto told the press:

Testing a nuclear device denotes that a country has acquired a nuclear weapon capabilty. But a nuclear weapon is not like conventional military weapons. It is primarily an instrument of pressure and coercion against nonnuclear powers. . . . We are determined not to be intimidated by this threat. I give a pledge to my countrymen that we will never let Pakistan be a victim of nuclear blackmail. . . . We will not compromise the right of self-determination of the people of Jammu and Kashmir, nor will we accept Indian hegemony or domination over the subcontinent.[34]

The United States put a damper on Pakistan's efforts to go nuclear when, as a part of his campaign for nuclear nonproliferation, President Carter pressured the French government not to assist Pakistan with building a nuclear reprocessing plant. While the French initially refused to submit to the pressure, they have now delayed the operation for an indefinite period. Despite that, however, it was revealed recently that Pakistan had assembled the technology to build a "centrifuge enrichment plant" which could produce weapons-grade enriched uranium.[35]

While it appears that Washington elected not to express openly undue alarm at this discovery, the speed with which the U.S. government reacted to this development indicates the seriousness of the situation. On April 6, 1979, the United States cut off military and economic aid worth nearly 90 million dollars to Pakistan, its budgeted amount for 1979–80. This will sting but can hardly stop Pakistan from accomplishing the goal it has in mind. Pakistan's military ruler, General Zia-ul-Haq, is said "to be determined to equip his country with a nuclear bomb to match the proved capabilities of neighboring India."[36]

Pakistan started its nuclear program as early as 1964. But it was in the fall of 1978 that information surfaced that Islamabad had acquired all the equipment and the technology to enable it to produce nuclear weapons. Western powers were shocked and embarrassed at the discovery that Pakistan reached this stage by securing the necessary material and know-how under various disguises from countries of West Germany, Britain, the Netherlands, and Switzerland. It was also learned that President Muammar el-Qaddafi of Libya had provided Islamabad with more than $30 million to finance the purchase of an enriched uranium plant now located at the town of Kahuta, southwest of the capital. Colonel Qaddafi is widely mentioned as interested in producing a "Moslem bomb" to enhance the power of every Islamic country.[37]

It is alarming for the Western powers to realize "that Pakistan has eluded not only the elaborate controls set up by the International Atomic Energy Commission, but also the newer export restrictions of the Nuclear Suppliers Conference, which was founded by seven atomic exporting countries" in 1974.[38] But this occurrence is even more alarming for the states of South Asia—and for Israel. They are apprehensive that Pakistan will possibly share the technology and the bomb with Qaddafi or some other messianic leader in the Muslim world. But what disturbs them most is the fact that under a highly tense situation, South Asia could face the threat of a nuclear war in the future.

Whether possession of the bomb would lead to an offensive capability in Pakistan's hands, or whether it will be an assured deterrent against India's intervention in Pakistan's internal affairs in the future, is uncertain. It is clear, however, that this development escalates tensions between the two countries. Political instability within Pakistan enhances the sense of fear generated by the new development.[39]

PAKISTAN THEN AND NOW: THE IMPLICATIONS

Between 1947 and 1958, Pakistan changed prime ministers seven times. None of them was removed through the electoral process. The first prime minister, Liaquat Ali Khan, was assassinated. The other six came to power and were ousted at the will of a military-bureaucratic elite group which has dominated Pakistani politics all along.

Since 1958 the country has experienced three military coups. The only general elections, held in 1970 under Gen. Yahya's regime to found a popular government, ended in a civil war and dismemberment, because the results of the elections were not acceptable to the ruling elites in the Western wing. The civilian rule of Prime Minister Z. A. Bhutto, who came to power in 1972 after the disastrous war, ended abruptly in 1977. Bhutto, accused and convicted for ordering the assassination of a political opponent in 1974, was hanged in April 1979. The country has been under martial law most of the time since General Zia took over the reins of government in a bloodless coup in 1977. The General has promised elections in November 1979. Whether this promise can be fulfilled so soon after the execution of one of most popular national figures is questionable. For while it is true that protest demonstrations after Bhutto's death were nowhere massive, it also happens that freedom of thought, expression, and assembly lie suspended. Were this restraint lifted for election purposes, there is fear that it could result in general chaos.

There is also widespread doubt whether in the absence of Bhutto, another leader of national standing exists who can muster popular support, consolidate the badly split nation, and control the military which has played a decisive role in Pakistani politics. The prospects then are that the present military regime will continue in power. Whether it can restore internal stability will depend upon its success in solving the perennial economic problems that have been the bane of earlier governments. It will also depend upon the success made in defusing the situation in the Northwest Frontier Province and Baluchistan, where movements for an independent Pukhtoonistan and Baluchistan threaten to further dismember Pakistan.[40]

Overwhelmingly dominated by the Punjabis, the central government of Pakistan has always enjoyed maximum support from only one of its four provinces, namely Punjab. The other three provinces, Sind, Baluchistan and the Northwest Frontier Province (NWFP) have manifested violent resentment against the center from time to time. In the case of Baluchistan and NWFP, the intensity of this resentment has reached the stage where peoples in revolt are demanding independent statehood.

Some 5 million Baluchis inhabit the mountain and desert areas of Western Pakistan, eastern Iran and southern Afghanistan. The majority of them live in Pakistan's province of Baluchistan. The language and the life style of the Baluchis is distinctly different from that of the rest of the Pakistanis. While the religion of Islam provides the common link, it is not enough to generate feelings of unity and loyalty toward the center. The result is that people of Baluchistan have risen in revolt. They are joined by their brethren on the borders of Iran and Afghanistan in their fight for a separate state—a People's Republic of Baluchistan.

The worst case of insurrection took place in 1974. While the government in Islamabad was successful in crushing the revolt, protracted guerrilla warfare did not abate until 1977. Since then an uneasy truce has prevailed in the area. It could erupt at anytime. Guerrilla leader Mir Hazar is quoted by Harrison as saying:

> If we can get modern weapons, it will never again be like the last time. . . . Next time we will choose the time and place, and we will take help where we can get it. In the beginning the Bengalis didn't want independence, but if Pakistan continues to use force to crush us, we'll have no alternative but to go that way.[41]

Lasting stability can come to this part of Pakistan only when the Central and the Provincial leadership find a formula which would satisfy the demand for maximum provincial autonomy without disrupting central control. But a successful solution is not in sight. General Zia's government, gripped with fears of further dismemberment, does not appear to be ready in the immediate future to take the risk necessary to handle this complex situation. Baluchistan, therefore, continues to present a threat to Pakistan's internal stability.

A somewhat similar situation exists in the Northwest Frontier Province. The Pushtu speaking people of this region, claiming a separate cultural identity, also desire to sever their link with Pakistan and establish an independent state of Pukhtunistan (also referred to as Pukhtoonistan). They receive encouragement and assistance from their fellow Pukhtoons in neighboring Afghanistan. The situation in this province, in addition to being related to internal stability, carries international ramifications.

Baluchistan and NWFP then present a serious challenge to General Zia's government. "The failure of the Zia regime to deal more effectively with its multiplying political and economic problems could open the way for separatist activity that would literally tear the country apart." [42]

The fact is that Pakistan not only believes that India supports the dissident elements on its southwestern and northwestern frontiers; it also suspects that India looks forward to further dismemberment of Pakistan, for that would present India with an opportunity to annex the portions adjacent to the Indian border. Because of the long legacy of mutual suspicions, India's repeated denials in this regard hold little value for the leadership in Islamabad. Prevailing circumstances, then, do not paint a very optimistic picture to permit a reduction of tensions between India and Pakistan. Given these conditions it appears that security and stability on the South Asian subcontinent will remain under stress for a long time to come.

BANGLADESH AND REGIONAL SECURITY AND STABILITY

The people of Bangladesh were successful in securing their independence on December 16, 1971. [43] But political stability and economic viability continue to elude them. The bitter struggle for order and peaceful daily existence has never ceased. External intervention and interest in the internal politics of the state by no means ended with liberation. The same will dictate the influence Bangladesh will have on regional security and stability in the future.

Nearly eight years after independence, the country has still to establish a stable regime that could begin to tackle the enormous problems of a grossly underdeveloped state. [44] Sheikh Mujibur Rahman, the leader of the liberation struggle imprisoned in March 1971 was released by Pakistan's new government of Prime Minister Bhutto in a gesture of goodwill and returned to take over power in January 1972. He failed to build a governmental foundation that could handle the task of relief and rehabilitation and introduce a program of rebuilding an economy which, while never being healthy, had been shattered by the separation of the two wings of Pakistan. The fact is that by 1974 he had lost control over his party, the Awami League, and had alienated the army. In December of that year he suspended the constitutional system and declared a state of emergency that permitted him to assume dictatorial powers.

Sheikh Mujib did not invoke martial law. He did not call upon the army to assist him to run the country because he did not trust the generals. He turned instead to Rakhi Bahini, a special military force he had put together for personal security and to crush the terrorism and violent opposition that had surfaced against his rule in the countryside. Resenting his actions, a segment of the Bangladesh army rose against him. Mujibur Rahman and all the members of his family were murdered in August 1975. In their surprise move, the group of young army officers who took over control also executed the entire leadership of the Rakhi Bahini, thus rendering it ineffective. They declared martial law but installed a civilian government headed by Khondakar Mushtaque Ahmed. The new regime promised to hold elections in January 1977 in order to establish a popularly elected government. This was never realized. A military junta headed by Major General Ziaur Rahman executed a countercoup in November 1975. While violence and blood-letting continued for sometime, General Zia finally succeeded in consolidating his power. By early 1977, he came to occupy the offices of the president of the nation as well as of the chief martial law administrator. He maintained stability by imprisoning all who opposed him and by severely punishing the violators of law and order. To legitimize his authority, he announced in April 1977 that he would hold a referendum to ascertain if the people had confidence in him. In May of that year the Bangladesh voters by a margin of nearly 99 percent approved of his rule.[45] However, it became clear that dissident elements were still alive when some military units attempted to overthrow General Zia in October 1977.

Although he was able to crush the rebellion quickly, it shook the morale of the military administration. Zia was under pressure to depoliticize the army so that the country could be immunized against periodic military coups. As one commentator had predicted, the middle class became sensitive to military indiscipline, and the demand for early elections to hand over power to civilian political leaders became difficult to resist.[46] President Ziaur Rahman held general elections in February 1979 in order to restore parliamentary rule.

The president's party, the Bangladesh Nationalist Party, won a solid majority of the seats and holds 237 seats in a House of 330 members. The party in parliament has selected Shah Azizur Rahman as the new prime minister of Bangladesh.[47]

The second parliament of Bangladesh held its first session in April 1979. While this development was welcomed in all quarters abroad, the political observers hoped that the life of the second parliament would be longer than that of the first one, which has been established by Sheikh Mujib in 1972 and was disbanded in 1974.

How much power President Zia is prepared to share with the representatives of the people in running the country has yet to unfold. But political stability will also depend on the ability of the new government to solve the difficult problems of the nation while functioning in an open atmosphere where the opposition is free to exploit dissent. The external forces involved in the birth of this new nation refrained from any interference in internal affairs during its independent existence. But they watch the developments very closely. Since an economically and militarily weak nation must rely on outside sources for survival, the question of which nations will play a major role in building the necessary economic and military foundation for Bangladesh is of great interest to outside powers and remains a potential source of rivalry among them.

The emergence of East Pakistan as the free state of Bangladesh was a plus for Indian foreign policy under the stewardship of Prime Minister Gandhi. Long-standing hostility between India and Pakistan made it necessary for India to hold the premise that she was threatened by Pakistan on two fronts, a problem that assumed grave proportions after 1962. As China and Pakistan began to close ranks in the 1960s, India feared that China might be permitted to use East Pakistan as the stage for creating overt action or internal disorder in India. While such a contingency never materialized, India expected the worst from both quarters.

Inasmuch as India made a total commitment to the cause of the liberation movement, the government believed that it could count on a close relationship between India and Bangladesh. In February 1972, Mrs. Gandhi and Sheikh Mujibur Rahman signed a 15-year treaty of friendship and cooperation that was modeled after the Indo-Soviet treaty. And despite her own massive economic problems, India promised substantial economic aid to Bangladesh. Given the nature of nation states, however, this pattern of relationship did not last long.

Large-scale smuggling operations on the border of the two countries created irritation in Dacca as well as New Delhi. There were border skirmishes between the troops of the two countries. And voices were raised in Bangladesh warning against the potential threat of Indian domination.

The close friendship between Prime Minister Gandhi and President Mujib prevented disruption of good relations. But after the assassination of Mujib, relations between the two countries began to deteriorate.

Soon after Ziaur Rahman came to power, there were reports of frequent skirmishes on the border between Indian and Bangladeshi troops. There was an attempt made on the life of the Indian high commissioner in Dacca. He escaped, but the incident resulted in a warning from the Indian government that unless terrorist activities stopped, they would be forced to take action.

The situation worsened in 1976. There was an increase in border incidents, which New Delhi blamed Dacca for initiating. General Zia in turn accused India of aiding and abetting the guerrillas and other forces in Bangladesh who were attempting to overthrow his regime. And Bangladesh not only raised the issue of Farakka Barrage again, accusing India of breaking an earlier agreement, but took it to the United Nations to generate world opinion against India. While Mrs. Gandhi's government was able to block a debate on the issue in the UN, India was stung by these actions.

General elections in India in March 1977 brought a new government to power. The occasion was seized by both the countries to prevent their relations from sliding any further. India's new prime minister, Morarji Desai, and the Bangladesh president met for the first time at the Commonwealth conference in London in June 1977. Using the opportunity, they held bilateral talks. They were able to resolve some of the outstanding differences causing tension between the two neighbors. They also stated that further negotiations would be held to settle the Farakka waters dispute. Finally, the two countries signed the Farakka agreement in November 1977.

The Farakka accord mandates that the two neighbors will equally share the waters from the eastern rivers, the Ganga and the Brahmaputra, during the dry season. The agreement extends over five years but can be renewed by mutual understanding. While Bangladesh saw most of its demands being met in this settlement, there was widespread criticism of the Desai government in the parliament and outside, especially in the state of West Bengal, for having yielded too much. But India's prime minister repeatedly defended the action in the name of promoting good relations with the next door neighbor. President Ziaur Rahman, for his part, demonstrated his country's approval of the new trend in relations between India and Bangladesh by paying an official visit to New Delhi in December 1977.

All this augurs well; but it is dependent upon a number of factors that are uncertain in character. How well they will work out in the long run will determine whether the present state of affairs has a lasting quality. Bangladesh wants an assurance that India will not shelter any rebels who enter as political refugees. While the Desai government has promised not to aid rebel elements, to what extent this can be enforced in the face of the cultural bond that exists between the eastern and the western Bengalis is questionable. The uproar over the Farakka Barrage settlement in India could affect the situation when the agreement comes up for renewal in 1982. This has significance since the Desai government will go to the polls in 1982 to seek a mandate from the people to stay in power for the next five years. And then again the course of Sino-Bangladesh relations and Pakistani-Bangladesh relations will always cast its reflection on future stability.

That relations between Bangladesh and Pakistan were put on a normal course despite the bitterness generated by the civil war between the two parties came as a surprise but was a matter of great accomplishment for the late Prime Minister Bhutto. He used the occasion of the pan-Islamic conference held in Lahore, Pakistan, in February 1974 to strike a new posture vis à vis Bangladesh. At his request, a delegation of foreign ministers of seven Islamic countries traveled to Dacca to persuade Mujibur Rahman to attend the conference. The intermediaries were not only successful in this venture, but they also negotiated a settlement of a thorny issue left over from the 1971 war. Earlier India and Pakistan had worked out an agreement on the issue of repatriation of prisoners of war. But Bangladesh still held 150 prisoners who were expected to be tried for war crimes. Through the good offices of the delegation of foreign ministers, it was arranged that Pakistan accord recognition to Bangladesh as a sovereign state in return for the freedom of the 150 prisoners. As one author put it:

> Bhutto killed three birds with a single stone: he got the war crimes trial dropped; he recognized Bangladesh without submitting to pressure from India; and he got Mujibur Rahman, despite his adherence to secularism, to share the Lahore platform with other leaders of the Islamic world.[48]

Prime Minister Bhutto, encouraged by his first advance toward Bangladesh, paid a personal visit to that country soon after the Islamic conference was over. He was warmly received. And although he failed to solve the foreign debts issue as well as the issue of compensation for damages in the war during his visit, he felt that he had established a new rapport between Pakistan and Bangladesh by invoking the theme that the two societies continued to be linked by the common tie of Islam. If India was disturbed by the sight of Mujibur Rahman warming up to Pakistan so soon after the liberation struggle, what followed in succeeding years was even more disconcerting. Mujib's death in 1975 opened up the possibility of an even closer relationship between Pakistan and Bangladesh.

The anti-Indian attitude of the rulers in Bangladesh who succeeded Mujib was welcomed in Islamabad. But closer ties did not develop because leadership in both Pakistan and Bangladesh was soon convulsed in political turmoil. It was toward the end of 1977 that the domestic political situation permitted the new rulers of the two countries to resume active contact. General Ziaur Rahman flew to Islamabad immediately after his December visit to New Delhi and met with Pakistan's chief martial law administrator, General Zia-ul-Haq, for two days. While this furthered the process of normalization and reconciliation, it could not have accomplished much more given the situation Zia-ul-Haq faced on the home front. Nonetheless, both leaders made statements to the effect that their meeting involved nothing that would disturb India.[49]

What has transpired thus far would suggest that Pakistan is no longer in a position to exert significant influence among the ruling circles in Free Bangladesh. Nonetheless, India watches with interest and concern any development which could lead toward such a situation.

RELATIONS WITH THE MAJOR POWERS

India is equally concerned with China's role in Bangladesh. The fact is that the prospect of a strong tie between those two countries would be viewed with alarm by India. Sino-Bangladesh relations did not begin on a happy note. Having decided to support Pakistan to the hilt in 1971, not only did China oppose the liberation movement, contrary to her philosophical beliefs, but she also gave military aid to Pakistan during the war. When the war was over, it was China who vetoed UN recognition of Bangladesh, presumably at the request of Pakistan.[50]

The anti-Indian stance of the government that came to power after the death of Mujibur Rahman was considered a proper signal by the Chinese to seek rapprochement with Bangladesh. The actions of the new regime manifested for Peking that they sought to vacate Indian and Soviet influence and presence from Bangladesh; they would therefore welcome the support of China. And so formal relations between the two countries were established in October 1975.

Subsequent to that, Peking supported Bangladesh in its claims against India in the Farraka Barrage dispute, signed a trade agreement, and even provided Dacca with a squadron of MIG fighters. One writer suggests that China's main objectives in Bangladesh are to deny the Soviet Union and India a primary role in the affairs of that nation.[51] Even if that is the sole motivating force behind China's support for Bangladesh, it is then clear that Peking's attempts to retain influence in

Dacca are a long term goal. Given that situation, stability in South Asia may well depend upon how astutely any Bangladesh regime can handle its relations with China and India, and beyond that with Pakistan and the Soviet Union, without unleashing the hostility that is latent in the rivalry among these nations.

The Soviet Union made an early bid to establish her presence and influence in Bangladesh; but the prospects for a long-term relationship faded out because of the abrupt changes in the governmental setup in the new nation. The USSR was one of the first to recognize Bangladesh in January 1972. She was also quick in inviting Sheikh Mujib to visit Moscow, which he did in March of that year. This was followed by trade and aid agreements, and even the handing over of some civilian and military aircraft to Dacca. But one particular action caught the attention of Washington and Peking. The Soviets agreed to clear the heavily mined harbors of Chittagong and Cox's Bazar at no cost to Bangladesh.[52] Not only did this bring parts of the Soviet navy into the Bay of Bengal, but it was clear that this free service could lead in time to a demand on the part of Moscow for a naval base. The clearing operations took two years. Not granted privileges to remain there any longer by the wary Bangladesh government, the Soviet navy left the area. Soon after the Mujib's government was overthrown. When General Ziaur Rahman assumed power, he left no doubt that his government looked with disfavor on any Soviet presence in Bangladesh.

Moscow has not pushed in the last few years to increase its influence in Dacca. It is understood, however, that were the events in Bangladesh to take a turn that was judged by India as threatening her security, the Soviet Union would support Indian actions to correct the situation.

As things stand now, the United States also maintains a relatively low profile in Bangladesh. This is partly due to the fact that there has been a shift in the emphasis of U.S. policy in Asia. It is also a result of the Sino-U.S. repprochement that permits the United States to rely on China to counter Soviet moves in this region.

Relations between the United States and independent Bangladesh started on a somber note. The United States did not play a direct or a positive role in the shaping of events that shook South Asia in 1971, despite the existence of US-Pakistani security pacts. Two factors influenced her conduct heavily in this regard. Washington gave priority to normalization of relations with China. Also, as the United States sought to bring her involvement in Vietnam to an end, she could hardly afford to be entagled in another conflict in a neighboring area. Possibly the United States would have welcomed a more active role on the part of China,[53] but the Indo-Soviet treaty ruled that out. Nonetheless,

Washington fully supported Pakistan's actions in dealing with the revolt in the eastern wing, and this was judged by Mujib and his supporters as opposition to their fight for freedom. And so both parties approached each other with caution when the war was over.

But the United States was not too far behind other nations in recognizing Bangladesh. Diplomatic relations were established between the two in March 1972. This was soon followed by bilateral agreements under which Dacca received substantial economic aid in succeeding years. In time it was manifest, however, that a close relationship with Bangladesh held no significance for U.S. vital interests. Under the circumstances, while Washington continues to support efforts towards uplifting Bangladesh's underdeveloped economy, The U.S. government exhibits no intention of playing a major role in the affairs of Bangladesh. This does not automatically guarantee for Bangladesh a policy of noninterference by other major powers. It leaves China and India as the primary contenders for influence in Dacca.

THE SUPERPOWERS AND THE SUBCONTINENT

The regional picture outlined above makes it clear that the superpowers are very much involved in matters relating to subcontinental security and stability. While they had nothing to do with the origins of the conflicts that afflict South Asia, the entry of the United States and the Soviet Union into the arena under the pressure of cold war tensions exacerbated the hostilities that were in the nature of things that appeared on the departure of the British. Strategic interests of the superpowers demanded a search for allies in the 1950s. Nations of South Asia, unable to resolve their disputes on a bilateral basis, sought outside support to strengthen their case vis à vis each other. Diversity of interests among partners notwithstanding, the situation produced a United States-Pakistan versus Soviet Union-India relationship over the years that instead of reducing the differences among the nations of the subcontinent, only multiplied them.[54]

Even though cold war has been replaced by détente[55], under the umbrella of détente, competition between the superpowers for influence in the capitals of the world and acquisition of bases to advance their respective strategic and economic interests has not ceased. They have not abandoned their efforts, therefore, to mold regional politics to suit their perceptions of what constitutes a proper balance. On the other hand, the nations of South Asia also, having failed to resolve outstanding issues among themselves; having failed to institute viable economies; and continuing to rely heavily on outside powers for economic and military aid, are unable to cut their close ties with one or the other superpower. No wonder then that actions of the United States and the Soviet Union continue to affect the security and stability of the area. China's entry in South Asian politics has made the picture more complex: if yesterday regional politics were affected by U.S.-USSR tensions, they are today influenced additionally by severe Sino-Soviet friction. It is now believed by many that China has to a degree replaced the United States in South and Southeast Asia, possibly under the impetus of America's move to seek regional influentials as partners in the drive to stem the tide of expanding Russian influence.[56] How valid this is need not be debated here. What must be noted, however, is that certain developments in states bordering the northwestern tier of the subcontinent concern the United States deeply. How Washington will respond to the unexpected changes that have occurred in that area will have significant effect on security and stability issues in South Asia.

Commenting on recent events which have taken place in West Asia and South Asia, President Carter's national security advisor, Zbigniew Brzezinski, is said to have observed:

> An arc of crisis stretches along the shores of the Indian Ocean, with fragile social and political structures in a region of vital importance to us threatened with fragmentation. The resulting political chaos could well be filled by elements hostile to our values and sympathetic to our adversaries.[57]

Among other occurrences what the United States finds most disturbing is the radical change in the character of governments in Iran and Afghanistan.

Events in Iran

Iran was ruled by Shah Mohammed Reza Pahlavi for more than three decades. The Shah was as fervent in his anticommunism as was the Secretary of State John Foster Dulles. Thus from the days of the cold war until his reign ended, the shah remained a steadfast ally of the United States in the battle against the spread of Soviet communism. The fact that Iran borders Russia, is strategically located on the Persian gulf, and is the fourth largest producer of oil in the world added immensely to the value of the country as a close friend. And so the United States spared no pains to return the compliment. The autocratic nature of the government notwithstanding, the shah enjoyed the total support of every American administration from Eisenhower to Carter. At the request of the monarch, the United States supplied Iran with the most sophisticated modern weapons and the latest in jet fighters and bombers, together worth more than $15 billion. Given these features, Iran became a formidable military power and the shah not only felt secure, he saw his influence extend from West Asia to South Asia. Recent events, however, revealed that underneath the glittering monarchy dissent simmered, since the benefits of billions earned from oil income never reached the people.

Iranian masses led by the religious leader Ayatollah Ruhollah Khomeini overthrew the shah's government in January 1979. Soon after coming to power the Ayatollah declared that Iran would be an Islamic Republic. And according to him Islamic values were threatened by Western presence. This meant cutting off all ties with the United States, ousting U.S. personnel who acted as military advisors, and scrapping of the intelligence base in Iran operated by Washington.

The consequences of Iranian revolution were damaging for the United States economically and strategically. Iran has supplied 13 percent of U.S. oil imports. She has also been the biggest supplier of oil for Japan and Western Europe. Additionally, as a formidable military power on the Persian gulf, she has guarded the narrow Straits of Hormuz,[58] thus assuring the passage of all oil traffic to its different destinations in the democratic industrial world. The policy of reduced oil production and "no favored customers" under the new regime has hurt the United States.

The loss of Iran as a strategic intelligence post is considered an even more serious blow by the U.S. policymakers. During the Shah's rule, the United States had established two intelligence posts near the Soviet border in Iran. From these listening posts, U.S. intelligence could watch the Soviet missile test flights and gather extremely sensitive data on their strategic weapons. Iran's new government forced the United States to abandon this base. In departing the U.S. personnel had do destroy some of the most sophisticated electronic equipment which could not be shipped back and which the United States could ill afford to have fall in unfriendly hands.

Under the Shah, Iran also served as a barrier against expansion of Soviet influence in the neighboring countries. A leftist rebellion in Oman was crushed with the help of the Shah. Iran as a supporter of Pakistan acted as a restraint upon the leftist regime of Afghanistan that was considered a security threat by Islamabad.

The loss of Iran as a close ally, then, creates a vacuum for the United States which her interests dictate must be filled. South Asians anxiously watch U.S. actions, for the alternatives she chooses would hold great significance for the subcontinent. Already Turkey and Pakistan are being mentioned as prime candidates for increased military

assistance to shoulder some of the burdens carried by Iran. To demonstrate that the United States would not tolerate any further uprooting
of friendly regimes and erosion of her influence in the area, in March
1979 President Carter decided to dispatch, without a Congressional
review of his action, 12 F-5E fighter planes, 50 armoured personnel
carriers, and 64 tanks to Yemen, which was engaged in a war with its
neighbor to the south. South Yemen has a Marxist regime and is
heavily supported by the Soviet Union with military equipment and
military advisers. The United States also plans to send some 300
military experts to Yemen over the next few years to train Yemeni
soldiers in the use of modern weaponry. Since Yemeni pilots are not
qualified to fly the fighter planes, it was expected that pilots would be
recruited from Saudi Arabia, Jordan, and possibly Pakistan to fill the
gap.[59] These are omens which spell a feeling of continued insecurity and
instability in the region of South Asia.

Events in Afghanistan

Similarly, the South Asian states also watch closely the developments in Afghanistan, where recent events have unfolded a picture that
engages the attention of the superpowers. The strategic location of
Afghanistan as it borders Iran on the west, Pakistan on the east and
south, and the Soviet Union on the north—there being a narrow strip in
the northeast that touches Indian Kashmir—and China's Sinkiang
region, makes it a key state. Ruled by General Muhammed Daud Khan
since July 1973, Afghanistan was considered as leaning toward Moscow
but not hostile toward the West. This orientation changed in April
1978, when Nur Mohammed Taraki overthrew President Daud in a
military coup. Espousing Marxist-Leninist ideology, the government of
Prime Minister Taraki makes no bones about its close ties with the
Soviet Union. The open presence of the Soviet military and political
advisers in Kabul leaves no doubt in the minds of the Western observers
that Afghanistan under Taraki is guided by Moscow and will do its
bidding.

Taraki visited Moscow in December 1978. While there he signed a
treaty of friendship and cooperation with the Soviet Union that
brought him increased military and economic aid. While this does not
build Afghanistan into a military power threatening her neighbors, it is
the prospect of Afghanistan being used as a base by the Soviet Union
for supporting leftist elements in unstable Iran and Pakistan that
frightens the West.

Demand for a separate state on the part of the Pushtu-speaking
people in the Northwest Frontier Province of Pakistan is seen as

presenting a situation which could be easily exploited by Afghanistan and the Soviet Union.

On the other hand, the government in Kabul maintains that the orthodox Muslim elements that oppose the Marxist regime are carrying on a guerrilla warfare in borderlands with the help of Iran and Pakistan. As Harrison observes:

> Deputy Prime Minister Amin indicated in an interview that Afghan handling of the borderlands would be determined by how Islamabad behaves toward the new regime. Charging that some circles in Pakistan have already been fomenting trouble in Pushtu and Tadzhik border areas by branding the revolutionary government as anti-Islamic, he declared that "we will fight fire with fire if necessary. . . . If we are provoked or attacked, we will defend ourselves. We hope that the United States will play a restraining role in the region, but if you choose to pour in arms, we will turn to the USSR, and they are so friendly to us they will give us whatever we need to deal with the situation".[60]

India and Afghanistan have always maintained and continue to maintain friendly relations, even though recently there have been governmental changes. Changes have been made by Pakistan that the two in collusion are aiding and abetting the separatist elements in the NWFP who demand an independent state of Pushtu-speaking people— Pukhtoonistan. New Delhi's assurances to the contrary notwithstanding, Islamabad fears that it faces further dismemberment, similar in character to Bangladesh's condition. Believing that the answer lies in increased military build up, it hopes that Washington will come to its assistance under the pressure of mounting international crisis.

The Broader Picture

Press comment in the United States reflects a widespread concern that Soviet influence is on the rise in Asia and Africa. Voices are being raised calling for action on the part of the Carter administration to counter this tide. In an interview with *Time* Correspondent Christopher Ogden, the former Secretary of State Henry Kissinger said:

> During all the postwar period, the countries bordering the Indian Ocean believed that the United States was strategically predominant in that area and that, therefore, that friendship with the United States assured their security, both internationally and, to some extent, domestically. The Soviet march through Africa, with Cuban troops, from Angola to Ethiopia, and the Soviet moves through Afghanistan and South Yemen, or at least the moves of Soviet clients, altered that

perception. That inevitably decreased the importance of friendship
with the United States and emboldened our opponents.[61]

Kissinger then suggested that the United States could halt the
Soviet advances, "by imposing penalties and risks that they [the Soviets]
are not willing to accept." Commentator Morton Kondracke, in an
analysis of the same situation, remarks:

> Overthrow of the shah would not necessarily lead to a cut off of oil or
> actual Soviet advances in the region, but any American administration
> obviously must be worried by the threats to what has seemed a stable
> status quo. This administration may be even more worried than
> others, because it already stands accused of presiding over a steady
> erosion of American power in the area. Afghanistan has been taken
> over by communists and its neighbor, Pakistan, has decided to
> transfer its ambassador, Yakub Khan, from Washington to Moscow as
> a demonstration of flagging confidence in the US. South Yemen, too,
> has fallen to pro-Soviet elements, and that causes nervousness in
> Saudi Arabia and other West-leaning countries in the region. It is not
> just Republicans and right-wing Democrats who accuse the Carter
> administration of not being tough enough in foreign policy; our allies
> do, as well.[62]

Washington failed to see the coming of the revolution in Iran, and
thus could not stop it. In the case of Afghanistan the political character
of the previous government made difficult the possibility of U.S.
intervention to block greater Soviet control. But U.S. response to the
Yemeni crisis indicates that Washington expects to take some measured
actions not only to mitigate the effect of Soviet gains but also to
discourage future adventurism by Moscow. Lack of speed in this regard
does not mean lack of resolution. Possibly, unsettled conditions in Iran
and Afghanistan warrant a "watch and wait" approach for the present.
But the thought of not knowing how long this will last and what will
follow thereafter not only creates uncertainty, it makes the governments of South Asia prepare for the worst.

The region seemed relatively quiet during most of the 1970s. It is
now experiencing a ripple effect from the revolution in Iran, arrival of a
government in Afghanistan which gives the appearance of accepting
Soviet satellite status and continued instability in Pakistan. China's
punitive strike at Vietnam, news of Pakistan's major progress toward
building a nuclear bomb, and the recent appearance of U.S. and Soviet
aircraft carriers in the Indian Ocean heighten the nervousness which
pervades the subcontinent currently. Collectively these events feed the
desire of the South Asian states for greater security through procurement of larger quantities of arms and more sophisticated weapons. In

the long run, that reduces the prospects for peace and increases the prospects for continued tensions and possible warfare.

NOTES

1. The slogan translated stands for, "Indians and Chinese are brothers."

2. An interesting account of this is offered by T. N. Kaul in *Diplomacy in Peace and War* (New Delhi: Vikas Publishing House, 1979). Kaul was India's Foreign Secretary for four years.

3. Neville Maxwell in his book *India's China War* (Bombay: JAICO Publishing House, 1970) makes a case that China was provoked. Indian scholars and statesmen unanimously reject this.

4. China's invasion of Vietnam in 1979 led to many a writer recalling similar action by China against India in 1962.

5. G. W. Choudhury, *India, Pakistan, Bangladesh, and the Major Powers* (New York: The Free Press, 1975), p. 206.

6. Details pertaining to developments in this regard are discussed in other articles in the book.

7. *Indiagram* (San Francisco: Consulate General of India), February 20, 1979, p. 2.

8. *Times of India*, February 22, 1979.

9. Ibid.

10. *The Statesman Weekly*, Calcutta, Feb. 24, 1979.

11. *India News* (Washington D.C.), March 5, 1979.

12. *Times of India*, Bombay, February 23, 1979.

13. *The Statesman Weekly* (Calcutta) March 17, 1979.

14. Ibid.

15. China's invasion of India in 1962 lasted for approximately a month; so did the action against Vietnam.

16. *Los Angeles Times*, March 17, 1979.

17. Inder Malhotra, "The Wrecked China Visit," *Times of India*, February 23, 1979.

18. *Indiagram* (Consulate General of India, San Francisco), May 1, 1978.

19. *Times of India* (Bombay), February 7, 1979.

20. Malhotra, "The Wrecked China Visit."

21. The war was brought to an end by a UN imposed ceasefire in 1949. After the ceasefire, under the United Nations' sponsorship, several attempts were made to settle the dispute. All these efforts failed for various reasons.

22. Subsequent to the signing of U.S.-Pakistani Treaty in 1954, the United States built a communications center at Badabar near Peshawar and an airfield not far from where the U-2 spy aircraft took off for intelligence missions over Soviet territory.

23. Choudhury, *India, Pakistan, Bangladesh*, gives a detailed and interesting account of these developments. It is worthy of note here that in March 1963, Pakistan signed a boundary agreement with China that gave it direct access to the strategically important areas in Kashmir.

24. The United States gave substantial military aid to India immediately after the Chinese attack in October 1962, overriding Pakistan's objections. However, the Pentagon made certain that India did not receive the sophisticated weapons, tanks and high powered aircraft supplied by the United States to Pakistan. For example, India's request for sidewinder air-to-air missiles and F-104 supersonic jets was turned down by Washington.

25. *Time*, August 23, 1971, p. 7.

26. Although the major powers did not participate in the combat, they gave arms assistance to their respective allies. The military aide to Pakistan suspended in 1965 was resumed by the US in 1970. China and Iran, Pakistan's ally in CENTO, also gave substantial arms aid to Pakistan. India received major military supplies from the Soviet Union. U.S. and Soviet navies made some moves in the Indian and Pacific oceans. But there was no naval engagement between the two. See Bhabani Sen Gupta, *Soviet Asian Relations in the 1970s and Beyond* (New York: Praeger, 1976). Also Choudhury, *India, Pakistan, Bangladesh*.

27. *Times of India* (Bombay), December 7, 1978.

28. *Times of India*, January 26, 1979.

29. The Sikkim question is treated in detail by me in *The Foreign Relations of India* (California: Dickenson Publishing Co., 1976).

30. *L.A. Times*, January 30, 1975.

31. *The Statesman Weekly* (Calcutta), February 15, 1975.

32. *The Statesman Weekly*, February 24, 1979; *Indiagram*, March 20, 1979.

33. Inder Malhotra, "Two Major Trouble Spots," *The Times of India*, January 18, 1979.

34. *Times of India*, May 23, 1974. On another occasion Bhutto said: "If India builds the bomb, we will eat leaves or grass, even go hungry but we will have to get one of our own."

35. *Los Angeles Times*, April 7, 1979.

36. *Los Angeles Times*, April 9, 1979.

37. David Binder renders a full account of how this happened in, "How Pakistan Ran the Nuke Round the End," New York *Times*, April 29, 1979, p. E5.

38. Ibid.

39. Foreign Minister Vajpayee told the Indian Parliament on March 30, 1979, that India would review its nuclear policy if a change in the international situation or developments in neighboring countries warranted the same. *The Statesman Weekly*, April 7, 1979.

40. For a detailed and penetrating analysis of this situation see, Selig S. Harrison's, "Nightmare in Baluchistan," *Foreign Policy* (Fall 1978).

41. Ibid., pp. 139–40.

42. Ibid., p. 155.

43. Anthony Mascarenhas, *The Rape of Bangladesh* (Delhi: Vikas Publications, 1972) and Subrata Roy Choudhury, *The Genesis of Bangladesh* (New Delhi: Asia Publishing House, 1972), are two accounts which provide a detailed picture of the tragic background of the birth of Bangladesh.

44. One of the most poverty stricken areas of the world, Bangladesh is often cited as an example of a nation in the "Fourth World."

45. In 1977 elections were held for village and city councils also. These were "partyless" elections, but the local population was aware of the political affiliation of the candidates.

46. See, M. Rashiduzzaman, "Bangladesh in 1977: Dilemmas of the Military Rulers," *Asian Survey* 18 (February 1978): 126–34.

47. Shah Azizur Rahman was Minister of Labor and Industrial Welfare under the President's rule.

48. Sen Gupta, *Soviet Asian Relations*, p. 148.

49. Lawrence Ziring, ed., *The Subcontinent in World Politics* (New York: Praeger, 1978), pp. 7–16.

50. S. M. Burke, *Mainsprings of Indian and Pakistani Foreign Policies* (Minneapolis: University of Minnesota Press, 1974), p. 218.

51. Shirin Tahir-Kheli, "Chinese Objectives in South Asia," *Asian Survey* 18 (October 1978): 1011.

52. Sen Gupta, *Soviet Asian Relations*, pp. 157–59.

53. See Choudhury, *India, Pakistan, Bangladesh*, p. 206.

54. While I disagree with the author on a number of points, Prof. Leo Rose presents an interesting and controversial analysis of this situation in, "The Superpowers in South Asia: A Geostrategic Analysis," *ORBIS* 22 (Summer 1978), pp. 395–413.

55. In his comments on the Iranian crisis during an interview, Henry Kissinger said: If it is not understood by the Soviet Union and if dètente becomes a kind of tranquilizer, then sooner or later a showdown is likely to occur with tremendous dangers for everybody. So the first necessity is to bring home to the Soviet Union that to us dètente means a restrained international conduct, and if we cannot achieve that, then we will have to confront expansionism where it takes place, however indirect it is. *Time*, January 15, 1979.

56. In an examination of the U.S. foreign policy under President Carter's administration, political analyst Herman Nickel observes: "Brzezinski envisages the building of a new international order that would in the end confront the Soviet Union with a choice to join or to compete . . . At the core of this world order would be the trilateral relationship between the advanced industrial democracies of the U.S., Western Europe, and Japan . . . To buttress this relationship, Brzezinski would assign special roles to the 'regional influentials'—his academic and ungainly jargon for local power centers around which neighboring countries could cluster and join the U.S. and its allies in common endeavor. The countries cited by Brzezinski for such regional leadership include Mexico, Venezuela . . . and very much China." *Fortune*, April 23, 1979, pp. 72–73.

57. *Time*, January 15, 1979, p. 18.

58. Some 71 percent of the oil consumed by Western Europe passes through this waterway.

59. *Los Angeles Times*, March 13, 1979.

60. Selig S. Harrison, "Nightmare in Baluchistan," *Foreign Policy* (Fall 1978): 150.

61. *Time*, January 15, 1979, p. 29.

62. *The New Republic*, November 18, 1978, p. 10.

· 7 ·

THE INDIAN OCEAN:
ZONE OF PEACE OR WAR?
Sudershan Chawla

The attention paid to the Indian Ocean today for its strategic and economic significance is of recent origin. Developments in the 1960s which might be considered mainly responsible for this phenomenon are: the withdrawal of the onetime great naval force of Britain from the area; the increased Soviet naval presence in the Indian Ocean; and the overwhelming concern with the free flow of Middle Eastern oil to Western Europe, Japan and the United States.

Britain exercised near monopolistic control over the Indian Ocean region and its waters for more than a century. During this period not only did the English dominate most of the littoral and hinterland states of the area; they were also successful in defeating the ambitions of other great powers who challenged their formidable naval forces. Interestingly enough, no major naval battles took place in the Indian Ocean in either of the two world wars. This picture changed radically soon after the Second World War ended. The empire fell apart as one colony after another won independent status. The strained economy, which took a long time to recover from the aftereffects of the war, forced the British government to reduce its defense commitments. The

---

This article is confined to an examination of the factors which raise security related issues for the littoral states of the Indian Ocean. For a detailed account of the historical background and current situation of the region as a whole see Terence A. Vali, *Politics of the Indian Ocean Region* (New York: The Free Press, 1976) and, Alvin J. Cottrell and R. M. Burrell, eds., *The Indian Ocean: Its Political, Economic, and Military Importance* (New York: Praeger, 1973).

then Prime Minister Harold Wilson declared in 1964 that his government had "inherited defense forces which are seriously overstretched
and in some respects dangerously underequipped." He announced in
January 1968 that Britain planned to withdraw its land forces and naval
units from east of Suez by the end of 1971.

Of significance is the fact that another occurrence coincided with
the announcement of the planned British withdrawal from the Indian
Ocean region. Before 1968 there was no regular Soviet naval presence
in the Indian Ocean. From that point on, however, there was a marked
increase in the presence and the activities of the Soviet navy in the
area.

A wide range of hypotheses has been put forward by different
authors to account for this occurrence.[1] According to Alvin Cottrell and
R. M. Burrell, Soviet entry into the Indian Ocean is simply a fulfillment
of the Russian desire entertained by rulers from the time of Peter the
Great to the present not only to find warm water outlets in the South,
but to use such facilities to extend Russian control and dominance
worldwide. The age old dream is being realized by the communist rulers
of today because the departure of the British created a "power vacuum"
in the area which the Soviets rushed in to fill. The two authors contend:
"The Kremlin's ultimate objective is immutable—the creation of a world
under Soviet paramountcy."[2]

As opposed to this, Graeme Gill maintains that the Soviet naval
expansion into the Indian Ocean came after the United States established communications facilities at the Northwest Cape in Australia and
at Asmara in Ethiopia that had the capacity to communicate with
submarines in the Indian Ocean. Since this was followed by announcements in December 1966 and June 1968 indicating that the United
States was ready to construct a logistic support base at Diego Garcia,
the Soviet Union assessed that Washington planned to deploy Polaris-
and Poseidon-type submarines in the area that could pose a threat for
the Russians.

> The Soviet deployment of vessels in the Indian Ocean was thus
> concerned to provide a counter to the possible presence of American
> craft in the region, and hopefully to neutralize it as a source of nuclear
> attack on the Soviet Union by making it less secure for the operation
> of offensive vessels than it otherwise would have been.[3]

Oles Smolansky, who has presented arguments similar to those
above to explain the presence of the Soviet navy in the Indian Ocean,
goes further to suggest that the Sino-Soviet conflict has reinforced the
Kremlin's belief that their security interests warrant impressive naval
presence in the area. He says:

While . . . the Soviet naval entry into the Indian Ocean has been strongly influenced by Washington's decision to deploy nuclear submarines in its waters, the Kremlin's extensive political involvement in the Indian subcontinent . . . has over the past few years, been dictated primarily by the exigencies of the Sino-Soviet dispute. . . . There may have been no direct initial relationship between the two in the sense that the budding Sino-Soviet rift would probably have dictated a political involvement by the U.S.S.R. in the affairs of the subcontinent even without the naval strategic considerations. In this particular instance, however, the two have been closely interwoven.[4]

As seen by the then U.S. Chief of Naval Operations, the Soviets have multifold objectives in mind as they augment their strength in the Indian Ocean. Testifying before the House Subcommittee on the Near East and South Asia of the Committee on Foreign Affairs in March 1974, Admiral Russell Zumwalt said that in his judgment the Soviets were attempting to expand their influence with the states of the area, enhance their image as a great power and check China's political influence and military power by bolstering their own on China's southern flank. He said further that

the Soviets recognize that any nation which has the capability to project substantial naval power into the Indian Ocean automatically acquires significant influence not only with the littoral countries but with those countries outside the area which are dependent on the free use of its sea lanes as well.[5]

While the views expressed above by no means exhaust the variety of perspectives on the motives behind the presence of the Soviet navy in the Indian Ocean, they are examples which exhibit a widespread concern in the United States about this matter. Not only has the Soviet activity in the area heightened American consciousness about the economic and strategic significance of those waters; it has raised demands in many quarters that the United States must match the Soviet strength in the region.

All indications are that even though U.S. interest in the Indian Ocean surfaced in the 1960s, it was not until the 1970s that serious thoughts were given by the policymakers in Washington toward building a permanent facility in the area which would serve the nation as a major naval and air base. The U.S. Navy entertained thoughts of replacing the British presence in the area in full force in the early 1960s. But neither the State Department nor the Defense Department supported this position.

The Pacific, Atlantic, and Mediterranean were perceived as areas of much higher priority. U.S. policymakers acknowledged that in the highly improbable event of a conventional conflict between the United States and the Soviet Union, the Indian Ocean was a most unlikely area of confrontation. The State Department and the White House did not believe that a major U.S. security interest would be served by an expansion of U.S. naval presence in the region.[6]

Talks between the United States and Britain did take place as early as 1964 with a view to building "an austere" communications facility on the island of Diego Garcia, a part of the Chagos Archipelago, located some 1200 miles south of the tip of India in the Indian Ocean—a facility which would add to a network extending from Asmara, Ethiopia, to the Northwest Cape of Australia. Negotiations were concluded in 1966 when the United States and the United Kingdom signed a 50-year agreement whereby the British-owned island was leased to Washington for joint defense purposes. These communications facilities could serve the purpose of permitting periodic patrols of Polaris and Poseidon submarines in the Indian Ocean. It appears that while the United States did not station the nuclear submarines in those waters at the time, parts of the ocean were used as patrol areas.

But even as late as 1972, the United States did not contemplate a major naval presence in the area. The then Defense Secretary Melvin Laird said at the time: "Our strength in the Indian Ocean lies not so much in maintaining a large standing force . . . but rather in our ability to move freely in and out of the Ocean as the occasion and our interests dictate."[7]

However, this posture encountered a sudden change in 1973. It was the Arab-Israeli war followed by the oil embargo imposed by the oil-producing countries of the Middle East that resulted in the adoption of a new approach to the entire region by the policymakers in Washington. The occasion also made more credible a possible threat from the increased Soviet naval presence in the area, for though the oil flow had been blocked by the land based nations this time, the same consequences would follow if the next time around the Soviet Navy selected to choke the sea lanes.

In the aftermath of the Middle East crisis, the Pentagon won grudging approval of $18 million from the Congress in 1974 to upgrade the facilities on the Diego Garcia island. Additional sums were appropriated in the succeeding years, leading some Congressmen to express the belief that the final bill could exceed the sum of $50 million.

Diego Garcia has a good harbor and a site for a major airfield. The U.S. Navy is undertaking a dredging of the harbor to create a turning basin that will be 2,000-by-6,000 feet and able to accommodate submarines and aircraft carriers. Available will also be a massive 640,000-barrel fuel storage capacity for ships and aircraft. The United States has constructed an 8,000-foot-long coral runway on the island, and U.S. C-130 and C-141 transport aircraft have been using the airstrip; it will ultimately accommodate personnel in the number of 600 or so. The airfield runways are to be lengthened from 8,000 to 12,000 feet, so that they are available for use by KC-135 refuelling aircraft. While the runways will be able to accommodate B-52 bombers, the chairman of the Joint Chiefs of Staff has told the Senate Armed Service Committee that that is not contemplated.[8]

In its approval of the initial budget, Congress stipulated that the president must provide testimony that the activity is in the U.S. national interest. A confidential memo from the State Department to Congress says:

> In our judgment, an adequate U.S. presence in the Indian Ocean provides a clear signal to the Soviets of our resolve to insure a credible military capability there ... the opening of the Suez Canal will obviously increase the Soviet ability to show force to influence events where major U.S. interests are at stake.

While specific U.S. interests have not been spelled out in any one place, it is becoming clear that the State Department and the Defense Department are now convinced that sufficient reasons exist to justify an impressive naval presence in the Indian Ocean. While Britain's resolve to pull out her military contingents from East of Suez pointed to the initial need for a U.S. entry in the area, protection of oil interests and other strategic interests which have surfaced since the Soviet navy became visible in the region now cause Washington to prepare for long term presence in those waters. As one author says:

> Britain's determination to reduce to all but a token force her overseas military contingents East of Suez, including in the Middle East and Southeast Asia, and particularly the announced termination of her security arrangements with the oil rich Arab states in the Persian Gulf have often been offered as the initial cause of U.S. strategic decisions to fill an anticipated defense "gap" in the Indian Ocean region. But U.S. State Department spokesmen have also pointed to the 1962 Chinese incursion into India's Northeast Frontier territory and Ladakh, the deteriorating Indian-Pakistan relationship, and the critical importance that "forward movement in economic development and toward political stability" be maintained in the no less than thirty states that belong to the Indian Ocean region.[9]

THE LITTORAL STATES

Interestingly enough, the 30 states of the littoral do not see eye-to-eye with either the Soviet Union or the United States on this issue. They see a situation developing where the Indian Ocean would turn into a seabed of nuclear weapons. And they are fearful that continued presence of the formidable navies of the superpowers off their shores would tempt the United States and the Soviet Union to interfere in the domestic and interstate affairs of the regional states, as they compete to extend their influence over governments in the area.

By no means are all the states whose shores are washed by the waters of the Indian Ocean of one mind on the subject. But they did join together in voicing their concern in September 1970 at the Nonaligned Nations Conference in Lusaka by adopting a resolution which urged all nations to consider the Indian Ocean as a zone of peace. The following year they carried their case to the United Nations.

The General Assembly adopted on December 16, 1971, a resolution sponsored by Sri Lanka and strongly supported by India and most of the littoral states, which declared that the Indian Ocean was designated for all times as a zone of peace.[10] In the main, the resolution called upon the great powers to enter into immediate consultations with some 30 littoral states of the Indian Ocean with a view to halting the further escalation and expansion of their military presence in the Indian Ocean. It also asked the major powers to eliminate from the Indian Ocean all bases, military installations, and logistical supply facilities; the disposition of nuclear weapons and weapons of mass destruction; and any manifestation of great power military presence in the Indian Ocean conceived in the context of great power rivalry.

Primarily, the Peace Zone declaration contemplates the establishment within the Indian Ocean area of a zone of peace free of nuclear weapons in which conditions of peace and tranquility would be ensured by the exclusion of great power rivalries and competition as well as the elimination of bases conceived in the context of such rivalries and competition.

The creation of a peace zone also obligates the states of the region to renounce the use of threat or force against any other state in that region. The resolution mandates that the littoral states must settle their disputes with one another by peaceful means only. The declaration does not deny the states the right of self-defense. If observed in letter and spirit, it would help the states of the region devote more attention to the task of economic and social reconstruction.

Then again, if abided by, the zone of peace declaration would guarantee freedom of the high seas and thus give commerce and merchant ships the right of free passage.

THE SUBCONTINENT

That India has been in the forefront of the campaign to restrict the presence of the superpowers in the Indian Ocean can only be understood if one recognizes that India's concerns with that waterway go back into ancient times. It is a tragic part of India's history that only since 1947 has she found it necessary and possible to publicly proclaim her interests in the Indian Ocean. It is also a painful part of India's history that even after independence, she has acquired but very limited ability to influence events in the Indian Ocean and to secure her interests in the area.

India has a coastline 4,000 miles long that borders on the Indian Ocean, a coastline as long as India's land frontier. It is the longest in the world facing navigable waters, and it is more vulnerable than the land frontier.

India's major trade and communication routes traverse the ocean. As a developing nation, India depends on exports of foodstuffs and raw materials (such as jute and jute products, tea, cashew nuts, ores and metals, shellac, oilseeds, and mica) to earn the foreign currency needed to import equipment and technology in such key areas as mining, electric power, railroads, oil drilling, and textile machinery. While her total import-export trade of some $7 billion may not be impressive by itself, when put in proper context the picture leaves no doubt in one's mind that trade routes of the Indian Ocean are the lifelines of India.

In the period following the first major increase in oil prices in 1973, industry was badly hurt for the reason that close to 90 percent of petroleum is used for essential industrial, transport, and agricultural services. It is clear that India's reliance on imported oil is impossible to waive and that, further, India will be forced to import two thirds of its oil for years to come. The post-1973 situation has emphasized as never before India's dependence on the sea-lanes for its life-giving supplies and the exports to pay for them.

In strategic terms, India is one country that needs no reminder that her fate as a truly sovereign entity is inextricably woven with the winds that will blow from the Indian Ocean. If the Indian Ocean is controlled by a single naval power, the will of that power will dominate India. That is what India suffered for two centuries and that is what India overthrew after a long and bitter struggle—not completely in 1947, but as late as 1961 in Goa. Thus India does not wish to see the Indian Ocean dominated by any single power.

On the other hand, if the Indian Ocean becomes an arena of superpower rivalries, this too will generate ill winds drawing India into the eye of a storm not within the means of this country to overcome. It will deal for India nothing but death and destruction. For the policymakers of India, Vietnam stands as a bold example of such a situation; the failure there of the peoples to weld unity within not only led to intervention by outside powers, but it led to Vietnam's becoming a battlefield where such senseless combat, bombing, and massacre prevailed that few could even articulate what interests and whose interests were being served in such a holocaust. Apparently, India's imagination is not running amuck in conceiving of a scenario like this as long as superpower rivalry is permitted to escalate in the Indian Ocean.

The Indian subcontinent continues to be highly unstable. Problems within the nations of the subcontinent and on their borders simmer with explosive situations. Bangladesh, China, India, and Pakistan are each riddled with disturbances within their borders. To top it off, there is no solution in sight for the Sino-Indian and Indo-Pakistani border conflicts. These unsettled conditions provide a natural ground for superpower rivalries to be transferred from the Indian Ocean to the subcontinental mainland. Given the facts that the United States and China support Pakistan, the Soviet Union supports India through a treaty of friendship and cooperation, and Sino-Soviet hostility is at its peak, it is not difficult to visualize that the subcontinent is ripe with opportunities for the Soviet Union and the United States to intervene.

Perhaps this scenario displays an element of cynicism and a fear that the superpowers are prone to act hastily in certain situations. But a moment of thought to what happened in 1971 and 1973 prepares one for the worst. In December 1971, as a result of the Indo-Pakistani war, the aircraft carrier *Enterprise* headed a task force including an amphibious assault ship, the *Tripoli*, with a battalion of 800 marines, three guided missile escorts, four destroyers, a nuclear-attack submarine, and an oiler. This force entered the Bay of Bengal and, as things turned out, was deployed in the Indian Ocean until January 1972. Early in 1972, the jurisdiction of the U.S. Seventh fleet was extended to the Indian Ocean.

When the Bangladesh war started in 1971, there were four Soviet warships in the Indian Ocean, the largest being a relatively old destroyer, none of which had any surface-to-surface cruise missile capability. This force was strengthened by 16 warships so that for a brief period in early 1972, there were 20 combatants present in the Ocean, 13 surface vessels and 7 submarines. Four of the extra Soviet ships, some with surface-to-surface missile capability, were sent into the Ocean after the U.S. Navy had dispatched a task force there headed by the aircraft carrier *Enterprise*. The Indo-Pakistani war led, therefore, to record force levels for both the United States and the Soviet Union.

SUPERPOWER RIVALRY

During the "global alert" called by President Nixon in October 1973, with a view to challenging a potential Soviet military intervention in the Middle East conflict, the United States dispatched to the Indian Ocean the aircraft carrier *Hancock* accompanied by four destroyers and an oiler. Present during the same period in the area were the aircraft carrier *Oriskany* with four destroyers and an oiler.

The Soviet navy, which had four to six war vessels in the area at the time, sent in additional ships to bring her force to a level of ten surface combatants and four submarines.

It is granted that these situations were not permitted to get out of hand; but what guarantee is there that if the naval buildup on both sides continues to grow without any check, the very same situations would not assume a different and a more volatile character? As one author says:

> There seems to be a common denominator for the political mood prevailing from Dar es Salaam to Djakarta: a growing mistrust of major powers who have used the pretext of regional conflicts to further their own political objectives, far too often to the detriment of weaker states. It would be shortsighted to underestimate the strength and political importance of these feelings, even if for the time being a number of states bordering on the Indian Ocean still prefer to secure for themselves the solid support of one of the major powers.[11]

The littoral states of the Indian Ocean do not individually or collectively command even the semblance of sufficient naval strength to act as a deterrent to the actions of any great power from the outside. While presently they must depend on the good sense and the goodwill of Washington and Moscow, it should be easy to see that they would rather rely on something more solid for a guarantee of regional stability and nonintervention of the superpowers than merely the words of those in power at any given time.

In this regard it must be noted that an outstanding feature of the international trade routes of the Indian Ocean is the dominance of European countries both as traders and ship owners. The United Kingdom, the United States, France, and the Soviet Union lead all the others. The fact is that among the littoral states, India is the only nation that appears in most league tables of world shipping tonnage. As late as the early 1970s India had some 2.5 million tons of oceangoing merchant shipping—or only some 1.2 percent of the world's tonnage.

It is manifest then that were the declaration of the zone of peace taken seriously by member nations of the UN, it would work not only to the advantage of those states on the Ocean coastline, but it would preserve the economic prerogatives of the Western maritime powers. In fact it would also deal effectively with the often stated problem that Soviet preponderance in naval power in the Indian Ocean could enable Russia to cut off oil supplies to Western Europe and Japan. U.S. interest in the oil supplies of the Arabian peninsula and the Persian Gulf is too obvious to deny or challenge. On the one hand, the United States wants the oil flow to continue toward its traditional destination points—as Western Europe and Japan cannot survive without it.[12] On the other hand, the United States can ill afford to lose its own oil imports (approximately 17 percent annually) as well as the nearly $3.5 billion invested by American companies in the oil fields of the Middle East. Undeniably then, the stakes are high. And so the question arises, would the Soviets dare to put on the oil squeeze which would not only threaten the life of Western Europe but also strike a heavy blow against U.S. economic interest?

It is difficult to conceive that if the Kremlin took such a step, the United States would stand idly by. What is more likely is that were a situation of this order to arise, the United States would react with full force, and leave the Soviet Union no choice but instant withdrawal or a nuclear war. Recent actions of Moscow strongly indicate that it does not want to engage in a nuclear war with the United States. They further indicate that the USSR prefers détente—for détente has brought the Soviet Union not only the Helsinki agreement that has extended her defensive line far beyond her borders, but détente has also realized for that nation a stabilized Western front, permitting it to concentrate more on tackling its problems vis-à-vis China. If the Soviets are rational enough to eat capitalist wheat without complaining of stomach pains, they are rational enough not to go too far in testing the iron will and the intestinal fortitude of the American policymakers by threatening what they know is vital U.S. interest.

In this regard it should be noted that the oil embargo experienced by the world in 1973 was imposed by the member states of the Organization of Petroleum Exporting Countries (OPEC), not by any outside agency. Which leads one to observe that oil flow and oil investment would be best protected if a permanent solution to the Middle East problem is realized to the satisfaction of all concerned.

Policymakers of the major powers, however, do not consider

circumstances compelling enough to accommodate such views at this time. For all practical purposes, they have shelved the Peace Zone Declaration as well as the subsequent recommendations prepared by a UN appointed ad hoc committee of experts in 1974. Their main objection centers on the contention that the UN proposal contradicts the prevailing international law on the freedom of navigation on the high seas for all ships. As *Pravda* stated it in February 1977 for the Soviet Union:

> The Soviet Union is prepared to participate with all interested states on an equal basis in the search for a favorable resolution of the question of creating a zone of peace in this region [Indian Ocean] ... However, such measures should take full account of the generally recognized norms of international law concerning freedom of navigation in the open sea and the associated need for business calls at the port of coastal states, as well as freedom of scientific research.[13]

When all is said and done, it becomes clear that the great powers wish to preserve "freedom of navigation in the open sea" because it is crucial to enable them to indulge in such strategic exercises as testing of sophisticated weapons, calls at ports of coastal states, and keeping a close watch on each other's activities to make certain that no threat exists to their interests as well as the interests of some of their client states. For as uncomfortable as the thought might be for some of the littoral states, it has to be recognized that constant bickering and even warfare among many of the coastal states has led to some of them readily accepting superpower client status. As Braun points out:

> There is, of course, more to it than meets the eye of the conventional strategist. The Indian Ocean, by its very geographical location, is of special significance to both superpowers with regard to the latest technological devices in military strategy, both under water and in the air, including satellites (such as the British-American Skynet communications system). Ships are part of this strategy of threat-deterrence-vigilance, and in such a context conventional bases such as Simonstown are likely to lose much of their importance.[14]

The significance of increase in Soviet naval activity in the Indian Ocean lies not only in the ship days logged by Soviet ships at sea but also ship days accumulated in ports. Figures provided by different sources make it manifest that the Soviet Union is far ahead of the United States in both these categories. Soviet ship day levels increased from 1,760 in 1968 to 8,543 in 1973. During the same period U.S. ship day levels rose from 1,688 to 2,154. For the same period Soviet port calls ranged from 42 to 153, while U.S. port calls varied from 71 to 115.[15] It is beyond the purview of this article to discuss the full implications of these statistics. What is important to mark is that both powers attach strategic value to this conduct. While a higher count of ship days enhances the ability of a state to take initiative, act on short notice, and carry out long range programs, it is the in-port days which have an even greater impact in terms of extending a nation's influence. Ship days spent in port result in direct contact between the naval power and the host country. They provide an opportunity to exploit a military, political, economic, or social situation if it presents itself. And as the Soviet navy commander in chief says:

> The friendly visits of Soviet navy men make it possible for the peoples of many countries to become convinced with their own eyes of the creativity of the ideas of Communism . . . They see warships as embodying the achievements of Soviet science, technology and industry.[16]

U.S. naval experts consider port calls equally significant. Even if Washington does not propose to match Moscow for every ship day at sea or in port, it can be expected that neither party would permit the other to hold a monopoly in this sphere. Consequently it can be assumed that the navies of the two powers will be much in evidence in the Indian Ocean in the foreseeable future. President Carter expressed interest in "complete demilitarization" of the Ocean in March 1977. Secretary of State Cyrus Vance discussed the matter with his hosts while visiting Moscow at the same time. This was followed by the setting up of a joint U.S.-Soviet commission which was handed the task of working out a plan to allow a gradual demilitarization of the Ocean. But so far nothing has surfaced to indicate that any progress is being made by the commission. One author suggests that this is partly due to the fact that the Pentagon is unable to determine what would constitute proper levels of U.S. naval presence in the area so that U.S. security interests are fully protected.[17] Since the superpowers appear in no hurry to change the status of things as they exist, such attitudes only guarantee continued rivalry and naval competition. The littoral states of the Indian Ocean see this as a potentially dangerous situation fraught with tension, conflict, and possibly warfare.

NOTES

1. Robert H. Donaldson provides an excellent analysis of the whole range of viewpoints rendered in this regard in "The U.S.S.R., the Subcontinent, and the Indian

Ocean: Naval Power and Political Influence," *The Sub-continent in World Politics*, ed. Lawrence Ziring (New York: Praeger Publishers, 1978), pp. 168–95.

2. "Soviet-U.S. Naval Competition," *Orbis* 18 (Winter 1975): 1109.

3. "The Soviet Union, Detente and the Indian Ocean," *Australian Outlook*, 31 (August 1977): 256.

4. "Soviet Entry into the Indian Ocean: An Analysis," *The Indian Ocean: Its Political, Economic and Military Importance* (New York: Praeger, 1973), pp. 346–48.

5. *Hearings Before the Subcommittee on the Near East and South Asia of the Committee on Foreign Affairs House of Representatives, Ninety-Third Congress*, (February-March 1974), p. 133.

6. Ibid, p. 89: The testimony of Gene R. La Rocque, Rear Admiral, U.S. Navy (Retired).

7. As quoted by Admiral La Rocque in his testimony, ibid., p. 90.

8. The testimony given by Dr. Earl Ravenal (who at one time served in the Defense Department and is now teaching at Johns Hopkins University, School of Advanced International Studies) before the House Subcommittee, already cited, is worthy of note in regard to some of the information supplied above. He said: "It is my impression from reviewing these proposals in the Defense Department in the late sixties that it has always been the ultimate intention of the Joint Chiefs of Staff and the Navy to create a major, complete, multi-purpose base, not just a naval base but a base that is also capable of housing mobile projection forces—Marines or airlifted Army divisions—and of course longrange bombing planes." In reference to B-52 bombers he said: "It is significant that the Pentagon is planning an air strip that is adequate to launch KC-135's, which have no other function but to refuel B-52's." Ibid., pp. 123 and 126.

9. Justus M. van der Kroef, "Strategic Importance of the Indian Ocean," *The Indian Review* (Autumn 1978): 61.

10. In the General Assembly 61 states voted for the resolution. While none voted against it, 55 states abstained. Britain, France, the U.S., and the U.S.S.R. were among those who abstained. For an analysis of the votes cast and UN deliberations on the subject see: K. P. Misra, "Developments in the Indian Ocean Area: The Littoral Response," *International Studies* 16 (January-March 1977), pp. 17–33.

11. Dieter Braun, "The Indian Ocean in Afro-Asian Perspective," *The World Today* 28 (June 1972): 250.

12. About 17 percent of the U.S. oil needs are met by imports from the Persian Gulf area, whereas 79.6 percent of Japan's oil and approximately 64 percent of Western Europe's is imported from the Middle East.

13. Donaldson, "U.S.S.R., Subcontinent, and Indian Ocean." p. 189.

14. Braun, "Indian Ocean in Afro-Asian Perspective," p. 251.

15. The statistics quoted here are from a report prepared in May 1974 by the Foreign Affairs Division, Congressional Research Service Library of Congress, for the House Subcommittee on the Near East and South Asia. Title of the report is: *Means of Measuring Naval Power with Special Reference to U.S. and Soviet Activities in the Indian Ocean*, pp. 4–7. For an excellent in-depth analysis of ship days and port calls see Donaldson, "U.S.S.R., Subcontinent, and Indian Ocean." Also see James M. McConnell, "The Soviet Navy in the Indian Ocean," in *Soviet Naval Developments: Capabilities and Context*, ed. Michael McGuire (New York: Praeger, 1973).

16. Donaldson, "U.S.S.R., Subcontinent, and Indian Ocean," p. 174.

17. Van der Kroef, "Strategic Importance of Indian Ocean", pp. 59–60.

· 8 ·

ASEAN IN REGIONAL DEFENSE AND DEVELOPMENT

Charles E. Morrison and Astri Suhrke

The five member countries of the Association of Southeast Asian Nations (ASEAN)—Indonesia, Malaysia, the Philippines, Singapore, and Thailand—form a vast land and archipelago arc around Indochina. This region's strategic importance derives from its geographical location, as it commands the sea routes between the Indian and Pacific Oceans, and its rich natural resources of tin, petroleum, and timber. Some 250 million Southeast Asians live in the five ASEAN countries, a population equal to that of the United States and Canada combined. Economically, the region is one of the fastest growing in the world, with gross national product (GNP) growth rates averaging between 6 percent and 10 percent annually. The combined GNP of the ASEAN countries is approximately $100 billion; and as a collective entity the five countries are the fourth largest trading partner of the United States (after Canada, the European Communities, and Japan).

Politically and economically, the ASEAN countries are oriented toward the Western world and Japan. Their largest trading partner is Japan, and the United States is second. All five are anti-Communist in terms of domestic policies; yet while all like to regard themselves as nonaligned in foreign policy, four of the five (Indonesia excluded) retain some form of formal security connection with either the United States or Great Britain. They have been increasingly concerned about the survival of their rather conservative regimes in the wake of the collapse of U.S. efforts to maintain anti-Communist regimes in Vietnam, about the increased tension between the Soviet Union and China, and about the growing military reputation of Vietnam following its displacement of the Pol Pot government in Kampuchea. As one means of helping to compensate for these developments, the ASEAN countries have strengthened their cooperation with each other on both political and economic issues in the context of the ASEAN organization.

The ASEAN organization was established by the foreign ministers of the five member countries in August 1967 and at first was formally limited to economic, social and cultural cooperation. However, almost all those who participated in its founding agree that their principal motives were diplomatic and political in nature. These motives were not identical, but a very important common thread was the desire to use their collective bargaining power to strengthen individual national governments and thus maintain political stability and the existing order of nation-states in the region. This preoccupation with national strength and internal stability among the member governments has had conflicting implications for the growth of the organization. On the one hand, it encourages greater cohesion stemming from shared problems and fears, but on the other it limits organizational development, since the member governments are unwilling to delegate any of their precarious national control to an entity with supra-national features in the name of the common good.

This chapter will examine both the ASEAN countries and the ASEAN organization. It will begin by looking at the security concerns of the ASEAN governments and the constraints on a more effective mobilization of domestic political and economic resources. Then it will turn to the ASEAN organization to examine how the ASEAN governments have attempted to use the organization to help fulfill political and economic needs.

THE ASEAN COUNTRIES

The five ASEAN countries range in size from the regional giant Indonesia—3,000 miles in length and with 140 million inhabitants—to tiny Singapore with only 225 square miles of territory and 2.3 million people. Indonesia and Singapore also represent the extremes in terms of economic resources and level of development. The former possesses rich natural resources but has the lowest GNP per capita in the region ($280 at 1976 market prices), while Singapore, which as is sometimes observed has no natural resources except its people and orchids, enjoys the highest GNP per capita of the ASEAN countries ($2,580 at 1976 market prices).[1] There are also marked differences in the countries' colonial experiences, the nature of their transition to independence, religious adherence, and cultural heritage.

Despite these differences, the commonalities in the perspectives of the ASEAN governments on basic political and economic issues have become increasingly apparent. All the ASEAN governments preside over states which have a relatively delicate national fabric, marked by visible or latent sociopolitical or class tensions and intraelite competition. With the exception of Singapore, all have "dual economies" with sharp contrasts between the modern and the traditional sectors, attendant socioeconomic tensions, and large income disparities between the urban centers and the rural hinterland. In most cases, awareness of nationhood is confined to a relatively small educated elite, and in some cases ethnic minorities are demanding that their own "nationhood" be recognized in the form of autonomy or independence (as in the case of the Moro National Liberation Front in the southern Philippines). Central political institutions are weak, and national symbols still have questionable saliency. Even in Thailand—the only Southeast Asian country that was not colonized by European powers and where the monarchy has long been a prominent symbol of national unity—there are signs that this symbol is losing its effectiveness in generating national consensus and unity. Finally, the ASEAN countries have had considerable continuity in their elite structure. The ruling elites are relatively narrowly recruited from the landed or industrial wealthy classes (as in the Philippines) or from these classes in combination with the old aristocracy (as in Malaysia) or in combination with the military (as in Thailand and Indonesia). Only in Singapore have technocrats and professionals achieved truly elite status, and only in Indonesia have there been claims that a sociopolitical revolution was attempted after independence and, according to critics, was subsequently aborted and betrayed.

Given this elite structure and the delicate national fabric of these states, it is not surprising that the ASEAN governments support cautious and pragmatic rather than revolutionary change. In economic policy, growth with distribution has been emphasized rather than *re*distribution of income and wealth. In political life, stability and order are stressed. The ASEAN governments employ a wide range of instruments to maintain domestic control, including the manipulation of symbols to develop broad national consensus around general concepts (such as Indonesia's *Panchasila*, Malaysia's *Rukunegara*, and Thailand's "nation-religion-king"); the establishment of constitutional procedures designed to permit some opposition representation without jeopardizing the position of the existing rulers; strong anticommunist and antisubversive laws (such as Malaysia's and Singapore's Internal Security Acts, and sundry martial law orders and the Anti-Communist Act in Thailand); various forms of press and media censorship; and of course military suppression of insurgencies. All the ASEAN governments, in their quest for security, use some authoritarian methods which have been severely criticized by human rights organizations such as Amnesty International.[2]

These characteristics reflect a general sense of insecurity as regards domestic affairs among the ASEAN governments. This was reinforced in the 1970s by a series of foreign policy developments in the region: the retrenchment of American military power following previous British military withdrawals from Malaysia and Singapore and the Communist victories in Vietnam, Laos, and Kampuchea. Vietnam, rather than China, came to be regarded as the main external threat to the ASEAN governments (particularly in Thailand) as Hanoi reunified Vietnam (and captured a great deal of American military equipment in the process), expanded its influence in Laos (where it maintains several thousand troops and a 25-year friendship treaty concluded with the Pathet Lao regime in July 1977), and invaded Kampuchea, where it installed the Heng Samrin government in January 1979. Added to this has been continuing apprehension among the ASEAN governments about the role of the major communist powers in the region. Their anxiety is partly based on ideological hostility, and this raises questions such as: How genuine is China's protestation of friendship with the ASEAN governments when China refuses to eschew party-to-party support for local communist insurgencies in the ASEAN countries? Has Soviet support for Vietnam, especially before and after the Sino-Vietnamese war of 1979, been designed to expand Soviet influence in the area to the detriment of the non-communist ASEAN governments? Even the open conflicts among the Communist powers have not served to allay such fears. Vietnam's invasion of Kampuchea was thus seen as increasing the power of ASEAN's rival and antagonist; China's attempted chastisement of Vietnam in the 1979 war raised fears that China might similarly assert its power in quarrels with non-Communist states as well. Moreover, the Sino-Vietnamese conflict appeared to stimulate Soviet presence in the region, reflected in the Soviet-Vietnamese friendship treaty of 1978 and reports of increased Soviet use of facilities at Cam Ranh Bay for servicing ships and reconnaissance aircraft.

Nevertheless, in viewing these developments the ASEAN governments do not consider a direct, external attack as a very likely immediate threat. Beyond this, their sense of insecurity is not very precisely defined in terms of specific threat perceptions. Rather, there is a diffuse, vague sense that the external environment has become more complex and less favorable and is likely to exacerbate the internal security problems, which remain the most important ones. In some cases, the link between internal and external forces is seen to be relatively direct, as in the verbal encouragement and suspected material support provided by China and Vietnam to local insurgents. Nor is the Soviet Union above suspicion in this regard, for we know that Moscow was identified as the source of aid and inspiration to two high Malaysian officials who confessed to be Communist agents in 1977. In other cases the links are seen as being more indirect; there are fears that ethnic Chinese in ASEAN countries will increasingly identify with China as China's status in the region and the world is enhanced and that the Communist victories in Indochina point to the strength of alternative models of political order and economic development while the reduced Western presence implies weakness of, and lack of external support for, the models of the ASEAN states.

The ASEAN governments recognize that challenges to their political order as well as the maintenance of existing regimes require an accelerated mobilization of their own political and economic resources. The magnitude of this task can perhaps best be appreciated by examining more closely the political and economic constraints on each ASEAN government.

Political constraints

In the Philippines, the freewheeling liberalism of the post-World War II period was abruptly terminated by the imposition of martial law in 1972. Since then, President (and concurrently Prime Minister) Ferdinand E. Marcos has been faced with a growing separatist/autonomy rebellion by Muslims in the South, with continued insurgency by the Maoist New People's Army, and with opposition from an assortment of church leaders, intellectuals, and political leaders from the pre-martial law period. Attempts to legitimize his regime by periodic referenda and elections for an interim national assembly have been more form than substance, as evidenced, for example, in the response of Manileños to the 1978 elections of holding a three-hour demonstration of pan-beating and horn-honking and the decision of some local opposition leaders to field a halfwit as a candidate in the 1979 regional elections in Mindanao. These responses, of course, also testify to the current impotence of the opposition to the regime.[3]

In Indonesia, the political and security picture appears in many ways more complex. One of the most significant fault lines in the body politic has been between the politically dominant and nominally Muslim Javanese (*abangan*) and the strongly Muslim minority which includes more religiously oriented Javanese (*santri*) but also a much higher proportion of non-Javanese.[4] Both the pre-1966 Sukarno government and the Suharto government that followed have regarded partisan Muslims as a principal threat to their secular regimes. Under the Suharto government, the Muslim-based political parties were forced to coalesce into a single, government-approved party (the Development Unity Party, PPP) which received 27 percent of the popular vote in 1971 and 28 percent in 1977. While its leaders have been largely coopted by the government, there remains a considerable degree of dissatisfaction with Suharto's "New Order" among the Muslim elite, many of whom continue to advocate an Islamic state. In 1978, the government arrested four prominent Muslim leaders and many Muslim students for opposing a third consecutive presidential term for Suharto.

The Suharto government has also been faced with criticism from younger military officers who are concerned about what they see as corruption and lack of professionalism among the older generation of military leaders who now wield power.[5] A more visible threat to the Suharto government, however, has come from university and high school students who are often tools in intraelite competition. In January 1974, for instance, there were violent protests during the visit of Japanese Prime Minister Kakuei Tanaka, encouraged by an ambitious deputy commander in chief of the armed forces, General Sumitro. Again, in the spring of 1978, there were significant student demonstrations against a third term for Suharto.

Student influence reflects the growth of the middle class, which is common to all the ASEAN countries. The political impact of the growth of this class and of the student population in particular is still unclear. In Indonesia, activist students have tended to be sharply critical of the existing order, but in Thailand both student and middle-class sentiments appear more polarized. Both groups supported the demise of the dictatorial and corrupt military regime of Thanom and Praphat in the October Revolution of 1973. But in the following three years of civilian rule, sizable segments of the new middle classes were alienated by continuing economic problems, price and wage effects of farmer and worker unrest, and governmental inefficiency and political violence (provoked by both the left and the right). As a result, they generally supported or tolerated the October 1976 military coup that followed the brutal suppression of Thammasat University students by right-wing vocational students and the police. Since then, there has been one abortive coup and one successful coup that placed General Kriangsak Chamanand in power.

As in the case of Suharto, Kriangsak faces problems of controlling the military and of coopting or intergrating civilian politicians in his government. In addition, labor unions have become increasingly organized and demanding as spokesmen of the urban poor; the militant opposition has gained new adherents as hundreds of students reportedly fled to the jungle to join the insurgency in the aftermath of the 1976 coup; and a self-proclaimed broad national (and clandestine) front of socialists, communists, farmers, workers, and intellectuals was subsequently announced.[6] Insurgency activity has increased in the South in the past few years, has continued to be a problem in the Northeast and has been compounded in areas adjoining Kampuchea since 1975. While few observers foresee major victories by the insurgents in the near future, the latter create a continuing sense of insecurity both in Bangkok and in the countryside and a feeling within the ruling circles that failure to deal effectively with other opposition groups and claimants to power may be exploited by the militants. From this perspective, it was certainly a defeat for the government that during the April 1979 elections, only about 20 percent of the Bangkok electorate was sufficiently committed to the existing political framework to bother to vote and that many independent candidates associated with Kriangsak were defeated.

In Malaysia and Singapore, threats to the political order are more latent and are largely derived from potentially explosive ethnic tensions between the Malay and the Chinese communities in both countries. The remnants of the Malayan Communist Party, which once led a major insurgency (the 1948–60 "emergency"), have been contained in the border region in southern Thailand for many years, unable to overcome internal factional differences or to broaden their base beyond a small, primarily Chinese constituency. The federal government in Kuala Lumpur remains very concerned about the insurgency, however, partly for fears that it could help stimulate or exploit a renewal of race riots, such as those that occurred after the elections in May 1969. The May 1969 riots, which left several hundred dead or wounded, remain indelibly etched in the Malaysian national consciousness a decade later. The Malaysian government prohibits open discussion of sensitive ethnic issues and maintains strong internal security laws.

The political party framework devised to deal with ethnic divisions has proved only partially successful. Political power rests with conservative Malays who, with conservative Chinese leaders, have worked out ethnic compromises on most sensitive issues. However, the Chinese component of this alliance (the Malayan Chinese Association) has lost much of its constituency support to more activist Chinese opposition parties (principally the Democratic Action Party), and there has also been opposition to the established Malay party (the United Malay National Organization). While the ruling alliance (*Barisan Nasional*) made stunning victories in terms of parliamentary seats in the 1978 federal elections—winning 131 of the 154 seats—the opposition parties gained a much larger percentage of the popular vote than their parliamentary seats indicate (1.34 million votes of a total of 3.61 million).[7]

Dissatisfaction with the existing ethnic compromise concerns a wide range of issues. Most central, perhaps, are education and economic issues, especially the government's efforts to improve the economic welfare of the Malays through its New Economic Policy. Malay critics claim that this policy tends to benefit the already rich Malays rather than the poor and, at any rate, is not being pursued vigorously enough; on the Chinese side, there is worry that the policy is being implemented too hastily and a suspicion that it will mean redistribution of existing wealth from the Chinese to the Malay community. The government also has to consider the potential divisiveness of a rather recent phenomenon: the growth of Islamic fundamentalism among Malay youth embodied in the *dakwah* movement. These groups emphasize religious values and hence underscore the differences and tension between the Muslim Malays and the Chinese.

By comparison with the other ASEAN countries, Singapore appears relatively stable and cohesive. The ruling People's Action Party (PAP) provides efficient government, has the opposition under firm control, and has won every parliamentary seat in the past three elections. As in Malaysia, there are significant restraints on the discussion of sensitive ethnic issues, but the internal social division most threatening to the PAP leadership in the past (the distinction between English-medium educated and Chinese-medium educated among the Chinese, who account for 75 percent of the total population) has become increasingly muted. Singapore's small size and the possibility that ethnic tensions in Malaysia could spill over into the adjacent city-state, however, make a stable external environment very important to domestic order. Moreover, the PAP has yet to develop "second generation" leadership with proven political skills.

Economic constraints

Sustained economic growth is regarded as a crucial element in regime survival by all the ASEAN governments. All subscribe to the case for economic growth as necessary for political stability, as succinctly stated in Singapore's case by its prime minister, Lee Kuan Yew:

In the 1950s, Singapore suffered high unemployment, slow economic growth, social and political unrest. Many bright, eager-beaver types joined the communist underground cells for guerrilla revolution. Strikes, riots, arson, and assassination were part of the dreadful repetitive calendar of weekly events. Today the same bright, eager-beaver types are in industry as young engineers and managers. Now communist recruitment has dropped in quality and in numbers. This political transformation would not have happened but for our rapid economic development.[8]

Of course, not all social and political unrest in the ASEAN countries is communist inspired or led, nor is aggregate economic growth in itself a sure remedy for unrest. A common experience among the ASEAN countries is that their rather impressive rates of growth of GNP per capita—averaging 6.8 percent in Singapore, 5.3 percent in Indonesia, 4.7 percent in Malaysia, 4.2 percent in Thailand, and 3.9 percent in the Philippines annually during the 1970-76 period—have created some new problems and not necessarily ameliorated old ones. Economic development has often been concentrated in export and urban manufacturing and service sectors, and this accentuates class and social problems in countries with marked dual economies. The opportunities for, and scale of, corruption multiplies. Ineffective taxation and budgetary systems fail to redistribute the benefits of growth even where such policies have been attempted, and in most cases deliberate policies of redistribution have been halfhearted at best. Growing numbers of young people with secondary or college eudcation fail to find professional or managerial jobs commensurate with their aspirations. Unskilled surplus labor from the countryside continues to pour into urban centers but often remain as poor and underemployed as when they lived in the rural areas.

In facing these problems, the ASEAN governments increasingly have promised to concentrate on development for the poorer segments of their populations. But while the declarations to this effect abound, the results so far appear much less impressive. In Indonesia, for example, despite a significant boost in national income resulting from the price increases for crude petroleum—Indonesia's most valuable export—there has been no significant reduction in the income gap. A comparison of the 1970 and 1976 National Household Expenditure Surveys indicates that there has been little change in the proportion of total consumption accounted for by the poorest 40 percent of the population (who accounted for slightly less than 20 percent of the total consumption expenditure in both years) and the richest 20 percent (who accounted for slightly more than 40 percent of total expenditure).

ASEAN leaders sometimes refer to their economic situations as analogous to riding a bicycle: if one slows down, it becomes harder to maintain balance. The current economic development plans of Malaysia, the Philippines, Thailand, and Indonesia target annual growth at rates of 8.5 percent, 7.7 percent, 7.0 percent, and 6.5 percent respectively. These plans are predicated not only on higher levels of domestic savings and capital formation, but also on sustained growth for exports, foreign investment, and official development assistance. Thus, all the ASEAN countries have a common interest in export earning stabilization programs, trade liberalization and, more specifically, improvements in the generalized systems of preferences (GSPs) of the developed countries, especially for manufactured and semimanufactured goods. They are interested in maximizing the flow of private capital, managerial skills, and technology from the industrialized world to the ASEAN region and in maintaining a high level of official development assistance.

THE FUNCTIONS OF THE ASEAN ORGANIZATION

As indicated at the outset of this chapter, the motives behind the creation of ASEAN were largely political and diplomatic in nature. Although the assoication's activities were initially limited to economic, social, and cultural cooperation, the Bangkok Declaration of August 8, 1967 that founded ASEAN referred to the determination of the member countries to "ensure their stability and security from external interference" and declared that foreign bases in the region were temporary.[9] The ASEAN governments have been at great pains to deny that ASEAN is in any way a military organization, and only in February 1976 was political cooperation among the members brought within the formal ambit of the organization. Nevertheless, from the outset ASEAN helped provide an intangible yet quiet significant security function by creating a sense of solidarity among like-minded governments keenly aware of their delicate internal power bases and the increasingly uncertain and complex external environment. In this way, ASEAN has given psychological reassurance to and symbolic support for the member countries—not as a traditional security alliance, but as a political entente among friendly governments.

It is a reflection of this function that the development of the ASEAN organization has been parallel to events suggesting the need for greater solidarity. During its first nine years, ASEAN functioned exclusively as a foreign ministers' organization. The annual meeting of the foreign ministers was the highest policymaking body of the organization, and although 11 permanent and several more ad hoc committees were established for economic, social, and cultural cooperation, ASEAN made little significant progress because of the lack of active involvement by the national policy-implementing ministries for these fields. The association was serviced by national ASEAN secretariats in each foreign ministry whose heads (secretaries-general) were the chief officials in the individual governments primarily concerned with ASEAN affairs. The most significant joint initiative, the call for a "zone of peace, freedom, and neutrality" in Southeast Asia in the November 1971 Kuala Lumpur Declaration, was undertaken outside the formal framework of the organization.[10]

Following the collapse of the non-Communist governments in Kampuchea, Laos, and South Vietnam in 1975, the ASEAN governments felt it was important to enhance their solidarity in a visible way by materially strengthening the ASEAN organization. This effort culminated in the first summit meeting of the ASEAN heads of government in Bali in February 1976 where several important new documents emerged. A Treaty of Amity and Cooperation in Southeast Asia set out general principles for relations among the ASEAN countries and outlined a procedure for the settlement of disputes; the Declaration of ASEAN Concord established a more specific program of cooperation—including political cooperation; an agreement was signed establishing a permanent ASEAN secretariat in Jakarta. The economics ministers were brought into the organization on an equal basis with the foreign ministers, and the heads of government meeting became the highest ASEAN decision-making body. The momentum toward greater cooperation slowed down, however, after a second summit in Kuala Lumpur in July 1977. It took new developments in Indochina in early 1979 to touch off an apparent renewed determination to enhance intra-ASEAN solidarity.

In examining ASEAN's political and economic functions more specifically, it should be kept in mind that while ASEAN and intra-ASEAN relations are important to the member governments, the most significant sources of tangible support come from large powers outside the region. Indeed, one of the main purposes of ASEAN is to augment such extra-ASEAN support. In the economic field, intra-ASEAN trade is relatively small (about 16 percent of the members' total trade), while trade links with Japan and in most cases with the United States and the European Communities are much more significant. Private capital investment and foreign aid of course come largely from the same outside countries. As for security support, the United States and European countries are the most significant sources of weapons and military assistance. The Philippines maintains a 1951 bilateral defense treaty with the United States, augmented by a military bases agreement most recently revised in early 1979. Both the Philippines and Thailand are signatories of the multilateral 1954 Manila Collective Defense Treaty; it is supplemented in the Thai-U.S. case by the 1962 Rusk-Thanat communique declaring that the United States interprets its treaty obligations as applying bilaterally, something which since then has been periodically confirmed. Malaysia and Singapore are members of the loose 1971 Five Power Defense Agreement, which links their security with Great Britain, Australia, and New Zealand; and Australia maintains two air squadrons in northern Malaysia.

POLITICAL FUNCTIONS OF ASEAN

Status and Identification

The ASEAN organizational machinery, declarations, and other activities have helped to give ASEAN a kind of collective identity which increasingly has received external recognition. In its early years, the association was roundly criticized by the Soviet Union and China as an imperialist-inspired organization, while the United States maintained a discrete, aloof posture. Now the organization engages in ministerial level dialogues with its principal trade and aid partners, receives rhetorical support from China, and has been informally approached by the Soviet Union regarding a possible ASEAN-USSR dialogue.

As ASEAN's stature grows, the organization serves to enhance the status and legitimacy of member governments. ASEAN gives some meaning to the "active" element of Indonesia's long-standing proclamation of having an "independent and active" foreign policy. The ASEAN foreign ministers' qualified endorsement in 1971 of the Malaysian proposal for the neutralization of Southeast Asia gave a political boost to the relatively new government of Tun Abdul Razak. For the Philippines, participation in the organization adds credibility to the government's claims of stressing its ethnic and geographical links with other Southeast Asian countries, an emphasis popular with domestic nationalists who resent the visibility of the close ties with the United States. For Singapore, ASEAN is an organization where it can deal with its much larger neighbors on a formal basis of equality.

Similarly, membership in ASEAN has enabled member governments to emphasize particular foreign policy identification at little cost. In the cases of Thailand and the Philippines, two former members of the Southeast Asia Treaty Organization (SEATO), their association in ASEAN with nonaligned Indonesia projected an image of foreign policy flexibility at a time when U.S. reverses in Vietnam made adjustments seem appropriate, but before the Manila and Bangkok governments were willing to take more substantial steps (such as the later phasing out of SEATO and normalization of their relations with China). The situation was the reverse for Indonesia, which in the early years of ASEAN was anxious to be associated with its neighbors who had long been in good standing with the principal donors of foreign aid to Indonesia. Membership thus facilitated a closer rapprochement with the United States and Japan without formally deviating from the principle of an "independent" foreign policy. Additionally, Indonesia's role in the establishment of ASEAN helped demonstrate to the other members that the Suharto government repudiated the aggressive confrontation policy of the previous Sukarno government. In the case of Singapore, participation in ASEAN underscores the determination of the government of this predominantly ethnic Chinese city-state to establish a Southeast Asian identity and thus alleviate fears on the part of its neighbors that it might become a third China.

The status and identification functions of ASEAN are continually being reinforced by the large number of ASEAN meetings and joint activities. It is undoubtedly beneficial at home that each member government appears to be playing an active role in the diplomacy of the region and is accepted as a legitimate government and full partner by its close neighbors. To assure that each government shares in the benefits of the prestige and publicity of ASEAN activities, the ministerial and summit meetings are held in successive capitals, the rotation going according to alphabetical order.

Collective Political Defense

In an increasingly complex international environment, "collective political defense" (a term coined by former Thai Foreign Minister Thanat Khoman) has become more important to the member governments. Collective political defense connotes solidarity and mutual support and can be useful in dealing with outside powers as well as defending foreign policy adjustments that are difficult to explain to domestic audiences. An example of the latter occurred after the fall of the anticommunist governments in Pnompenh and Saigon in early 1975, when the ASEAN countries coordinated their recognition of the new governments. The recognition of the successor Communist regimes was not popular in some conservative circles in the ASEAN countries, but each member government could defend its necessity by referring to a collective ASEAN position that, of course, it had to respect. Similarly, since the invasion of Kampuchea by Vietnam in early 1979, Thai Prime Minister Kriangsak has defended his government's decision not to recognize the new Heng Samrin government in part by referring to the need to wait until the ASEAN members are prepared to take a common position.

In external bargaining, political solidarity among the ASEAN countries has undoubtedly helped enhance individual members' bargaining positions in bilateral negotiations with larger powers. In bargaining with China, each ASEAN member's position was strengthened by the fact that the Chinese knew that the other ASEAN countries were watching China's responses closely, and would draw appropriate conclusions for their own relations with China. Similarly, before making a March 1979 visit to the Soviet Union, Kriangsak consulted other ASEAN heads of government. A Thai newspaper appropriately editorialized that "by consulting with the leaders of Singapore, Indonesia, and Malaysia, General Kriangsak will have his hand strengthened when he goes to Moscow next week so that he would be able to talk for ASEAN rather than for Thailand alone."[11]

Other illustrations of "collective political defense" abound. The willingness of the ASEAN governments to support the Malaysian government by endorsing its regional neutralization proposal has already been noted. In 1975 and 1976, the ASEAN countries, with the partial exception of Singapore, supported Indonesia's invasion of East Timor. More recently, after the January 1979 Vietnamese invasion of Kampuchea, the ASEAN foreign ministers held a special meeting in Thailand, the country nearest "the firing line," to help reassure the Thais and warn the Vietnamese of their collective disapproval. As Thai Foreign Minister Upadit Pachariankul reported afterwards, "with the help of our ASEAN partners, we feel sure that nothing will happen to Thailand."[12] Beginning in March, there were reports of Vietnamese hot pursuit of Pol Pot forces across the Thai-Kampuchean border into Thai territory. However, reports indicated that Upadit's assessment was correct: the Vietnamese seemed concerned to minimize any direct threat to Thailand and to limit the possibilities of border clashes, partly because of their desire not to further alienate the ASEAN countries as a whole.[13] The ASEAN nations similarly responded in a concerted fashion when the Chinese invaded Vietnam in February by presenting a joint ASEAN resolution for the consideration of the United Nations Security Council.

These events also point to the limitations of collective ASEAN action. Although they demonstrated a common diplomatic response to unsettling events in the region and may have been psychologically comforting to the member governments, ASEAN had no perceptible impact on the Sino-Vietnamese conflict nor did they deter the Vietnamese from invading Kampuchea. As for the Thai government, its major responses to the extension of the military power of its traditional rival Vietnam into Kampuchea involved large power diplomacy, as was evidenced by Kriangsak's trip to Moscow, by his February 1979 visit to Washington to appeal for more military aid, and by his government's close contacts with China throughout the crisis.

Collective political defense has also been evident in another major

206 • SECURITY AND STABILITY IN ASIA

issue facing the ASEAN governments, how to respond to the massive influx of refugees from Indochina. Thailand and Malaysia have by far borne the brunt of the refugee inflow—Thailand as an alarmed recipient of land refugees (primarily from Laos and Kampuchea) and Malaysia as a possibly even more reluctant recipient of "boat" refugees, largely consisting of Vietnamese of Chinese ethnic origin. The refugees are not only a burden on the social services and economies of the receiving countries; they are also perceived as a potential security problem, and especially in Malaysia, they aggravate ethnic tensions. Although the other ASEAN governments were less affected, they felt it appropriate that ASEAN make a collective effort to relieve the burden on the most seriously impacted countries. The major thrust of ASEAN efforts was to seek more international attention to the problem and a greater willingness from the United States and other countries to accelerate their admissions of refugees. These efforts culminated in an international conference on the subject held in Jakarta in May 1979, which was attended by Vietnam, the ASEAN countries, the United Nations High Commissioner for Refugees, and the major receiving countries. Another element in the ASEAN response has been an attempt to share the refugee burden a bit more equitably. Indonesia offered an island as a temporary shelter for refugees already accepted by the countries of ultimate asylum. This offer, which was not uncontroversial in Indonesia, was explicitly intended to contribute to the stability of Malaysia by helping to relieve the burden on that country. Clearly, however, with a maximum capacity of only 10,000 refugees, the Indonesian island offer was more a symbolic gesture than a substantial contribution to a growing problem.

Rights of consultation

It is generally understood within the ASEAN group that a government should consult with other members before undertaking any major initiative that might affect their interests, and that it likewise has a right to ask other members to consult. This understanding is formalized in the Treaty of Amity and Cooperation in Southeast Asia (1976), which specifies that members "shall maintain regular contact and consultations with one another on international and regional matters with a view to coordinating their views, actions and policies."

Consultations contribute to group solidarity and the containment of intra-ASEAN tensions. Indeed, one side effect of the growth of an ASEAN identity has been that individual members fear being associated with a foreign or domestic policy of another member which they find undesirable. This gives the member governments a greater stake in the policies of other members than if ASEAN did not exist. As a result, there is an impetus toward ensuring through consultations that no one member will take unilateral actions with which the others are uncomfortable. The earliest instance of policy coordination came at the time of the 1971 Kuala Lumpur conference, when the member governments agreed to consult on their policies toward China. When Malaysia became the first ASEAN country to propose normalizing relations with China in 1973, it consulted with Indonesia and delayed recognition for a year to accommodate Indonesian urgings for less haste.

More recently, there was a series of bilateral ASEAN summit consultations in early 1979 as the result of considerable strains within the ASEAN group regarding their appropriate responses to the events in Indochina. All members felt a need to present similar responses, but Thailand believed that as the most affected country, it should have the lead in formulating ASEAN's posture and the other members should support Thailand. On the other hand, Malaysia and Indonesia were disturbed by reports that Thailand was permitting China to resupply Pol Pot forces through its territory and feared Thailand was involving itself too deeply in Indochina on the Chinese side. While Malaysia and Indonesia were unhappy about Vietnam's invasion of Kampuchea and alliance with the Soviet Union, they were also deeply skeptical of China's motives in attacking Vietnam. They believed a more neutral and less involved Thai course would better serve the interests of Thai stability and feared that Thailand's actions could give ASEAN as a whole the appearance of a pro-China and anti-Vietnam tilt that would be embarrassing for their own foreign policies.

Consultations within the purview of the organization are also designed to prevent conflict among the members on political issues that are principally of interest to ASEAN members alone and thus contribute to stability in the region. Since ASEAN was established, there have been relatively few such conflicts among the member states. The most enduring ones relate to the Philippine claim to the East Malaysian state of Sabah and the Muslim rebellion in the southern Philippines which have been sources of tension in Philippine relations with Malaysia. These conflicts have been contained partly because the ASEAN members realize their potentially disruptive effect on ASEAN and wish to protect the organization and partly because the very existence of ASEAN has legitimized more direct mediatory efforts. Thus the Indonesian government interceded on several occasions in the Philippine-Malaysian quarrel during the time when Sabah's Chief Minister, Tun Mustapha, channeled aid to the Moro National Liberation Front in the southern Philippines. Tun Mustapha was invited to Jakarta at least twice to be advised of the guidelines for correct neighborly behavior.

Despite Tun Mustapha's political downfall in 1975 and Marcos' pledge to Hussein Onn at the second ASEAN summit in August 1977 to take steps to shelve the Sabah claim, some difficulties remain between the two countries—as does Indonesian interest in the situation.

ECONOMIC FUNCTIONS OF ASEAN

Bargaining for external support

ASEAN has proved to be far more important to its member governments as a vehicle for bargaining with outside powers for greater external support than for promoting development through economic cooperation within the group. Indeed, the ASEAN members have relatively little to offer each other in economic exchanges. All are interested in market access for their products in the developed countries, increased investment and foreign aid flows into the region, and stabilization of their export earnings from primary products. The ASEAN countries are of course members of the developing nation Group of 77 and actively participate in UN Conference on Trade and Development (UNCTAD) meetings on North-South economic issues. But they have found that their more specific interests can be addressed more effectively in separate discussions with the developed countries. For this purpose, ASEAN has initiated a number of dialogues where it promotes the members' economic interests and seeks symbolic support for the ASEAN organization as well as endorsements of broader Group of 77 demands, such as the establishment of an Integrated Commodity Program including a Common Fund.

The ASEAN dialogues began with negotiations with the European Communities (EC) in 1972 and a series of discussions in 1973 and 1974 with Japan on its synthetic rubber exports, which competed with ASEAN natural rubber. Informal meetings also began with Australia in 1974 and New Zealand in 1975. With the full participation of the economics ministers in 1976 came a much more vigorous effort to use the dialogues to further the member-countries' economic interests. The existing discussions with the EC, Japan, Australia, and New Zealand were placed on a more formal, regularized basis, and in 1977 new dialogues were initiated with Canada and the United States. Specific ASEAN countries were assigned the coordinating role for specific dialogues, making use of traditional ties (for example, the Philippines was assigned the United States and Canada, Malaysia was assigned Australia, and Indonesia was assigned Japan and the EC).

The results of joint bargaining through the dialogues and in other forums have been mixed. Rhetorical and symbolic support for the ASEAN organization has been generous, and certainly the ASEAN countries have commanded more attention acting jointly than they would have on an individual basis. The August 1978 ASEAN-U.S. ministerial dialogue required more than a day of the personal time of the U.S. secretary of state and was attended by more than half the cabinet, while a November 1978 dialogue with the EC was the first that the Communities had ever conducted with another regional organization on the ministerial level. More tangible support has been much more limited. There has been some trade liberalization on specific items (such as plywood, canned pineapples, shrimp, and palm oil), and the EC and Japan have facilitated imports from ASEAN by accepting the "group of origin" principle in their preference systems, and the U.S. will apparently follow suit.[14] The dialogues have also resulted in efforts to increase the flow of private investment capital into the region. Following the 1978 ASEAN-U.S. dialogue, missions led by the American Overseas Private Insurance Corporation and the Export-Import Bank were dispatched to the region, and there have been two large ASEAN-EC investment conferences in 1977 and 1979 designed to bring together businessmen from the two regions.

ASEAN has been most successful with the countries for which the five member-countries have the most significance—Japan, Australia, and New Zealand. In 1977, the ASEAN countries invited the prime ministers of these three countries to meet with the ASEAN heads of government following the Kuala Lumpur summit. None of the prime ministers could easily afford to reject an invitation from a group of countries so diplomatically and economically important to their own. (For example, for Japan, the ASEAN countries account for 11 percent of that country's trade, 20 percent of its overseas investments, and more than 40 percent of its official development assistance.)[15] Each of the visiting prime ministers was expected to meet separately with the ASEAN leaders; each would be judged on the basis of his receptivity to ASEAN requests.

The meetings were quite successful from the ASEAN point of view. In addition to the expected statements of support for ASEAN and ASEAN positions in the North-South dialogue, there were agreements by Japan and Australia to substantially increase their foreign aid to the ASEAN region. Japanese prime minister Takeo Fukuda pledged $1 billion to support ASEAN's proposed large-scale industrial projects (provided the feasibility of each was demonstrated and it was fully accepted as a joint project by the organization). Japan also promised to consider ASEAN's proposed export earning stabilization proposal (STABEX), which has been rejected by other developed countries, and subsequently agreed to represent ASEAN points of view at the economic summit meetings of the leaders of the industrialized countries. A side effect of Japanese interest in and support for ASEAN is that it does stimulate some degree of competitive interest on the part of the United States and EC, as evidenced by the appearance of the U.S. secretary of state as well as Japan's foreign minister at the June 1979 ASEAN ministerial meeting.

Intra-ASEAN economic cooperation

Internal cooperation within the ASEAN group has had only a negligible impact on the development programs of the member countries. It has helped, however, to give credibility to the ASEAN organization and its objectives and has symbolic importance far beyond its economic significance.

According to Dr. Widjojo Nitisastro, Indonesia's chief economic planner, "only since 1976 has economic cooperation between the ASEAN countries become meaningful."[16] Before the 1976 Bali summit, intra-ASEAN economic cooperation, then under the supervision of the foreign ministries, consisted of little more than periodic meetings of governmental personnel with little follow-up and subsequent recommendations for additional exchanges or endorsements of ongoing national projects. This was a period, however, in which personal contacts among policymaking personnel in the five countries were built up, facilitating later cooperation. Also of longer-term significance was ASEAN's request to the United Nations to undertake a study of means to enhance economic and trade cooperation among the member countries. The 1972 report of the UN team suggested selective trade liberalization on a product-by-product basis, industrial complementarity schemes, and large-scale industrial projects to attract new kinds of industry that no single ASEAN market could support. These recommendations formed the basis for intra-ASEAN economic cooperation in later years after the economics ministries became fully involved.

To date, the most significant form of intra-ASEAN economic cooperation has been in the area of trade liberalization. In February 1977, the ASEAN countries signed an Agreement on Preferential Trading Arrangements (PTA) that envisaged tariff preferences, long-term quantity contracts, purchase finance support at preferential rates of interest, and other forms of commercial advantages. Preferences on 71 items (14 contributed by each country except for 15 by Indonesia) were implemented in January 1978; 755 items were added in September 1978; and another 500 were agreed upon in December 1978. These preferences are exchanged in a way that permits each country to argue its own national economic interests. For example, the Indonesian news agency noted that in the first two rounds, Indonesia had received concessions on 688 items, while making concessions on only 138 items.[17]

The developmental impact of the ASEAN PTA has so far been minimal. Intra-ASEAN trade itself has only been 15–17 percent of the members' total trade during the 1970s, and a major proportion of this has been entrepôt trade between Singapore, Malaysia, and Indonesia. Moreover, many of the tariff "concessions" have either consisted of promises not to increase rates (that is, "binding" rather than actual reductions) or have been reductions on rates already of nominal significance. On the items where there have been meaningful concessions of more than half a percent in rate, only about 12 percent of the ASEAN countries' imports come from other member-countries.[18] Nor has there been any significant progress in eliminating nontariff barriers to trade among the five.

A second form of proposed intra-ASEAN cooperation has been in the development of large-scale industries, which would be jointly owned by the ASEAN countries and the products of which would receive duty-free treatment within the group. In March 1976, the economics ministers agreed on an initial list of one large-scale plant for each country—urea for Indonesia and Malaysia, superphosphates for the Philippines, soda ash for Thailand, and diesel engines for Singapore. These projects required further feasibility studies, and one of them— Singapore's—almost immediately became embroiled in controversy because Indonesia and other ASEAN countries had existing small diesel engine manufacturing plants and planned to enlarge them. Singapore eventually withdrew from the large-scale industry program, except for a nominal 1 percent equity participation in the other four projects. In December 1978, the economics ministers initialed agreements on the two urea projects and also accepted the Thai soda ash project. The Philippine project is reportedly under reconsideration.

In contrast to the large-scale industrial projects, ASEAN complementarity arrangements within a single industry (whereby components of a product may be manufactured in different ASEAN countries and freely traded) were basically left to the private sectors to formulate under the general aegis of the ASEAN Chambers of Commerce and Industry (CCI). In November 1975, the ASEAN-CCI established a Working Group on Industrial Complementation which a year later called for the formation of ASEAN industry clubs. By the end of 1978, some 12 clubs were formed (e.g., the ASEAN Automotive Federation, the ASEAN Federation of Cement Manufacturers, and the ASEAN Pulp and Paper Industry Club) and six more were in the process of formation.[19] The numerous hurdles any scheme must overcome as it passes through national and regional industry clubs, ASEAN-CCI institutions, and intergovernmental ASEAN committees suggest that even the formulation of complementarity proposals will be a very difficult process. Several projects have reportedly been proposed through this complicated network of private and intergovernmental institutions, but the failure of the economics ministers to agree on detailed guidelines for ASEAN complementarity projects has so far prevented final approval of any.

For ASEAN's private sector, cooperation within the association has been a slow and often frustrating process. Chomkiet Meedej of the Thai Chamber of Commerce has remarked that "problems dog us and multiply at every step we take concerning multilateral cooperation—be it in the planning or the implementing stage."[20] And David Sycip, a Filipino businessman who is an active proponent of an ASEAN economic community, is more blunt: "We have really not moved beyond square one."[21] Among the governments, Singapore and the Philippines have pressed hardest for more rapid economic cooperation including across-the-board tariff concessions.

As in the case of political cooperation, each ASEAN government looks at each proposal in terms of its perception of its own national interest. Indonesia has been the most reluctant to engage in broad-scale trade liberalization for several reasons. First, as the least industrialized country of the five Indonesia fears that many of its smaller-scale "infant industries" will be overwhelmed by more established and economically efficient industries in such countries as the Philippines and Singapore. Secondly, Indonesians believe that since theirs is the largest ASEAN market, new industries locating in the region would tend to gravitate toward Indonesia in the absence of trade liberalization; with trade liberalization, these industries are likely to be attracted to countries with more highly developed infrastructures.

Officials connected with ASEAN defend the slow nature of ASEAN internal economic cooperation as a necessary stage to build up a psychology of cooperation permitting more rapid cooperation later. As Indonesian Industries Minister Soehoed has put it: "Once people get used to this sort of package idea, the benefits will gradually be understood. And then we can move into a more sophisticated system of operation. It is only a matter of development."[22] According to this argument, large initial steps would require expensive and painful national adjustments, and this would result in a political backlash against further cooperation.

CONCLUSIONS

In assessing ASEAN, one should be careful not to put up straw men by judging its performance against such criteria as an integrated economic community or a military security pact. The member governments did not have such encompassing intentions when establishing the organization and—for good and obvious reasons—have continued to entertain much more limited objectives. Their primary goal has been to strengthen national governments. They do not have the solid internal power base nor the economic cushion to make immediate sacrifices and adjustments that transfers of power to a supranational entity or more wide-ranging economic cooperation would entail. Moreover, their major security concerns are internal in nature and therefore require concentration on the mobilization of domestic, political, and economic resources. Where external resources are important, sympathetic large powers rather than other ASEAN members remain the primary source of help.

In light of these qualifications, ASEAN can be seen as a relatively successful endeavor. Given the delicate internal fabric of the ASEAN societies and the fears of member governments that internal tensions may be exacerbated from the outside, the essence of ASEAN's contribution is that by projecting an image of political solidarity, it warns the outside world that interference with one ASEAN government will be a matter of concern for all five. It thus raises the political costs of hostility against any particular ASEAN regime. Simultaneously, the member governments enjoy the psychological comfort of being associated with like-minded parties. In economic matters, the key function again is solidarity. The members use their collective weight in seeking meaningful concessions from their major aid and trade partners and hence increase the costs to the large powers of not responding adequately to ASEAN's interest and demands.

ASEAN is not the principal solution to the many political and economic challenges its members face. The survival of their present political order, and of the ASEAN organization, depends most immediately upon their ability to mobilize their internal resources in an efficient and equitable manner or—to paraphrase an Indonesian slogan—to establish their national resilience. Cooperation within ASEAN is a useful adjunct to these efforts by generating support from other sources, providing reassurances among the five, and defending against overt external interference.

NOTES

1. International Bank for Reconstruction and Development, *World Bank Atlas* (13th edition, 1978).
2. *Amnesty International Report* 1977 (London: Amnesty International Publications,

1977). See also Department of State, *Report on Human Rights Practices in Countries Receiving U.S. Aid* (Washington: Government Printing Office, 1979), and *Thailand Update*, February 1979.

3. See Kit Machado, "The Philippines 1978: Authoritarian Consolidation Continues," *Asian Survey* 19 (February 1979): 131–40.

4. See Donald K. Emmerson, *Indonesia's Elite: Political Culture and Cultural Politics* (Ithaca, N.Y.: Cornell University Press, 1976).

5. Harold Crouch, *The Army and Politics in Indonesia* (Ithaca, N.Y.: Cornell University Press, 1978), pp. 304–6.

6. Committee for Coordinating Patriotic and Democratic Forces, *News Service*, June 1978. For a sociological analysis of Thai developments in the 1973–1976 period, see Ben Anderson, "Withdrawal Symptoms: Social and Cultural Aspects of the October 6 Coup," *Bulletin of Concerned Asian Scholars* 9 (July-September 1977): 13–30.

7. R. S. Milne and Diane K. Mauzy, "Ethnicity, Elections and Democracy in Malaysia: 1969-78," Paper presented at the annual meeting of the Association of Asian Studies, Los Angeles, 1979. For a more general treatment, see the same authors' *Politics and Government in Malaysia* ((Vancouver: UBC Press, 1978).

8. Lee Kuan Yew, "Extrapolating from the Singapore Experience," (Lecture, October 5, 1978). Published by the Publicity Division, Ministry of Culture, Singapore. p. 27.

9. For more detail, see Charles E. Morrison and Astri Suhrke, *Strategies of Survival: The Foreign Policy Dilemmas of Smaller Asian States* (New York: St. Martin's Press, 1979), pp. 268–72.

10. On the Malaysian neutralization proposal, see Morrison and Suhrke, pp. 156–160. Since ASEAN was limited to economic, social, and cultural cooperation until 1976, the Kuala Lumpur conference was a meeting of the foreign ministers of the member states, but not an ASEAN meeting.

11. *Nation Review* (Bangkok), March 16, 1979.

12. *Bangkok Domestic Service*, January 13, 1979.

13. *Far Eastern Economic Review*, May 11, 1979, p. 9.

14. Authorization for the U.S. to use the "group of origin" principle was contained in mid-1979 in congressional recommendations to the president for legislation to implement the results of the GATT Multilateral Trade Negotiations.

15. Makoto Ikema, "Japan's Economic Relations with ASEAN," Paper presented at the Tenth Pacific Trade and Development Conference, Australian National University, Canberra, March 22, 1979.

16. "Widjojo Nitisastro: Clearing the Jungle," in "Indonesia: the Awakening Giant," *Euromoney* supplement, January 1979, p. 9.

17. *Antara*, September 9, 1978.

18. Yasukichi Yasuba, "The Impact of ASEAN on the Asian-Pacific Region," Paper presented at the Tenth Pacific Trade and Development Conference, Australian National University, Canberra, March 19, 1979.

19. For a description of the industry clubs and their work, see ASEAN-CCI Secretariat, *ASEAN-CCI Handbook 1979*.

20. *Bangkok Bank Monthly Review* 18 (April 1977): 154.

21. Quoted by the Baltimore *Sun*, September 6, 1978. For a more optimistic statement by Sycip, see his article on "Industrial Development and Regional Cooperation in the ASEAN," *1978 Fookien Times Philippines Yearbook* (Manila, 1978), pp. 146–49.

22. Corazon M. Siddayao, ed., *ASEAN and the Multinational Corporations* (Singapore: Institute of Southeast Asian Studies), p. 65.

· 9 ·

VIETNAM'S QUEST FOR SECURITY
D. R. SarDesai

With the dramatic Communist victory in South Vietnam and Cambodia in the spring of 1975 and the "silent revolution" that pushed Laos fully into the Communist orbit in December of that year, the strategic-political balance seemed suddenly to have improved in favor of the Communist world. Of the three countries of former French Indochina, Cambodia was the least expected site for a Communist take-over. The Communist movement there, never known to be strong before Sihanouk's overthrow in 1970, had been accelerated within a short span of time, there being no long germinating period as in the two other countries of Indochina; and therefore the movement had lacked sustained mass support or an entrenched institutional structure. In any case, one would have assumed that the Communists would regard the three victories as the culmination of the liberation movements in the Indochinese peninsula and devote themselves, at least in the short run, to the tasks of domestic reconstruction without the major distraction of defense development. Even those noncommunists who believed in the two-decades-old domino theory and saw its practical fulfillment in the fall of the three capitals in rapid succession regarded the phenomenon as peculiarly applicable only to the states of the Indochinese peninsula because of their common history of French rule. After the immediate period of panic and grave apprehension among the states of the Association of Southeast Asian Nations (ASEAN), for example, there followed a sigh of relief that there would be more than a breathing spell before the new Communist states would be ready or willing to assist actively the mostly clandestine Communist organizations in the rest of Southeast Asia.[1] Hardly anyone, even in the non-Communist world, expected at that time such fissures to develop among the new Communist states as would provoke large-scale interstate warfare culminating in the Vietnamese blitzkrieg into Cambodia at the turn of 1978 and the Chinese march across its southern border in February–March 1979, and so revive the region's instability and vulnerability to major outside influence.

These recent events will undoubtedly have a long-term bearing on the geopolitics of the region far more consequential than the events of 1975. The involvement of China and the Soviet Union (which will be discussed in detail later in the chapter), accusing each other of hegemonistic ambitions in Southeast Asia, has important implications for the region's future. The containment policy seems to have been revived with more than one country crying encirclement; and China has apparently—ironically—begun believing in the domino theory. The situation would be downright amusing if it was not for its grave impact on the development plans of the new Indochinese Communist states, and for its larger consequences for global peace. Though the conflict's characterization by the U.S. national security advisor, Zbigniew Brzezinski as a "proxy war" between rival protagonists in the Sino-Soviet dispute may be an exaggeration,[2] the growing involvement of the two major Communist powers in the region is a reality with serious potential for making Southeast Asia tragically once again one of the most explosive tinderboxes in the world.

Although such larger considerations have been a factor in the most recent fighting in Southeast Asia, both the conflicts—Sino-Vietnamese and Khmer-Vietnamese—can be understood better in terms of historical hatreds between neighboring peoples, a virulent nationalism that has overwhelmed ties of international communism and rival ambitions of two local powers, namely China and Vietnam, to dominate Southeast Asia. The relevance of such a conceptual context to the reevaluation of future defense needs of Indochinese states is obvious. They have an even greater and long-term significance for the local dreams of socio-economic development and, indeed, the entire region's political stability.

ECONOMIC DEVELOPMENT AND DEFENSE EXPENDITURES

Reconstruction

In the first flush of victory over South Vietnam in April 1975, it was Hanoi's expectation that funds would flow in liberally from all over—from socialist countries as well as from the United States, Japan, and Western Europe—that would be used for development purposes. The new international situation would permit defense expenditure to be kept at a minimal level and would not obstruct development projects. The Vietnamese leadership girded itself for the long-needed social and economic reconstruction of the country on the level of a moral equivalent of a war. As it happened, however, economic reconstruction was hampered by poor climate, paucity of foreign aid, and the need to deal with substantial pockets of resistance to Communist rule.[3] The creation of special economic relocation zones on the Cambodian border would eventually exacerbate relations with Cambodia and China, involve heavy defense expenditure, which in turn would affect the developmental outlay. Additionally, the strained relationship with China would dry up economic aid from that quarter. By 1977, economic and political goals, domestic and international, became once again entwined enough to make economic development and defense competitive choices for the new Vietnamese government. In the spring of 1975, the Hanoi leadership could afford to concentrate its energies on the tasks of reconstruction of the South. Indeed, North Vietnam had suffered tremendously in physical terms, much more than its southern counterpart, during the seven years of American "strategic" bombing (1965–72). As the Report of the United Nations Mission to Vietnam points out, the U.S. bombing raids had blasted out of existence the North Vietnamese infrastructure in all the fields of economy: industry, agriculture, transport, and communications. Railroads had been blown out of commission for long stretches of several miles on various lines as most of the bridges (in particular the large- and medium-size ones on the Hanoi-Lang Son and Hanoi-Vinh lines) has been blown up several times. Tongking's dyke system, built over two millenia, had suffered grievously as 183 dams and canal areas and 884 water installations had been damaged. Of the 30 provincial capitals, 21 were damaged and nine of them completely destroyed. Thousands of villages were damaged and several dozens completely destroyed.

In the 28 months between the cessation of U.S. bombings of North Vietnam and the Communist victory in the South, Hanoi had in particular restored its infrastructure, including its dyke system. Based on the information broadcast by the Voice of Vietnam, Professor Huynh Kim Khanh has assessed that by the end of 1975,

> several industrial centers and installations had been rebuilt or otherwise enlarged, including those in the industrial suburbs of Hanoi; the numerous enterprises in the Haiphong industrial center (cement, glass, dockyards, etc.) the chemical enterprises in Viet-Tri industrial

zone; the steel complex in the Thai Nguyen industrial centre, etc. All the destroyed bridges had been rebuilt.[4]

Though the South had not physically suffered as much, the damage done there was qualitatively such as to require much more time, money and imagination to repair. To quote Professor Huynh,

> The Legacy of the U.S.-Thieu regime was an economic and social malaise of unknown proportion: an economy that was on the verge of bankruptcy; a threatening famine in the northern provinces of Central Vietnam; more than three million unemployed people, excluding an army of one-half million prostitutes about to be out of work; six to seven million refugees who had been forced by wartime activities to flee their native villages into the cities, etc.[5]

The new government inherited an economy in which more than 50 percent of the GNP was generated by a service sector almost completely dependent upon a U.S.-funded war and in which imports were twelve times the exports.[6] The industry was 85 percent dependent on foreign countries for raw materials and 100 percent dependent on foreign machines and fuel.[7] Moreover, fleeing officials and bankers had stolen most of the country's foreign exchange reserves.[8] The new government also had to do something about an estimated 1.1 million Army of the Republic of Vietnam (ARVN) troops and an additional 1 million including police (125,000), militia (500,000), and civil service officials (350,000), only some of whom could be relied upon for their loyalties to the Communist regime. Given the ideological context,[9] reconstruction in the South meant for the Provisional Revolutionary Government (PRG) and Hanoi not only rehabilitation but relocation and "reeducation" of several million individuals, practically one third to one half the population of South Vietnam.[10] Another important consideration in relocation would be a large number of handicapped from out of an estimated 2.2 million war casualties, some of whom could not be expected to contribute to the rebuilding of the economy at full strength and who, in fact, might need state assistance of some kind for periods of time.

The greatest damage in the South had been caused to its ecological balance. As the Report of the United Nations Mission to Vietnam pointed out, chemical warfare had created a large number of "blank zones." The ruinous impact of defoliation and total destruction of trees on rainfall, soil erosion, and consequently on the productive abilities of the land was incalculable. Le Anh Tu has estimated that South Vietnam's timber supply for the next three decades (based on current demands) had been destroyed and that it would take "anywhere from five years for the fruit trees to a century or so for the rare timber trees to become productive again."[11] During the war, South Vietnam, a longtime exporter of rice, had become an importer of food to the extent of about 400,000 tons annually to feed a large population that could not attend to agriculture, had been conscripted in the army, or had simple fled to urban centers.

The short-term strategy of the Provisional Revolutionary Government (PRG) was to restore the industrial capacity of the Saigon-Cholon area and to relocate a large number of the urban population to the countryside for intensive agricultural activity. It estimated an immediate additional employment for 1 million people in agriculture by bringing more than half a million hectares of fallow land in the Mekong delta under cultivation. The new slogan since mid-1975 was: "Break with the past, return to the countryside to work for production."[12] As in the postrevolutionary China, the new program had its sadistic overtones in compelling the city-bred, soft-lived intellectuals, civil service officials, and vast numbers of army officials of the former government "to work with their hands like the rest of the proletariat" in a reeducation program.[13] On the other hand, where the early Maoists had distrusted technology claiming it would be deleterious to socialist values, the Vietnamese had never feared any "contradiction between the construction of an advanced economy and the creation of the socialist man."[14]

The reunified Vietnam aimed at a "triple revolution"—collectivization and nationalization of industry and agriculture, ideological transformation, and scientific and technological revolution.[15] It appeared, however, that it would be prepared to sacrifice ideological purity to the altar of a technological transformation of the country. It is this aspect of Vietnamese policy that made for a broad, open-minded approach in international relations and a domestic policy based on compromise and pragmatism. The new leadership consequently welcomed outside investment of finance and technology on a joint venture basis, Vietnam supplying the labor, allowing remission of profits, and assuring that the new enterprises would not be expropriated. To prove its bona fides, Vietnam enthusiastically joined the International Monetary Fund unlike most Communist countries (with the significant exception of rebel Yugoslavia and Rumania) that had either refused to join the international body or had withdrawn from it.[16] Vietnam also joined the World Bank and the Asian Development Bank while remaining only an observer of the Moscow-dominated COMECON International Investment Bank.[17] It should be noted, however, that despite such efforts to attract capital from non-Communist countries in the varied fields of oil exploration, mining of tin, tungsten, apatite, phosphate and anthracite coal, the foreign interest, with very few exceptions, has so far been mostly limited to oil.[18] A major snag has been Hanoi's refusal to honor the former South Vietnamese government's debt obligations and its own action immediately after the takeover of Saigon in nationalizing all foreign enterprises.

For the kind of technological revolution to which Vietnam aspired, it needed and expected massive economic assistance from everywhere, this being part of the reason why the North Vietnamese leaders had agreed to the Paris Accords on cease-fire in exchange for an American promise to give 3.2 billion dollars in reconstruction aid. By the forcible capture of South Vietnam in April 1975, the North Vietnamese had, in the American official view, violated those accords and absolved the United States of that promise. Vietnam, however, continued to hope through 1976 that some U.S. assistance would be forthcoming, particularly after the advent of the Democratic Administration and as a part of the solution of the MIA question. Meanwhile, the assistance from socialist countries dropped or as in China's case, altogether dried up, making Vietnam's foreign exchange problems acute.[19]

Second Five-Year Plan

Despite such handicaps, Vietnam (formally reunited on July 2, 1976) adopted a five-year plan (1976–80) at the Fourth Congress of the Communist Party in December 1976.[20] It should be noted that the Democratic Republic of Vietnam's (DRV's) economic planning had practically been in abeyance since 1965 and the Second Five-Year Plan (1976–80) constituted a hurried revision of a plan formulated only for North Vietnam in 1974 and then expanded to include projects for South Vietnam as well. Hence the late announcement of the plan in December 1976, allowing only four years instead of five to meet its targets.

With its projected outlay of 7.5 billion dollars for a population of 48.8 million (1976 estimate), to increase at an annual rate of about 3 percent, the plan has not been deemed overambitious by knowledgeable critics.[21] It stressed the primary sector of the economy though it aimed also at laying the groundwork for heavy industry. Thus, 30 percent of the total outlay was earmarked for agriculture in the expectation by 1980 of a food production of 21 million tons, not including meat and saltwater fish (1 million tons each) and other fish and fishmeal (about 450,000 tons total). Accordingly, the country was expected, after feeding its population, to have a surplus of 3 million tons of rice for export. Most of this agricultural development was to be achieved in the South by reclaiming 2.6 million hectares of land mostly in the Mekong delta—something which, in the opinion of economists Ta Huu Phuong and Guy Ta, could be beyond the financial and technological resources of the country.[22] The large-scale collectivization of agriculture which the plan envisaged, was to be achieved through the creation of some 500 giant agrofarms each employing about 100,000 persons in South Vietnam alone. This would release some 4 million people who would be settled in the New Economic Zones in both parts of the country.[23] In addition to this, half the population of the Saigon-Cholon-Gia Dinh area as well as from the densely populated Red River Delta would be relocated in the New Economic Zones (NEZs). The authorities expect to remove in the next two decades about 10 million people from overcrowded areas like these to the mountainous zones in the north and west that border all three of Vietnam's neighboring countries. From the Red River delta and the central coast alone, about 4 million would be resettled in the mountainous zone, Mekong delta, eastern coast and offshore islands, particularly the Spratlys, "in order to build the economy and consolidate our national defense."[24] As a concept, the NEZ was earlier adopted in North Vietnam in 1970, creating 23 NEZs in 14 provinces. In the South, however, the motives for the establishment of the NEZs were not purely socioeconomic. In the words of a critic, Douglas Pike, they were also aimed at population control (facilitating the work of the internal security police); and the strategic purpose of peopling the under-populated region along the border with unfriendly Cambodia.[25] Presumably, the NEZs will also be centers for light industry, which has been given a great priority under the plan, helping to produce articles of consumption not only for the domestic population long deprived of consumer goods essentials but also help exports. Vietnam expects its foreign trade to increase annually by 10 percent, a goal that may not be realistic in view of the fact that its trade is mostly bilateral with socialist countries, themselves desperately short of foreign exchange. The plan's prospects are summarized by Ta Huu Phuong and Guy Ta thus:

> The individual sector's targets of the Plan although seemingly within reasonable limits may not be achieved during the Plan period, possibly because of the transformation lag that is required when structural changes are introduced into the economy. Secondly, they may not be obtained for lack of funds that cannot presently be generated domestically.[26]

Significant in this regard are the shortfalls in the expected foreign aid. Thus far, the Soviet Union has come up with 2.6 billion and the Eastern European countries 700 million. Vietnam expected 600 million from China, which has since mid-1975 stopped any grants and from mid-

1976, any new loans to Vietnam. Besides, Vietnam's expectation of U.S. reconstruction aid, probably ranging between 1 to 3.2 billion, has failed to materialize. Thirdly, the drought (South Vietnam), floods (Central Vietnam),[27] and severe winter (North Vietnam),[28] during 1976–77 severely affected the food production, necessitating imports of over 1 million tons of grains during 1977 alone. Inadequate managerial performance and confusion over plans to collectivize agriculture in the South were additionally responsible for the agricultural shortfalls.[29] From June 1977, rice was rationed to a level matching the lowest point of supply in North Vietnam during the war.

Defense

The Second Five-Year Plan which was principally a development plan has discounted defense development. This probably implied the existence of an excellent state of defense preparedness and/or reliance on external military assistance in case a serious threat to the national security presented itself. Vietnam certainly expected a long period of peace after the liberation of Indochina in 1975, and it assumed that defense would no longer need the priority that it had during the previous three decades and thus allow the unfettered pursuit of economic goals of reconstruction and development. [As will be seen in subsequent sections of this article, such hopes were belied partly by domestic dissidence but more so by the military conflicts with its Communist neighbors: Cambodia and China. The prospect of continuing tension in the area is not very promising for the continued economic development of the much-battered country.]

Vietnam's successful march into Cambodia in a 17-day war that began during Christmas 1978 has confirmed the long-held view of military analysts of the high morale and efficiency of the Vietnamese military machine. (Its performance against the Chinese will be analyzed later in the chapter.) In 1975, before the fall of Saigon, the North Vietnamese forces were estimated by the U.S. Defense Department at 583,000,[30] the air and naval elements being responsible for 14,000 and the bulk belonging to the army. Estimates of the National Liberation Front (NLF) forces have varied by a wide margin; details of their integration into the reunified Vietnam's armed forces are sorely lacking. The figure given by the usually well-informed London-based International Institute of Strategic Studies (IISS) of 615,000 (army: 600,000) appears an underestimate by at least 100,000.[31] Additionally, there are about 70,000 frontier, coast security, and Peoples' Armed Security forces aside from Armed Militia of about 1.5 million.

The army is organized into 25 infantry divisions, plus 2 training divisions, 1 artillery division (10 regiments), 4 armored regiments,

15–20 independent infantry regiments, 35 artillery regiments, 40 AA artillery regiments, 20 SAM regiments (each with 18 SA-2 launchers), with one engineering command. The army's equipment was plentiful, varied, and substantial thanks to Russian supplies of heavy equipment, China's supplies of light weapons, and a rich assortment of U.S. hardware that fell into Communist hands in April 1975.[32] The IISS gives the details of equipment of the Vietnamese armed forces in 1978–79, as follows:

> 900 T-34, T-54 and T-59 med, PT 76, Type 60 1t tks; BTR-40/-50/-60 APC; 75-mm, 76-mm, 85-mm, 100-mm, 105-mm, 122-mm, 130-mm, 152-mm, 155-mm, guns/how; SU-76, ISU-122 SP guns; 82-mm, 100-mm, 107-mm, 120-mm, 160-mm mor; 107-mm, 122-mm, 140-mm RL; *Sagger* ATGW; 23-mm, 37-mm, 57-mm, 85-mm, 100-mm, 130-mm towed, ZSU-57-2 SP AA guns; SA-2/-3/-6/-7 SAM.[33]

The Air Force has 300 combat aircraft; one light-bomber squadron with 70 MiG-19/F-6, 70 MiG-21F/PF; eight fighter bomber squadrons with 120 MiG-17, 30 SU-7. Transports included 20 An-Z, 4 An-24, 12 Il-14, 4 Il-18, 23 Li-2 and 20 Mi-4, 10 Mi-6, and 9 Mi-8 helicopters. There are about 30 trainers including Yak-11/-18, MiG-15 UT 1/-21 U.[34]

In contrast, Cambodia (Kampuchea) and Laos have limited strength, though under the Pol Pot regime, Kampuchea had far more equipment per capita than Vietnam. Pol Pot's army was about 70,000, organized into four divisions and three independent infantry regiments and had AMX-13 H tanks; 10 BTR-152, 200 M-113 APC. Its weaponry estimated by IISS at 300 105-mm, 122-mm, 130-mm guns/howitzers; 107-mm, 120-mm mortars; 57-mm, 75-mm, 82-mm, 107-mm RCL, 40-mm AA guns, was augmented considerably during 1978 by heavy supplies from China.[35]

An extremely important factor in evaluating the military strength of any country is, apart from its manpower and equipment, the proven fighting performance, discipline, and morale of its troops. The Vietnamese score the highest points in all three categories, equaling the best anywhere in the world with a record of successive victories sometimes achieved ahead of schedule. In terms of the present armed strength of Vietnam, however, one has to keep in mind the actual deployment of about 100,000 of its armed forces in Cambodia and 40,000–50,000 in Laos. Further, Vietnam planned to divert substantial numbers of its armed personnel to peacetime reconstruction tasks. Recent military involvement in Cambodia and on its own northern borders with China will certainly lead to revision of such plans for use of the army in the country's economic development.

HISTORICAL HATREDS

Vietnam and China

Vietnam's ambition for a regional leadership through assistance to Communist movements and domination of governments could be attributed to reasons other than purely ideological. Its desire to create a strong, independent, center of power is partly a quest for enhanced security born of a traditional fear of Chinese domination of Vietnam. Historically, Vietnam has been a fiercely freedom-loving country and at the same time apprehensive of its northern neighbor's expansionism. Vietnam's several revolts during the thousand-odd-year Chinese rule extending over the first millenium (111 B.C.–A.D. 939); its successful overthrow of the Chinese rule again in the fifteenth century (1407–28); its readiness to sign an agreement to allow the return of the French only to get the Chinese occupation troops out in 1946; and its reluctant acceptance of the cease-fire along the 17th parallel in 1954 at Geneva thanks to Chinese insistance—these events all demonstrate Vietnam's intense distrust and suspicion of China, whether under imperial, nationalist, or Communist governments.

During the greater part of the three-decade-long struggle which ended in 1975, the Viet-Minh and later the DRV and the NLF had to maintain cordial relations with China because of the much needed military assistance. While no reliable figures of Chinese aid to North Vietnam exist—even official Chinese estimates varying from 14 to 21 billion dollars[36]—there is no doubt that the Chinese economic and military assistance was crucial for the Communist success in South Vietnam. Despite such dependence, Hanoi retained its political independence; it refused, for instance, to enter into a formal military alliance with China and politely declined to "invite" Chinese Volunteer Forces to aid the Vietnamese liberation movement. Until 1965, there was a greater commonality in Sino-Vietnamese thinking on strategy and tactics, the Vietnamese being more appreciative of the Chinese than of the Soviets because of the former's support to wars of national liberation. Also, the Chinese aid to Vietnam up to that time was far more, almost double that proffered by the Soviet Union. The situation changed, though, in early 1965 with the U.S. strategic bombing of North Vietnam and the latter's need of more sophisticated defense equipment including surface-to-air missiles (SAMs), which could be supplied only by the Soviet Union. Thus far, the North Vietnamese had relied more on guerrilla warfare and much less on mobile warfare to carry on the struggle in the South. In mid-1965, the North Vietnamese strategists judged the time had come to switch to mobile warfare and in some instances even to positional warfare. Such an advanced war strategy was not appreciated by the Chinese, who preferred a protracted warfare in which the Vietnamese would depend for indefinite periods of time on Chinese assistance in the form of small weapons. Lin Piao's celebrated doctrine of the "wars of national liberation" launched on September 3, 1965, emphasized a policy of self-reliance and less external military aid that was indirectly an exhortation to reduce dependence on the Soviet Union.

During the years of the Cultural Revolution, the Chinese authorities acted deliberately to impede the flow of Soviet military aid to North Vietnam. For example, the Soviet Union was asked to pay in U.S. dollars the freight for transporting armaments by Chinese railroad wagons, and their availability would be inordinately delayed. The Soviet Union had consequently to supply by sea both large and small weaponry, which included SAM, MiG aircraft, bombers, helicopters, antiaircraft batteries, a radar defense system, and all kinds of transport vehicles and heavy weapons during most of the war (1967–75). The annual Soviet military aid to North Vietnam soon surpassed the Chinese figure.

The more recent phase of Sino-Vietnamese differences began in 1971 with Sino-American moves toward a rapprochement. American efforts to end the Vietnam conflict by asking the Chinese to cease assisting the North Vietnamese, and subsequent Chinese emphasis on a struggle against revisionism rather than Western imperialism, were regarded by Hanoi as a Chinese game to subordinate Vietnamese interests to those of China. In 1954, at the Geneva Conference, the North Vietnamese had reluctantly agreed to the partition of their country at the instance of the Chinese as a part of the global Communist policy of peaceful coexistence. Now in the early 1970s the Vietnamese suspected that China did not want to see a strong, reunified Vietnam to emerge as a "potential competitor for influence in Southeast Asia."[37] Additionally, they found themselves on the opposite side of the Chinese in regard to the U.S. presence in Asia, which China regarded as a desirable counterbalance to Soviet ambitions in the area.[38]

Vietnam and Cambodia

On the other hand, Vietnam's Southeast Asian neighbors, notably Cambodia, have reason to suspect Hanoi's expansionism. Cambodians, the proud inheritors of a glorious legacy of empire once extending over the southern belt of mainland Southeast Asia, have historically hated the Vietnamese, who deprived them of the rich Mekong basin in the eighteenth century and then shared with Thailand the suzerainty over what was left of the Khmer Empire. Several conflicts with the Vietna-

mese, notably the often remembered guerrilla war of the 1840s reinforced the hostility. Cambodia is the only country in Asia whose
identity was saved as a result of Western imperialism—in the form of a
French protectorate established over it in 1867.[39] In 1954 at the Geneva
Conference, the Cambodian delegation openly expressed its fears and
suspicions of domination by the Viet-Minh, which had already occupied
portions of Cambodia in April 1954.[40] And recently taking advantage of
the unsettled conditions following the U.S. Vietnamese invasion of
their country in 1970, the Cambodians massacred thousands of Vietnamese civilians on the pretext that they were all Viet-Cong, and sent
their corpses floating down the Mekong to their home country. The
hostility is mutual. The South Vietnamese forces treated the country as
a "military playground, with any Cambodian fair game." To quote
William Showcross:

> South Vietnamese air force pilots, until then very lazy, actually paid
> bribes for the privilege of flying seven days a week over Cambodia.
> For weeks the 495th ARVN battalion rampaged around Takeo Pro-
> vince and according to one CIA report from Phnom Penh, its com-
> mander, Captain Le Van Vien, constantly called in airstrikes to drive
> the people from their villages. His men would then seize the livestock
> and force the villagers to buy it back.[41]

Suspicions of Vietnamese were not limited to non-Communists or
anti-Communists. As early as 1930, the Vietnamese Communists had
betrayed their "imperialistic" ambitions. In January of that year, Ho Chi
Minh succeeded in uniting the three Communist parties of Vietnam
into the Communist Party of Vietnam. Later in October, the party was
renamed the Indochinese Communist Party (ICP) to include Cambodia
and Laos, probably to suit comintern convenience of threating all of
Indochina as a national section of the Communist International.[42] Until
1951, when the ICP technically divided itself into three national parties
for the practical reason of organizing better resistance against the
French, there was no separate Cambodian Communist Party as such.
The ICP early advocated a federation of Vietnam, Cambodia, and Laos
after the liquidation of French rule, although subsequently the ICP did
pass resolutions providing for each nation's right to join such a federation. Nevertheless, the Cambodian Communists never abandoned their
fear that Vietnam would, by virtue of its size, numbers, educated
manpower, economic and military strength, some day compel Cambodia
and Laos into such a composite polity under Vietnamese domination.

Differences between Khmer Rouge and Vietnamese Communists
originated in 1954 at the Geneva Conference on Indochina. There,
presumably under the pressure of Moscow and Peking, which were

eager to arrive at a settlement as part of their global policy of peaceful coexistence, the North Vietnamese did not press the cause of Khmer Rouge, but instead agreed that it be disbanded and that its cadres retreat to Hanoi. The Khmer Rouge never forgot or forgave the Vietnamese Communists for this "betrayal," which in effect made of the Cambodian Communist movement something "dissolving into the air."[43] About 5,000 of the Khmer Rouge, to be conveniently labeled "Hanoi-Khmers," withdrew to North Vietnam; the small band of the radicals that stayed behind, styled "Khmer Viet-Minh," were reinforced by individuals like Ieng Sary, Khieu Samphan, Hou Yuon, Hu Nim, and Saloth Sar (later known as Pol Pot).[44] They had been trained in France, mostly in law or economics—and not by ICP—and they organized and fought in the maquis against Sihanouk's government in the late 1960s.[45] They were all fiercely anti-Hanoi because of the latter's friendship with Sihanouk, who had used force to all but eliminate the Khmer Rouge in the late 1950s. The North Vietnamese were quite contented with Sihanouk's cooperation in allowing the flow of men and materiel along the Ho Chi Minh Trail across Eastern Cambodia and from the port of Sihanoukville (Kompong Som) into South Vietnam and, most importantly, in permitting the establishment of extensive, secret base camps inside the Cambodian border for the Vietnamese National Liberation front. By 1969, there were an estimated 40,000–50,000 North Vietnamese and NLF troops in the Cambodian sanctuaries.

This was, indeed, not the first time that a Communist state for tactical reasons and, even more so, for its own national interest, sought and received assistance from a non-Communist government at the expense of a "fraternal" Communist party. The Khmer Rouge have, however, alleged a diabolical plot on Hanoi's part in deliberately weakening the former so as to eventually bring Cambodia under its own control as a part of a projected Indochinese federation. In a rewriting of the history of their party, a favorite communist sport, the Khmer Rouge have gone so far as to disassociate themselves completely from the Vietnamese, claiming the birth of the Cambodian Communist Party ocurred in 1960 instead of the actual date, 1951, when the ICP had been split and separate national parties were created.

It was, therefore, only natural that the Khmer Rouge distrust of the North Vietnamese would continue even after a tactical alliance between the four regional communist groupings of Pathet Lao, Lao Dong, NLF, and Khmer Rouge was established soon after Sihanouk's overthrow in early 1970. Significantly, the Khmer Rouge's immediate goal was "not to marshal military strength for an assault on the presumed common enemy in Pnompenh, but to secure undivided, if hidden, control of the coalition."[46] Indeed, Hanoi needed the Khmer Rouge's cooperation in keeping the supply lines to South Vietnam open by harassing the forces of Lon Nol, the United States and South Vietnam in eastern Cambodia. The tension between Cambodia and Vietnamese Communists was such that the former insisted on having an upper hand in the operations and that without Vietnamese manpower assistance. On the other hand, even as the North Vietnamese were contributing substantially to the growth and training of the Khmer Rouge during the early 1970s, they did not want the latter to develop independence and the ability to frustrate the long-term North Vietnamese ambitions to dominate all of Indochina. In order to ensure a pro-Vietnamese position, the North Vietnamese sent about 6,000 Khmer Rouge kept in reserve by them in Hanoi ever since their withdrawal from Cambodia in 1954. These "Hanoi-Khmers," as they came to be called, clashed with the homegrown Khmer Rouge under the leadership of Pol Pot and Khieu Samphan. In 1973, many Hanoi Khmers were purged or killed by the Pol Pot group.[47]

By 1972, the Khmer Rouge numbered well over 50,000, and were mostly young Cambodians, not necessarily Communist, with varying grievances against the U.S.-backed Lon Nol regime. There evidence of superior training, discipline, fighting power, and ability to handle Chinese, Soviet and American weapons supplied to them by the North Vietnamese, was noted in the successive skirmishes with Lon Nol's troops but also in the successful maintenance of the supply lines to South Vietnam. In early 1973, the Khmer Rouge were confirmed in their suspicions of the North Vietnamese when the latter repeatedly pressured them to accept a cease-fire that was presumably the precondition for American grant of reconstruction aid to Hanoi. Henry Kissinger was no better informed than most of the mortals who believed that the Khmer Rough was Hanoi's puppet, which could be made to dance to its master's will. Despite Hanoi's cutting off of military assistance and the U.S. saturated bombardment, the Khmer Rouge continued the offensive that brought the downfall of the Lon Nol regime, a full fortnight before Hanoi's victorious march into Saigon.

The Khmer Rouge would not easily forget the North Vietnamese subordination of Cambodian interest to their own in 1973, in a repetition of their previous experience of 1954. Equally, they would not forget the timely, massive military assistance they received from Peking starting in mid-1974. The Chinese leaders had attempted unsuccessfully to encourage an American dialogue with Prince Sihanouk, who since his ouster in 1970 had been in exile in Peking. Finally, they threw in their lot with the Khmer Rouge, and in place of the North Vietna-

mese became the principal suppliers of automatic weapons, ammuni-
tion, and mines. This equipment was used in the final siege of Pnompenh and its capitulation, achieved partly through mining the waterway
and cutting off the capital's food supply.

Tension between the Cambodian and Vietnamese Communists
continued after the overthrow of the Lon Nol regime in March 1975. In
addition, the Cambodian government remained divided at least into
four factions, one of which was certainly—though clandestinely—
linked with Hanoi, while yet another advocated rapprochement with
Vietnam on pragmatic grounds. The government was a coalition, the
core of which consisted of the Khmer Viet-Minh and the student groups
which had produced leaders like Pol Pot, Ieng Sary, and Khieu Samphan. They allied with moderates, led by Prince Sihanouk and other
non-Communists, who were intensely nationalistic, suspicious of Vietnamese expansionism, pro-Peking, in agreement with Teng Hsiao-
ping's analysis of international affairs and, therefore, in advocacy of
rapprochement with the United States. Except for the last point, the
core group agreed with the moderates in their international attitudes.
Foremost in their links with Vietnamese Communists were obviously
the Khmer-Hanois, the ICP group led by Chea Sim, the present
minister for the interior who was strongly suspected and even detested
by the core group. Last was a smaller group who styled themselves the
constructionists and advocated for pragmatic reasons accommodation
with Vietnam. Its leader, Heng Samarin, now president of the new
Cambodian government, became the clandestine conduit of top secret
decisions of the Pnompenh government to his allies in Hanoi.[48]

The leadership of the 1975 revolution has told the world through
Premier Pol Pot's five-hour speech in September 1977 that Hanoi all
along had harbored plans to compel Cambodia into an Indochinese
federation as the first step toward its annexation.[49] The Pol Pot regime
was certainly justified in attempting every means to avert Cambodia's
conversion to a Vietnamese satellite. But it should have been realistic
enough to appreciate the immensely superior Vietnamese military
machine and should have, therefore, acted in such a way both domestically and internationally as not to give an excuse for the alleged
Vietnamese expansionism to succeed. As it was, Cambodia launched the
most brutal, insensate, domestic programs (which could be spelled
"pogroms") which had the effect of dislocating, decimating, and
alienating the bulk of the population to the shock and dismay of the
entire civilized world. It is not my purpose to go into the controversial
aspects of those policies,[50] though they continue to have some relevance
for the present-day security problems facing the new Cambodian
government and its Vietnamese overlords. Suffice it to say that the Pol

Pot regime made any aggression by an external power to terminate the horrible condition prevalent in the pre-1979 Cambodia look less culpable than otherwise. Further, it did create a large exodus of Khmer people into Vietnamese sanctuaries in Eastern Cambodia and inside Vietnamese borders where they could be organized by the Vietnamese into an alternative rallying point for overthrowing the anti-Hanoi Pol Pot regime. And internationally, instead of playing the Vietnamese against the Chinese so as to maximize their own diplomatic maneuverability, the Cambodian government chose to adopt adventurist policies which were certain to provoke Vietnam to an eventual showdown. First, they took the initiative to attact the border provinces, beginning in April 1977, and particularly the new economic zone in Tay Ninh with a view to bring pressure on the Vietnamese to vacate the sanctuaries inside Cambodia. And secondly, they allied themselves with Vietnam's enemy, China, and invited several thousand Chinese military and technical personnel in what Vietnam called a bid to encircle it. Such policies, internal and international, could ensure neither Cambodia's domestic stability nor reduce its vulnerability to Vietnamese aggression. The Vietnamese march into Cambodia at the back of the newly born Kampuchea United Front for National Salvation occurred at a time when Vietnam could not have chosen to do so but for the Pol Pot government's ill-conceived and compelling tactics.

Cambodia-Vietnam Conflict: The Issues

The new leadership of Cambodia felt that its fears of Vietnamese expansionism had been confirmed by the Vietnamese refusal to quit the sanctuaries on Cambodian soil allowed them by Prince Sihanouk since the mid-1960s. In addition, within two weeks of the Communist victory in Saigon, the new government opened an old sore between the two countries by claiming some islands in the Gulf of Thailand. That led to the first clash between the two Communist governments and although Hanoi recognized Pnompenh's claim to Poulo Wai, the Vietnamese questioned at the May 1976 bilateral meetings the entire maritime boundary with Cambodia that had been settled by the Brevie Line in 1939 during the French rule. The incident helped to strengthen the Cambodian government's apprehensions of Vietnamese expansionist aims. An attempted coup in September 1976, sparked in all likelihood by the government's domestic policy excesses, was alleged to be a Vietnamese plot to overthrow the government through Khmer-Hanoi army units.[51] The Pol Pot regime took advantage of the situation to liquidate the remnant of the Hanoi-Khmers, which included five members of the 20-member party central committee. The regime's attitude toward

Vietnam hardened. The Pnompenh government refused to hold talks with Vietnam until the latter completely moved out of all territories claimed by Cambodia.

Thereafter, the Cambodians obviously decided that offense was the best form of defense, an attitude in which they did not initially receive the full support of their Chinese allies. Beginning in January 1977, and escalating their activity between April and September, 1977, Cambodian forces moved not only into the sanctuaries but also several miles into the Vietnamese province of Tay Ninh, where a NEZ for relocation of Saigon population was being established. The attack would achieve the multiple purpose of weakening Vietnam's economy, keeping military pressure on Vietnam so as to secure the complete evacuation from the sanctuaries, and frustrating an alleged Vietnamese plan to integrate Cambodia into a Vietnamese-dominated Indochinese federation.

If the Vietnamese indeed had any such plans, they were not in a hurry to implement them because of their preoccupation with problems of economy and domestic dissidence. Their policy of conciliation with Thailand since 1977 and their apparent readiness to endorse the ASEAN concept of a neutral zone in Southeast Asia free of any big-power influence are indicative of their desire to demonstrate even to their non-Communist neighbors that Vietnam sought peace and had no plans of military intervention in other states at least for several years.

If Vietnam wanted to live within its self-imposed constraints, China and Cambodia seemed determined not to allow it that kind of luxury. Since the conclusion of the Vietnam war, China had emphasized in its relations with Southeast Asian nations that the Soviet Union represented the "present strategic danger to Southeast Asia,"[52] and cautioned them to beware of "the tiger at the back door while repelling the wolf through the front door."[53] Therefore, as noted elsewhere in this article, China began to exert pressure on Vietnam from mid-1975 to condemn Soviet hegemonism, by holding back further economic aid and building up Cambodian military strength. Thus, between 1975 and 1978, China supplied Cambodia with 130-mm mortars, 107-mm bazookas, automatic rifles, transport vehicles, gasoline and various small weapons, enough to equip 30–40 regiments totaling about 200,000 persons.[54] There is no way of knowing how much economic assistance was additionally provided beyond the initial gift of $1 billion made at the time of Sihanouk's return to Pnompenh. An estimated 10,000 Chinese military and technical personnel were sent to Cambodia to improve the latter's military preparedness, which in the political circumstances then could have been directed only against Vietnam; for China had bent over backward in the postwar period to become friendly with Thailand, the only other neighboring country that could be a threat to Cambodian security. As noted elsewhere, Vietnam has alleged that such Sino-Cambodian measures were designed to destroy Vietnamese economy and encircle that country militarily.

An all-out war with Cambodia was not suited to Vietnam at that point for several additional reasons. Apart from the diplomatic damage it would cause by destroying the new self-image of sweet reasonableness Vietnam was attempting to create among its Southeast Asian neighbors, a belligerent act of those dimensions would certainly frustrate efforts to secure economic aid from other countries, particularly the United States. Secondly, in the absence of a militarily strong Cambodian movement in opposition to the Pol Pot regime, sizable Vietnamese forces would be locked up in direct combat with the Cambodian army, supported by China. Vietnam did not want a "Vietnam" on its hands in the form of a protracted guerrilla warfare in Cambodia. The Vietnamese leadership, therefore, attempted to negotiate with the Cambodians, directly and indirectly through the Chinese governments, but to no avail. They then resorted to large-scale fighting for three months beginning in October 1977, with the limited purpose of securing a Khmer-Vietnamese border treaty. Vietnam thus proposed in January 1978 that both sides withdraw their troops to five miles from the existing border and submit themselves to an internationally supervised truce commission. In May 1978, Cambodia agreed to peace talks that would begin in 1979 after Vietnam had demonstrated its genuine desire not to integrate Cambodia into an Indochinese federation under Vietnamese control. However, much had happened in early 1978 to cause Vietnam doubt of the genuineness of Cambodia's offer, particularly because of the internationalization of the conflict, brought about by Peking's overt and firm commitment to Pnompenh and the general deterioration in Sino-Vietnamese relations.

VIETNAM-CHINA DISPUTE

With the end of the war in South Vietnam, it was only a matter of time before the two halves of the country would unite to make one state. China was certainly not happy over the prospect of the emergence of a strong state on its southern borders. It would certainly not be a spectator to Hanoi's suspected ambitions to dominate Laos and Cambodia and lend assistance to fraternal communist parties all over Southeast Asia, traditionally an area of China's political influence. In order that Vietnam itself assume the historical role of China's vassal state, the Peking leaders insisted that Hanoi join them in condemning the Soviet Union of hegemonism. Thus, in October 1975, when Le

Duan, secretary general of the Vietnamese Lao Dong Party, visited China to seek economic aid for reconstruction, the latter made any further aid conditional on Vietnam condemning Soviet hegemonism. Consequent to Le Duan's refusal to do so, there was no joint communique nor a customary Vietnamese return banquet and no further grants-in-aid from China to Vietnam.[55]

Vietnam alleged that China thereafter attempted to contain it by organizing a coalition of the United States, Thailand, Cambodia, and itself as a "counterweight" to Vietnamese influence on mainland Southeast Asia.[56] Until late 1977, China continued to apply pressure on Vietnam in an effort to obtain the latter's loyalties in its conflict with the Soviet Union. That interregnum witnessed the steady deterioration of Sino-Vietnamese relations apparently because of three specific issues: the offshore islands, Vietnamese of Chinese ethnic origin, and border claims. The real issues were political, centering around the question of political hegemony in the short run, over Indochina and eventually over all of Southeast Asia.

The Islands Issue

No sooner had the PRG assumed authority in Saigon and attempted to occupy the offshore Spratly Islands, then it came into conflict with the People's Republic of China. The Spratly and Paracel Islands had been the subject of disputed claims between China and Vietnam in the nineteenth century. Apart from their strategic location in the South China Sea on the maritime artery between the Indian Ocean and the Western Pacific, these uninhabited islands suddenly became valuable in the early 1970s in the eyes of China, the Philippines (only the Spratly group),[57] and South Vietnam because of some preliminary geological surveys indicating rich oil deposits.[58] When the South Vietnamese government officially incorporated the Spratly islands through a special decree in September 1973 and China contested its claim,[59] the DRV and the NLF had maintained silence although Hanoi had previously expressed territorial claims on the archipelago.[60] Peking took naval and air action in January 1974 to occupy, interestingly enough, only the Paracel Islands which are closer to Chinese naval bases, not the Spratlys 550 miles further south. The Chinese short-range missile firing boats based on the naval base of Yulin on the Hainan islands showed a clear superiority over South Vietnam's coast guard cutters, destroyer escorts, and patrol boats in the engagements of January 19–20, 1974. The Spratlys were, in any case, beyond the range of Chinese air support, which could be why the Chinese took no action to prevent South Vietnamese occupation of those islands. Peking's occupation of the Paracel group was important also because of the presence of a Chinese naval complex and sophisticated radar facilities on one of the islands since 1971.[61]

Both groups of islands—the Spratlys and the Paracels—continue to be an issue between Hanoi and Peking. After the fall of Saigon, the PRG proceeded to occupy the Spratly islands, which are closer to its borders and only 280 miles northeast of the Cam Ranh Bay. Vietnam's interests in the Spratlys are both strategic and economic; this country is eager to continue the offshore oil exploration begun under the previous government and for which the present government is seeking American, Norwegian, and Indian financial and technical assistance. There is no doubt that the islands' worth is crucial to Vietnam's economic future and its plans for self-reliance in oil. Since 1975, however, Hanoi's efforts to negotiate the future of the islands with Peking have proved fruitless largely because of the latter's refusal even to answer Vietnamese communications on the subject,[62] which as of now is left for China to reopen at its convenience.

Though the Sino-Vietnamese relations continued to be cool, outwardly they could only be interpreted as correct. Perhaps Peking expected its coolness toward Hanoi to sway the latter toward its side and against the Soviet Union. Its action in September 1975 of withholding outright grants to Vietnam was followed two years later by its decision not to make any loans either. The Vietnamese gently pointed out that the late premier Chou En-lai had made a commitment in June 1973 to continue economic and military aid at the then existing level for five years. The Chinese explained that a prior "agreement between Chou En-lai and Ho Chi Minh called for termination of aid after the Vietnamese war ended."[63] China did not make an exception even on humanitarian grounds. Thus, when Vietnam was hit by severe food shortages during 1976-77 because of adverse weather conditions, China did not choose to alleviate human misery by sending food grains across its southern borders. In contrast, the Soviet Union supplied 450,000 of the 1.6 million tons of food rushed to the country.

The factor that eventually led to an open rift between Vietnam and China was the former's role vis-à-vis Cambodia. Hanoi's refusal to take sides in the Sino-Soviet conflict could at best be taken as a sign of timidity in not wanting involvement in the big-power conflict. It could even be a mark of gratitude to both the powers for the economic and military largesse over the previous two decades. But Hanoi's military action during September–December 1977 well inside the Cambodian borders, whether it was a punitive or expansionist action, was inexcusable in Peking's eyes and could only be construed as a direct blow to China's prestige insofar as the latter's revolutionary role in contrast with Russia's in Cambodia since 1970 was well-known. In December 1977, the Chinese leadership decided, possibly with some split opinion, to give open support to Cambodia. Peking dispatched Teng Ying-chao, a Central Committee member and widow of Premier Chou En-lai, to Pnompenh in January, 1978 to show solidarity with the Pol Pot regime. Additionally, China made large-scale arms shipments, which included long-range 130-mm and 150-mm artillery, to Cambodia in early 1978 even after the Vietnamese forces had completely pulled back from Cambodian soil. Hanoi's intelligence sources indicated Chinese resolve at this point to support Cambodia in what Peking expected and perhaps hoped would be a protracted war.[64]

The Ethnic Chinese Problem

What seemed at that time a separate matter was Peking's decision to open a united front of overseas Chinese to drum up support for itself vis-à-vis Taipei. In this regard it will perhaps never be known if Peking's new policy of open support to Cambodia precipitated Hanoi's resolve to end the special status of ethnic Chinese in the spring of 1978. The links between the Chinese overall policy in regard to the overseas Chinese, Vietnamese policy toward its ethnic Chinese, and China's declared support to Cambodia against Vietnam are none too clear. What was evident for everyone to see in the spring of 1978 was the deterioration of Sino-Vietnamese relations marked by exchanges of abusive language in the stepped-up propaganda offensive in China and Vietnam directed against one another.

The overseas Chinese in South Vietnam were as much hated by the local people as they were elsewhere in Southeast Asia because of their superior economic standing. After the Communist victory in Saigon, the large Chinese population here, which was noted for its industry and wealth, received special attention from the new government. The community's cooperation was vital for keeping the economy going until the government gradually moved to eliminate the private sector. By 1977, such cooperation was badly needed. The Vietnamese Chinese were then grouped together with intellectuals, devout Buddhists and Catholics as potential opposition to the spread of socialism. Although the Vietnamese Chinese were not specifically singled out as capitalist opponents of the new government, the frequent characterization of the areas in which the Chinese predominantly lived as the cesspool of black-marketing and corruption was an indirect condemnation of the community. In the campaign for ideological certification of the "misfits," the Chinese were progressively moved to the New Economic Zones in the countryside, which included the border province of Tay Ninh. There, the Chinese would serve additionally as a buffer between the Vietnamese and the Cambodians.

In March 1978, the Vietnamese government came down most openly against the Chinese community. In a bid to carry out rapid socialization of the economy, the government raided the Cholon area of the twin city of Saigon, where the Chinese lived, and ordered their assets frozen. Of note was a change in the Vietnamese official reclassification of the Vietnamese Chinese in May 1978 as an ethnic minority abolishing the special-category status the Chinese had enjoyed thus far. The change was to indicate the government's firm resolve to integrate the Chinese community along with other ethnic minorities in the national community. The Chinese community was thus faced with choosing one of two unpleasant alternatives: "either accept the burdens of Vietnamese citizenship or suffer the handicaps of alien status."[65] The large-scale hardship and discontent the new policy caused to the Chinese led to a hue and cry, and many of them—the estimate is about 100,000—fled the country. A puzzling point of this exodus was that a substantial number of Chinese from North Vietnam also crossed the land border into China, which indicates that the causes for this feeling of insecurity were probably political and had permeated the Chinese community throughout Vietnam.

It is doubtful if the Chinese government was genuinely concerned over the plight of the overseas Chinese in Indochina. To be sure, China had all along maintained its interest in the overseas Chinese but never enough to go to war with any country in Southeast Asia. As for South Vietnam, China had specifically protested against the South Vietnamese government's legislation in 1955 compelling the Chinese community to accept the Vietnamese citizenship. In 1965, North Vietnam agreed with China to settle the question in consultation with each other after the "liberation" of South Vietnam. In practice, the Chinese government had done little to protect the overseas Chinese, whether in Indonesia during the second half of the sixties or in Cambodia both before and after the Communist takeover. It could further have been assumed that the persecution of the Vietnamese would not ordinarily move Peking. Of the 1.5 million Vietnamese Chinese, 90 percent lived in the south, and had amassed fortunes even through exploiting the prolonged situation created by the second Indochina war and were generally supportive of the capitalist way of life. The indignation of the Chinese government over the racially discriminatory treatment to Vietnamese Chinese can be explained only in political terms as an attempt to find an additional excuse to attack Vietnam. This is reinforced by the halfhearted manner in which China tried to evacuate the Vietnamese Chinese. Thus in June 1978, China sent two ships—

Minghua and Changli—to Saigon and Haiphong to evacuate the Chinese. The two ships remained off the coast during the six weeks of fruitless negotiations with Vietnamese officials over an acceptable evacuation procedure. Meanwhile, the Chinese authorities would accept across the land borders only those refugees who could produce exit visas issued by the Vietnamese government as well as repatriation certificates from the Chinese embassy in Hanoi. Such strict adherence to documentation once again demonstrated that the Chinese government's concern for the Vietnamese Chinese was not genuine.

By the opening of the monsoon season of 1978, Sino-Vietnamese relations had sunk to such a precipitous low that armed action between these countries could not be ruled out once the fair weather opened in October. At the same time, Chinese military assistance to Cambodia was mounting so rapidly as to make Hanoi contemplate a quick military action to liquidate the Pol Pot regime and install one subservient to its wishes. In a series of diplomatic actions, Vietnam moved decidedly closer to the Soviet Union to bolster its own security against China in case the latter attacked its northern borders to coincide with Vietnamese action in Cambodia. On June 29, 1978, Vietnam joined the Moscow-dominated Council for Mutual Economic Assistance, COMECON, the Communist equivalent of the Common Market and, in October, signed with Moscow a full-fledged treaty of friendship and mutual cooperation.

China retaliated against the first of these actions by formally terminating on July 3, 1978, all of its economic, military and technical assistance to Vietnam and ordering the Chinese personnel there to head home.[66] In the previous month, Vietnam had rejected Chinese requests to open consular offices in Saigon, Da Nang and Haiphong, while the Chinese government asked Vietnam, in a reciprocal action, to close its consular establishments in Canton, Nanning, and Kunming.[67] Not coincidentally, the Chinese floated a deliberately false rumor which attained worldwide circulation that the Soviet Union had secured from Vietnam the former U.S. base in the Cam Ranh Bay and was planning to build a missile base there. A commentary in the *People's Daily* elaborated on the alleged grand strategy of the Soviet Union:

> Indochina lies midway between the Indian and the Pacific Oceans. From its foothold in Indochina, the Soviet Union may pass the Straits of Malacca and reach the Red Sea and the Horn of Africa by way of the Indian Ocean; it may also gain access to the Pacific and Oceania. The Soviet Union will thus be able not only to control the important oil transport lines leading to West Europe, the United States and Japan, *but also to form an arc of strategic encirclement*. For all their efforts to find an outlet to the sea and gain access to the Indian Ocean, the old

Tsars succeeded only briefly during the Russo-Japanese war in bringing their warships to anchor in the Cam Rahn Bay, but the new Tsars in the Kremlin have moved far more ambitious.[68] Peking also alleged that the Soviet Union and Vietnam had a three-part plan to "encircle" China: first, by removing the Vietnamese Chinese from positions of authority; second, by compelling Laos and Cambodia through military threats into an Indochinese Federation nominally under Vietnamese control but in fact under Soviet domination; and last, by implementing the Brezhnev Plan for an Asian security system, which would bring all of Southeast Asia into the Soviet sphere of influence.[69] China accused Vietnam of being the "Cuba of Asia," a satellite of the Soviet Union helping the latter to achieve its strategic aims in Asia.

THE SOVIET UNION AND SOUTHEAST ASIA

Towards the end of 1978, the only party that stood to gain from major conflicts in Indochina was the Soviet Union. From the evidence presently available, it would seem that the Soviet Union deliberately precipitated the Vietnamese military actions against Cambodia, which in turn made the Chinese invasion of Vietnam "inevitable." Particularly disturbing to the Soviet Union was the growing Sino-American friendship subsequent to the announced normalization of relations between the two countries. Moscow's actions in the second half of 1978 to draw Vietnam closer to the Soviet Union politically, economically, and militarily should be seen in the context of its dual policy to weaken the Sino-American friendship and frustrate Chinese ability to augment its influence in Southeast Asia. The Soviet policy was in fact a continuation of its decade-long, diplomatic offensive to win all the countries of South and Southeast Asia to its side or at least wean them away from Peking. Such efforts were supplemented by an increasing military activity, particulary in the Indian Ocean, though decidedly in a low key.

The steadily increasing diplomatic and naval activity of the Soviet Union in South and Southeast Asia since 1968 in the context of American withdrawal from the region and the growing Sino-American friendship has been noted elsewhere in this volume. Traditionally, Southeast Asia has never figured importantly in the Russian ambitions for exercise of power. Yet, the Soviet Union being partly an Asian country cannot countenance exclusive domination of any other major power, particularly China, over the whole region. Additionally, Moscow has regarded it most important not to allow its ideological rival, Peking, the "status and prestige of the standard-bearer and protector of the ranks of revolution not only in Southeast Asia but throughout the world."[70]

However, the Soviet Union was and is far from being eager to become the "policeman" of Asia, an ambition any power geographically distant from the region should be able to desist after the glaring failure of the United States. Even during the Vietnam conflict, the Soviet Union grudged the heavy costs of assisting North Vietnam and the NLF in the form of war materials and sophisticated equipment. The Soviets were also far from happy over the Vietnamese situation impinging upon the progress of their talks with the United States, which were on a wide range of topics aimed at a détente. Moscow was, therefore, most interested in pushing Brezhnev's "system of collective security for Asia,"[71] first propounded in 1968 just a month before the Nixon Doctrine. Initially, the Brezhnev Plan aimed at some kind of a military alliance system in which the resources could be found locally and supplemented by the Soviet Union. No Southeast Asian nation, including North Vietnam, hurried to join the proposed system because they did not want to gang up against China,[72] although Moscow denied its plan sought "to contain the PRC and eliminate the Western presence east of Suez."[73]

It seems that the long-term interests of the superpowers, both of them geographically distant from the Southeast Asian region, would lie in denying all major powers including themselves and China an opportunity to dominate the area and to achieve such a goal through promotion of a regional balance of power. In the short run, however, the Sino-U.S. rapprochement, the almost complete withdrawal of American forces from Southeast Asia and the Sino-Soviet race to win the allegiance of the new Communist regimes in Indochina have been compelling factors in the acceleration of Soviet involvement in the region.[74] Russia had no leverage with the Pol Pot regime because of Moscow's recognition of the Lon Nol regime up to its downfall in April 1975. In Vietnam and Laos, it was a different story. As noted earlier, the Vietnamese leaders were forced by China to make a choice between Moscow and Peking in October 1975, when the general secretary of the Vietnamese Communist Party, Le Duan, was asked during his visit to China to condemn Soviet hegemonism and refused. Then, as noted elsewhere, China stopped any further aid to Vietnam, while Russia came forward generously to support the Vietnamese dependence on the Russians was thereby even more enhanced because they were already fully dependent upon Moscow for the supply of heavy, sophisticated, military hardware.

During 1978, Moscow apparently persuaded the Hanoi leadership to think that a continuing state of tension between a Chinese-backed Cambodia and Vietnam would constitute a festering economic sore for Vietnam. Already heavily dependent on the Soviet Union, Vietnam in

1978-79 was in dire need of food assistance amounting to 4.3 million tons because of successive crop failures. It was this desperate economic situation that made Vietnam finally succumb to Soviet pressures to join the Council on Mutual Economic Assistance (COMECON), the pro-Soviet communist Common Market, in June 1978. After the U.S. announcement of normalization of relations with China, the Soviet Union stepped up its pressure on Vietnam for a formal military alliance against China. There is reason to believe that "an open anti-Chinese alliance was the price Moscow demanded for bailing Vietnam out of its economic crisis."[75] The 25-year Russo-Vietnamese Treaty of Friendship and Mutual Assistance signed on November 3, 1978—barely six weeks before the Vietnamese march into Cambodia—was clearly aimed at China. This is clear from article 6 of the treaty:

> In case either party is attacked or threatened with attack, the two parties to the treaty shall immediately consult each other with a view to eliminating that threat, and shall take appropriate and effective measures . . ."[76]

The treaty, indeed marked a high point of Moscow's diplomatic success in Indochina.

RECENT WARFARE IN INDOCHINA

In retrospect, it seems clear that having armed itself with a treaty with the Soviet Union, Vietnam was preparing for a brisk war aimed at toppling the Pol Pot regime and installing one favorable to itself. Its propaganda against the Pol Pot regime's excesses was augmented both to arouse international opinion and to win the sympathies of the population inside Cambodia. Secondly, in order to make the planned march into Cambodia politically palatable to the world, Vietnam helped the birth of the 14-member committee called the Kampuchean United Front for National Salvation (KUFNS), which was under the leadership of the dissident pro-Hanoi Khmer Communists like Heng Samarin and Chea Sim, but which included some exiled Cambodian intellectuals and monks. An important element in the new front would be the support of Khmer Krom, the Cambodian minority of more than one-half million people resident in Cochin-China. Parenthetically, if that minority moved out of Vietnam, it would partly alleviate the food shortages in the country.

Unlike the NLF, the KUFNS did not command large-scale popular support because of its Vietnamese patrons. It was clearly a Vietnamese smoke screen created on the eve of the Vietnamese invasion to legitimize it in the eyes of the world. The success of the 17-day Vietnamese "blitzkrieg" on Cambodia beginning Christmas Day, 1978, owed little to KUFNS or its few supporters inside Cambodia. If the new Cambodian government has not met serious opposition in most of Cambodia, it is because of the public relief over the extinction of the oppressive Pol Pot regime with its vexations of regimented life, communal kitchens, broken families, and hard, unending labor, not because of any enthusiasm for KUFNS. The lack of resistance (except in Western Cambodia) also significantly owes to the presence of an estimated 100,000 Vietnamese occupation troops who are not likely to brook any measures to crush a serious public opposition. On the other hand, the continued presence of Vietnamese troops on Cambodian soil will, in time, arouse the fiercest animosities among Cambodians against the Vietnamese-backed government.

China, indeed, expects a long-drawn-out peoples' war in Cambodia between the Pol Pot faction supplied by Peking and the new Cambodian government nominally under Heng Samarin but in fact controlled by Vietnam. There is no doubt that the new government's existence will continue to be precarious and vulnerable to popular resistance as long as it is supported by the hated Vietnamese. An alliance of core Khmer Rouge, Sihanouk moderates and Khmer Serei is already in force in the pockets of territory held by the Khmer Rouge, particularly in the western provinces of Battambang and Siem Reap. An airstrip built in Siem Reap is capable of receiving large transport planes and is therefore a likely facility for continued air shipments from China. The latter has also claimed that Thailand has been cooperating in the passage of Chinese assistance across its territory. Such a conduit has obviously disappeared with Laos' fully coming under Vietnamese domination and the request to Chinese personnel of all types that they return to China. There is indeed some possibility that the Khmer Rouge guerrillas are receiving Chinese supplies that are being smuggled along the 450-mile Cambodian coastline. The Pol Pot loyalists are, ironically enough, receiving the support of the Khmer Serei, who had been pushed either across the Thai border or into the hideouts of the Cardamom mountains by the Khmer Rouge in 1975. The Khmer Serei's hatred of the military occupation of their motherland by the ancient enemy, Vietnam, far surpasses their antipathy toward the Khmer Rouge. Even so, it is doubtful if the antigovernment resistance can achieve its aim of overthrowing the Vietnam-backed government in a short time, a realization that may have been responsible for the precipitate Chinese invasion of Vietnam in February 1979.

CONCLUSION

The two wars at the turn of 1978 in Indochina have made that portion of Asia once more an area of instability and insecurity. There have been several losers—all three Indochinese states and China—while the Soviet Union, a nonregional nation has benefited, though indirectly, in augmenting its influence in the region. Cambodia was the greatest loser of all, as its political independence and integrity have been badly compromised and its domestic disorder enhanced by a new civil war in which the two sides are supported by China and Vietnam. Neighboring Laos has finally and fully moved into the Vietnamese orbit, while Vietnam and China themselves have lost on several grounds. Vietnam's military and political domination over the rest of Indochina has been achieved at tremendous costs to its own security and stability. Its five-year plan (1976–80) has practically been scrapped as the government has set new priorities in defense outlay and postponed the development of the new economic zone as well as resettlement plans for the population of the northern, mountainous, border provinces. The country's military and diplomatic dependence on the Soviet Union and Eastern European countries has become as complete as its isolation from the rest of the Third World. Moreover, its chances of getting developmental assistance from the United States, Western Europe, and Japan have practically disappeared. Additionally, Hanoi's new stance has drastically diminished its credibility among ASEAN states as a nation committed to carving a zone of peace in Southeast Asia. Finally, Vietnam's control and domination over Laos and Cambodia will depend on its ties with the Soviet Union, and this dilutes the hard-earned independence of Hanoi itself to make it Moscow's agent for acquisition of power and influence in Southeast Asia and for the containment of China.

If Vietnam's victory was pyrrhic in a variety of senses, the Peoples Republic of China cannot even have that type of satisfaction. The month-long border hostilities have not established China's clear military superiority over its much smaller southern neighbor. From all accounts, Hanoi did not even commit its crack regiments to the border war, most of the fighting being carried out by its militia forces. If anything, the conflict has laid bare severe weaknesses in the Chinese military machine, which had not seen action since the border war with India in 1962, had not fully recovered from its severe discipline problems experienced during the Cultural Revolution, and perhaps had lacked certain categories of equipment supplied by the Soviet Union prior to its rift with China.

In terms of equipment, Vietnam enjoys an edge of superiority over

China, because of the highly sophisticated U.S. weaponry that fell into its hands in addition to modern, advanced supplies from the Soviet Union over the last two decades. Peking was certainly not successful in "teaching a lesson" to Hanoi inasmuch as the latter did not feel compelled to reduce its commitment to Pnompenh or to withdraw substantial numbers of troops from Cambodia. By late March, the Vietnamese in fact completely disregarded the possibility of Chinese retaliatory measures, as they undertook airlifts of men and material into the western Cambodian provinces of Battambang and Siem Reap, where the forces loyal to the ousted Pol Pot regime have demonstrated their strength.

China's only gain from the recent war has been the maintenance of tension over its southern border, which has adverse consequences for the Vietnamese economy. But such a policy is like a double-edged weapon in that it is certain to drain the Chinese economy and likely to necessitate revision in the much publicized modernization program. Further, the leadership differences over Vietnam policy that had been overcome in late 1978 are likely to surface again, possibly in the form of questioning Teng Hsiao-ping's direction of foreign affairs. In Southeast Asia itself, some damage to China's diplomacy has already become evident in the concern of ASEAN states with China's new aggressive stance, a shift that has been responsible also for reintroducing great power rivalry into a region desperately hoping for a peace reprieve.

In the short run, the Vietnamese ability to develop a third center of international communism that would provide leadership to the Communist movements in all of Southeast Asia is most questionable. As noted earlier, its desire and ambition to establish itself as a regional power capable of standing against China are an outgrowth of its historical fears of Chinese domination and a device of enhancing its own national security. A long-term dependence on the Soviet Union can hardly be a solution because of several reasons: geographical distance, alterations in Soviet international priorities, and above all, the necessary consequence that the country's hard-won independence will be eroded. A fiercely independence-loving people like the Vietnamese are not likely to play second fiddle to any country, even the Soviet Union, for long. Vietnam's search for long-term security is not likely to rest until it has discovered a self-reliant solution for extension of political influence in the region as a means of bolstering its national defense against potential Chinese aims to dominate it. Until then, Vietnam is likely to follow its own prescription of 1946, at which time the nationalist Ho Chi Minh agreed to welcome back the French to North Vietnam only to get rid of the Chinese army of occupation. He was rightly hopeful that he could liquidate the French imperialism in his lifetime far more easily than that of the historically dominant, geographically close Chinese. Hanoi's recent behavior in helping Moscow to acquire dominant political influence in Indochina may be deemed such a temporary expedient to keep Peking away until the time when Vietnam can muster its own economic and military strength enough to establish an independent center of international communism in its own backyard.

NOTES

1. For a detailed analysis see, Bernard K. Gordon, "Asian Perspectives on Security: The ASEAN Region," *Asian Forum* 8 (Autumn 1976): 62–76.

2. New York *Times*, January 10, 1978.

3. Leo Goodstadt, "South Vietnam: A Lingering Threat to Security," *Far Eastern Economic Review* (FEER), November 7, 1975; also Premier Phan Van Dong's statement, *FEER*, December, 12, 1975.

4. Huynh Kim Khanh, "Year One of Post-Colonial Vietnam," *Southeast Asian Affairs, 1977* (Singapore: Institute of Southeast Asian Studies, 1977), p. 291.

5. Ibid., p. 294.

6. The problem of reconstruction in South Vietnam in the context of withdrawal of U.S. aid is best examined by an anti-Thieu politician. Le Hoang Trong, "Survival and Self-reliance: A Vietnamese Viewpoint," *Asian Survey* 15 (March 1975): 281–300, particularly 294–98.

7. Gareth Porter, "The Revolutionary Government of Vietnam," *Current History* (December 1975): 243.

8. *The Guardian*, September 24, 1975.

9. Gareth Porter, "Vietnam's Long Road to Socialism," *Current History* (December 1976): 209–18.

10. The PRG expected some of these to spend up to three years in reeducation camps; *FEER*, May 14, 1976.

11. Le Anh Tu, "Vietnam: The Legacy of the War," *Indochina Chronicle* (May-June 1976), quoted in Huynh, op. cit., p. 290.

12. Nayan Chanda, "Vietnam: Back to the Land," *FEER*, June 27, 1975, p. 34.

13. For a French correspondent's eye-witness account of the "reeducation" program, New York *Times*, Feburary 8, 1976.

14. For a discussion of the role of ideology in Vietnam see, William J. Duiker, "Ideology and Nation-Building in the Democratic Republic of Vietnam," *Asian Survey* 17 (May 1977): 413–31

15. Nayan Chanda, "The East-West Touch," *FEER*, December 17, 1976, p. 20.

16. Nayan Chanda, "Vietnam's Joint Venture Plan," *FEER*, September 24, 1976, p. 55.

17. *FEER*, November 12, 1976, p. 13.

18. Susumu Awanohara, "The Rush for Vietnam's Oil," *FEER*, February 20, 1976, p. 36.

19. Francois Nivolon, "Hanoi's Next Victory," *Atlas* (June 1976): 23–25 (reproduced from *Le Figaro*) outlines some of Vietnam's economic problems including those of foreign exchange.

20. Details of the plan in *Summary of World Broadcasts*, December 18, 1976, and *Foreign Broadcasts Information Service*, January 24, 1977. This was an extremely important meeting, the Third Congress having met in 1960 significantly to resolve to liberate South Vietnam and reunify the country.

21. Ta Huu Phuong and Guy Ta, "The Post-war Economic Planning and Development of Vietnam," *Southeast Asian Affairs, 1978* (Singapore: Institute of Southeast Asian Studies, 1978), p. 311.

22. Ibid., p. 308.

23. By early 1978, some 82 NEZs had been established; FEER, March 3, 1978.

24. Nayan Chanda, "Hanoi Takes the Campaign Behind the Lines," *Feer*, March 3, 1978, p. 34.

25. Douglas Pike, "Vietnam in 1977: More of the Same," *Asian Survey* 18 (January 1978): 71.

26. Ta and Ta, "Post-war Economic Planning of Vietnam," p. 311.

27. These cyclonic floods were regarded the worst in a century.

28. North Vietnam recorded the lowest temperatures in two decades during February 1977.

29. Pike, "Vietnam in 1977," p. 68.

30. *Defense and Foreign Affairs Handbook, 1976-77* (Washington, D.C.: Copley, 1977), pp. 524-25.

31. *The Military Balance 1978-79* (London: International Institute for Strategic Studies, 1978), pp. 68-69.

32. About 500 aircraft of all types, 600 tanks, about 470 helicopters, 1,200 armored personnel carriers and 1.6 million rifles; *Time*, January 23, 1978, p. 54.

33. *Military Balance 1978-79*, p. 68.

34. Ibid., pp. 68-69; details of the dates of some of these arm supplies are provided in Stockholm International Peace Research Institute (SIPRI), *Arms Trade Register, The Arms Trade with the Third World* (Cambridge, Mass.: MIT Press, 1975), pp. 27-28.

35. Ibid.

36. Teng Hsiao-ping gave these two figures in June 1978 in separate meetings with journalists. *Wen Wei Po* (Hongkong), June 6 and 10, 1978, quoted in Yin Ch'ing Yao, "Peiping-Hanoi Conflict: Origins and Development" Issues and Studies 14 (October 1978): 31.

37. Robert G. Sutter, "Communist China's Strategy in Asia following the U.S. defeat in Indochina," *Issues and Studies* 14 (September 1978): 56.

38. Ibid., pp. 43-44.

39. Roger Smith, *Cambodia's Foreign Policy* (Ithaca, N.Y.: Cornell University Press, 1965), pp. 10-15.

40. Great Britain, Foreign Office, *Further Documents Relating to the Discussion of Indochina at the Geneva Conference, June 16-July 21, 1954*, London, HMSO, 1954, p. 11.

41. William Shawcross, "The Third Indochina War," *New York Review of Books*, April 6, 1978, p. 16.

42. Cedric A. Sampson, "Nationalism and Communism in Vietnam, 1925-1931" (Ph.D. dissertation, University of California at Los Angeles, 1975), p. 284.

43. Pol Pot's speech, September 28, 1977, and his subsequent press conference in Peking on October 3, 1977, quoted in *BBC Summary of World Broadcasts*, and NCNA, Oct. 3, 1977.

44. John Barron and Anthony Paul, *Murder of a Gentle Land: The Untold Story of Communist Genocide in Cambodia* (New York: Reader's Digest Press, 1977), pp. 43-45, provides brief biographies of the eight most prominent members of the Khmer Rouge High Command.

45. For details, see Bernard K. Gordon, "Cambodia: Following the Leader?" *Asian Survey* (February, 1970); FEER, September 4, 1969, pp. 611-613.

46. Barron and Paul, *Murder of a Gentle Land*, p. 55.

47. Timothy M. Carney, ed., *Communist Party in Kampuchea (Cambodia): Documents and Discussion*, Cornell University Southeast Asian Program, data paper no. 6 (Ithica, N.Y., 1977), p. 7.

48. Portions of this paragraph are based on an oral presentation by Stephen Heder of Cornell University, at the annual meeting of the Association for Asian Studies, Los Angeles, March 30, 1979.

49. Phnom Penh Radio, September 28, 1977, and December 30, 1977 in *FBIS* (Foreign Broadcast Information Service).

50. For an excellent review of books disputing the Cambodian internal conditions during 1975–77 see, William Shawcross, "The Third Indochina War," pp. 15–22. The books in question: Timothy M. Carney, ed., *Communist Party in Kampuchea*; John Barron and Anthony Paul, *Murder of a Gentle Land*; George C. Hildebrand and Gareth Porter, *Cambodia: Starvation and Revolution* (New York: Monthly Review Press, 1977). Also important are Francois Ponchaud, *Cambodia, Year Zero* (New York: Holt, Rinehart and Winston, 1977); and, U.S. House of Representatives, *Hearings before the Sub-Committee on International Organizations*, May 3, 1977, "Human Rights in Cambodia" (Washington, D.C.: Government Printing Office, 1977).

51. Anthony Paul, "Plot Details Filter Through," *FEER*, May 19, 1978.

52. Teng Hsiao-ping's speech at the banquet to Thai prime minister, Pramoj Kukrit, June 1975, in *New China News Agency (NCNA)*, June 30, 1975.

53. *Straits Times*, July 31, 1975.

54. *Le Monde*, March 30, 1978.

55. Sheldon Simon, "Peking and Indochina: the Perplexity of Victory," *Asian Survey* (May 1976): 403.

56. Gareth Porter, "China and Vietnam, Asia's New Cold War," *The Nation* 227 (September 9, 1978): 210; same author's "The Sino-Vietnamese Conflict in Southeast Asia," Current History 54 (December 1978): 193.

57. Hungdah Chiu and Chhon-ho Park," Legal Status of the Paracel and Spratly Islands," *Ocean Development and International Law* 3 (1975): 1–28, concludes that China's claim to the islands are "relatively stronger" than those of Vietnam.

58. The islands are also known for their guano and phosphate deposits.

59. *NCNA*, January 11, 1974; *FEER*, January 28, 1974, p. 32.

60. Carlyle A. Thayer, "Vietnamese Foreign Policy Orientations," in *Southeast Asian Affairs, 1977* (Singapore: Institute of Southeast Asian Studies, 1977), p. 310.

61. This portion of the paragraph is based on S. K. Ghosh, "Rivalry in the South China Sea," *China Report* 13 (March–April 1977): 6.

62. Gareth Porter, "China and Vietnam" p. 210.

63. Yin, "Peiping-Hanoi Conflict" p. 31.

64. Gareth Porter, "China and Vietnam," p. 211.

65. Leo Goodstadt, "Vietnam Stakes in the Conflict with China," *Economic and Political Weekly* (Bombay) 13 (July 29, 1978): 1213.

66. *NCNA*, July 3, 1978.

67. *NCNA*, June 21, 1978.

68. Quoted in Denzil Peiris, "Peking-Hanoi Clash over Cambodia," *The Times of India*, January 26, 1979. Emphasis added.

69. *Wen Wei Po* (Hong Kong), June 19, 1978, quoted in Yin, "Peiping-Hanoi Conflict," p. 40.

70. Coral Bell, "Southeast Asia and the Powers," *The World Today* 21 (April 1965).

71. Text in *International Affairs* (July 1969): 3–21. For recent commentaries on the changing nature of the Soviet plan see Howard M. Hensel, "Asian Collective Security: The Soviet View," *Orbis* 19 (Winter 1976): 1564–80 and Arnold L. Horelick, "The Soviet Concept of Asian Security," *Asian Forum* 8 (Autumn 1976): 44–49.

72. In fact, only Afghanistan and the Mongolian People's Republic have the Brezhnev Plan.

73. Hensel, "Soviet Concept," p. 1564.

74. On Soviet Relations with Southeast Asia during the 1970s, see Robert C. Horn, "The Soviet Perspective" in *Southeast Asia and the Balance of Power*, ed. S. Chawla, et al. (New York: Praeger, 1974), also Horn, "Soviet Influence in Southeast Asia: Opportunities and Obstacles," *Asian Survey* (August 1975): 656–71; and Geoffrey Jukes, "The Soviets and Southeast Asia," in *Southeast Asian Affairs, 1977* (Singapore, Institute of Southeast Asian Studies, 1977), pp. 64–72.

75. Nayan Chanda, "The Soviet-Chinese Equation, A Moscow 'Friendship' Agreement Unfriendly to China," *Atlas World Press Review* 26 (January 1979), p. 38.

76. Quoted in ibid., p. 37.

INDEX

ABOUT THE EDITORS
AND CONTRIBUTORS

SUDERSHAN CHAWLA is professor of political science at California State University, Long Beach. He received his B.S. from Delhi University and his M.A. and Ph.D. from Ohio State University. He served as research associate for the UN project with the Massachusetts Institute of Technology in 1957-58. Dr. Chawla also was associated with the Peace Corps India projects at Ohio State University and the University of Illinois. He has been the recipient of a Danforth Fellowship. In 1974 he edited, with Mel Gurtov and Alain Marsot, *Southeast Asia Under the New Balance of Power*. He is the author of *The Foreign Relations of India* (1976).

D.R. SARDESAI is professor of history at the University of California, Los Angeles. He received his B.A. Honors and M.A. from the University of Bombay, and his Ph.D. from University of California, Los Angeles. He is a Fellow of Royal Historical Society of Great Britain. In 1955 he was the recipient of the William Wedderburn Prize. He also has been the recipient of an American Institute of Indian Studies Fellowship, a John R. Dora Haines Foundation Fellowship, and a Watumull Foundation Fellowship. Dr. SarDesai is the author of *Indian Foreign Policy in Cambodia, Laos and Vietnam 1947-64* (1968), *Trade and Empire in Malaya and Singapore 1869-74* (1971), and *British Trade and Expansion in Southeast Asia 1830-1914* (1977).

ROBERT C. HORN is professor of political science and Asian studies at California State University, Northridge. He received his two M.A. degrees and Ph.D. from the Fletcher School of Law and Diplomacy. Dr. Horn has taught at the University of Massachusetts. He has been the recipient of a Shell Foundation Fellowship. He has published several articles on Soviet relations with Asian countries in *Asian Affairs, Asian Survey, ORBIS*, and *Pacific Affairs*. He is the author of the forthcoming volume, *The Soviet Union and India: The Limits of Influence*.

KAREL KOVANDA has been in Peking since July 1977, working as a Czech language specialist with Radio Peking. He received his undergraduate training in Czechoslovakia, and his Ph.D. in political science from the Massachusetts Institute of Technology in 1975. Dr. Kovanda has taught at University of California, Los Angeles, and California State University, Long Beach. He was a member of the MIT Corporation Joint Advisory Committee in 1973. He was recipient of a Pittsburgh Council for European Studies Research Grant in 1972. He has published numerous articles on Czechoslovakia and China in *Far Eastern Economic Review*, *New York Review of Books*, and *Soviet Studies*.

CHARLES E. MORRISON is professorial lecturer at Johns Hopkins School of Advanced International Studies. He received his Ph.D. from Johns Hopkins University. He is currently serving as a legislative assistant to Senator William V. Roth, Jr. He is the author of *Strategies of Survival: The Foreign Policy Dilemmas of Smaller Asian States* (with Astri Suhrke; 1978).

NORMAN PALMER is professor of political science at the University of Pennsylvania. He received his Ph.D. from Yale University. In 1973-74, he was visiting distinguished professor of political science at Duke University. Dr. Palmer has been a senior associate of the Foreign Policy Research Institute, and is a former president of the International Studies Association. He is the author of *International Relations: The World Community in Transition* (with Howard C. Perkins; 1953, 1957, and 1969), *The Indian Political System* (1971), *South Asia and United States Policy* (1966), *Sun Yat-sen and Communism* (with Shao Chuan-leng; 1961), and *Elections and Political Development: The South Asian Experience* (1975).

ROBERT A. SCALAPINO is Robson research professor of government, editor of *Asian Survey*, and director of the Institute of East Asian Studies at the University of California, Berkeley. He received his B.A. from Santa Barbara College, and his M.A. and Ph.D. from Harvard University. He is a fellow of the American Academy of Arts and Sciences. Dr. Scalapino is currently a member of the Visiting Committee of the Brookings Institution; Member, Policy Planning Committee, United Nations Association; Founder, First Chairman, and now a member of the Board of Directors of the National Committee on U.S.-China Relations. He has been the recipient of a number of research grants, including the Social Science Research Council, Guggenheim, National Endowment for the Humanities, and Luce Foundation fellowships. He has written over 110 articles and more than 14 books or monographs on Asian politics and U.S.-Asian policy. His most recent works include, *Asia and Major Powers* (1972), *American-Japanese Relations in a Changing Era* (1972), *Elites in the People's Republic of China* (editor and contributor; 1972), *Communism in Korea*, 2 Vols. (with Chong-Sik Lee;

1972), *Asia and the Road Ahead* (1975), and the *Foreign Policy of Modern Japan* (editor and contributor; 1977).

ASTRI SUHRKE is associate professor at the School of International Service, American University. She received her Ph.D. from the University of Denver. She has been a research fellow at the Department of International Relations, Australian National University. She co-edited *Ethnic Conflict in International Relations* (1977), and is the author of *Strategies of Survival: The Foreign Policy Dilemmas of Smaller Asian States* (with Charles Morrison; 1978).

MARTIN E. WEINSTEIN is associate professor of political science at the University of Illinois. He received his B.A. from the University of Southern California, his M.A. and Ph.D. from Columbia University. In 1969–70, he was assistant director of the East Asian Institute at Columbia University. In 1973–74, he was research associate at the Brookings Institution. In 1975–77, Dr. Weinstein was special assistant to the U.S. Ambassador in Japan. He is the author of *Japan: The Risen Sun* (Foreign Policy Association; 1970), *Japan's Postwar Defense Policy 1947–1968* (1971), and the monograph *The U.S.-Japan Alliance: Is There an Equivalent for Mutual Indispensability?* (1975).